The Cultural Wealth of Nations

The Cultural Wealth of Nations

Edited by Nina Bandelj and Frederick F. Wherry

Stanford University Press
Stanford, California

Stanford University Press
Stanford, California

Printed in the United States of America on acid-free, archival-quality paper

Library of Congress Cataloging-in-Publication Data
  The cultural wealth of nations / edited by Nina Bandelj and Frederick F. Wherry.
    pages cm
    Includes bibliographical references and index.
    ISBN 978-0-8047-7644-8 (cloth : alk. paper) — ISBN 978-0-8047-7645-5 (pbk. : alk. paper)
      1. Culture—Economic aspects. 2. Cultural property—Economic aspects. 3. Heritage tourism. 4. Economic development—Social aspects. I. Bandelj, Nina, editor of compilation. II. Wherry, Frederick F., editor of compilation.
    HM621.C8947 2011
    306.309—dc22

                                                          2011011736

Typeset by Thompson Type in 10/14 Minion

Contents

List of Figures   vii

Acknowledgments   ix

Contributor Biographies   xi

Introduction: An Inquiry into the Cultural Wealth of Nations
Nina Bandelj and Frederick F. Wherry   1

Part I   Empirical and Theoretical Motivations

1   The Political Economy of Cultural Wealth
     Miguel A. Centeno, Nina Bandelj, and Frederick F. Wherry   23

2   Bringing Together the Ideas of Adam Smith and
     Pierre Bourdieu
     Richard Swedberg   47

Part II   Constructing Cultural Wealth

3   When Cultural Capitalization Became Global Practice:
     The 1972 World Heritage Convention
     Alexandra Kowalski   73

4   Selling Beauty: Tuscany's Rural Landscape since 1945
     Dario Gaggio   90

5   Impression Management of Stigmatized Nations:
     The Case of Croatia
     Lauren A. Rivera   114

Part III   Converting Cultural Wealth into Economic Wealth

6   The Culture Bank:
Symbolic Capital and Local Economic Development
Frederick F. Wherry and Todd V. Crosby   139

7   Converting (or Not) Cultural Wealth into Tourism Profits:
Case Studies of Reunion Island and Mayotte
Madina Regnault   156

Part IV   The Cultural Wealth in Global Value Chains

8   Constructing Scarcity, Creating Value:
Marketing the *Mundo Maya*
Jennifer Bair   177

9   Creating and Controlling Symbolic Value:
The Case of South African Wine
Stefano Ponte and Benoit Daviron   197

10   Cultural Brokers, the Internet, and Value Chains:
The Case of the Thai Silk Industry
Mark Graham   222

Notes   241

References   247

Index   275

Figures

1.1	Global income distribution (by country)	28
1.2	Global income distribution (by region)	29
1.3	World Heritage Sites (by region)	31
1.4	Global distribution of brands (2010)	33
1.5	Distribution of prestige exports (2007)	34
1.6	Distribution of global chocolate trade (2007)	35
1.7	Distribution of study abroad (2008)	38
1.8	Distribution of tourism by region (2008)	39
4.1	Landscape in the Florentine Chianti	101
4.2	Cypress-lined road in the Orcia valley	110
5.1	Number of tourists in Croatia by year and origin	120
7.1	A traditional wedding ceremony in M'tsapéré (Mayotte)	160
7.2	A tour guide explaining Lazaret history	165
7.3	A retail outlet of handicrafts made in Madagascar	172
8.1	Young man of Mayan descent	190
10.1	Simplified representation of a value chain	224
10.2	Partially disintermediated chain	225
10.3	Disintermediated chain	225

Acknowledgments

THIS VOLUME WAS SUPPORTED by the American Sociological Association's Fund for the Advancement of the Discipline (FAD), co-sponsored by the American Sociological Association and the National Science Foundation. The Center for the Study of Democracy at the University of California, Irvine, and Office of the Vice President for Research at the University of Michigan also provided generous funding.

The chapters in the volume were compiled and refined over the course of two years. We thank Ulrike Schuerkens and Melissa Forbes for helping us bring together many of the contributors to this volume at meetings in Barcelona and Ann Arbor and Mark Mizruchi, George Steinmetz, Dan Hirschman, Stephan Bargheer and Claire Whitlinger for their contributions to the discussion. We gratefully acknowledge additional funding we received from the University of California, Irvine, Sociology Department, the University of Michigan Sociology Department, and the following units at the University of Michigan: the College of Literature, Science, and Arts; the Institute for the Humanities; the International Institute; Asian Languages and Cultures; German Languages and Literatures; the Museum Studies Program; the Center for Southeast Asian Studies; and the Center for European Studies. Fabio Rojas invited us to blog about our work on orgtheory.net, and a number of research institutes invited us to present our findings. The volume's contributors were generous with their time and their expertise. To them we owe a great debt. Thanks are also due to our editor, Kate Wahl, as well as Joa Suorez at Stanford University Press, and to the two reviewers who provided constructive suggestions for the volume's revision. Margaret Pinette carefully edited the manuscript.

Finally, we thank Viviana Zelizer and Alejandro Portes for their visions of an economic sociology that enfolds culture and development into its core.

Nina Bandelj
Irvine, California

Frederick F. Wherry
Ann Arbor, Michigan
November 2010

Contributor Biographies

Jennifer Bair is Assistant Professor of Sociology at the University of Colorado, Boulder. Her research in political economy, comparative historical sociology, and development studies, with a regional focus on Latin America and the Caribbean, has been published in *World Development, Global Networks, Economy and Society, Signs,* and *Environment and Planning A.* She is the coeditor of *Free Trade and Uneven Development: The North American Apparel Industry after NAFTA* (2002) and editor of *Frontiers of Commodity Chains Research* (2009).

Nina Bandelj is Associate Professor of Sociology at the University of California, Irvine. Her research on the social and cultural bases of economic phenomena, determinants and consequences of globalization, and social change in postsocialist Europe has been published in the *American Sociological Review, Social Forces, Theory and Society,* and *Socio-Economic Review,* among others. She is the author of *From Communists to Foreign Capitalists: The Social Foundations of Foreign Direct Investment in Postsocialist Europe* (2008), coauthor of *Economy and State: A Sociological Perspective* (2010), and editor of *Economic Sociology of Work* (2009).

Miguel A. Centeno is Professor of Sociology and International Affairs at Princeton University. His work on political economy, global capitalism, and comparative historical sociology has been widely published. His latest book publications are *Global Capitalism* (2010) and *Discrimination in an Unequal World* (2010).

Todd V. Crosby is cofounder of the Culture Bank and continues to work in cultural heritage and tourism development in Africa and Asia. A graduate of the University of Chicago, he presently lives in Dakar, Senegal.

Benoit Daviron is Senior Researcher at the Centre de Coopération Internationale en Recherche Agronomique pour le Développement (CIRAD) in Montpellier, France. His research on issues of food policy, agriculture in developing countries, and tropical commodity chains has been published in *Journal of Agrarian Change, Development Policy Review*, and *Journal of Global History*, among others. He is coauthor of *The Coffee Paradox: Global Markets, Commodity Trade and the Elusive Promise of Development* (2005).

Dario Gaggio is Associate Professor of History at the University of Michigan, Ann Arbor. His research on the interdisciplinary study of environmental and social change, with a focus on modern Italy, has been published in *Enterprise and Society, Social History* and *Technology and Culture*, among others. He is the author of *In Gold We Trust: Social Capital and Economic Change in the Italian Jewelry Towns* (2007).

Mark Graham is a geographer and Research Fellow at the Oxford Internet Institute, University of Oxford. His work on the economic, social, and spatial effects of technology has been published in over twenty articles and book chapters, including in *Progress in Development Studies, Journal of Economic and Social Geography, Geography Compass, Environment and Planning A*, and *Environment and Planning B: Planning and Design*.

Alexandra Kowalski is Assistant Professor at the Central European University, Budapest. She is interested in the social-historical sources of historic preservation and its contemporary transformations in postwar Europe and is currently revising her dissertation, *From Cathedrals to Teaspoons: The General Inventory and the Cultural Wealth of the French Nation* into a book manuscript.

Stefano Ponte is Senior Researcher at the Danish Institute for International Studies, Copenhagen. His research on the changing role of developing countries in the global economy has been published in *World Development, Third World Quarterly*, and *Economy and Society*, among others. He is coauthor of

Trading Down: Africa, Value Chains and the Global Economy (2005), *The Coffee Paradox: Global Markets, Commodity Trade and the Elusive Promise of Development* (2005), and *Brand Aid: Shopping Well to Save the World* (2011).

Madina Regnault is PhD candidate at the Ecole des Hautes Etudes en Sciences Sociales (EHESS), Paris. Her research on heritage, identity, tourism, development, and ethnicity has been published in the *Revue Juridique de l'Océan Indien* (2009) and as a book chapter in *Mise en scène des territoires musicaux: tourisme, patrimoine et performance* (2011). She is finishing a doctoral dissertation on cultural policies in Reunion Island and Mayotte, while co-editing a book on local cultural heritage and local development.

Lauren A. Rivera is Assistant Professor of Management & Organizations at Northwestern University's Kellogg School of Management. She has published on status signaling and evaluation and on hiring and promotion in elite corporations in the *American Sociological Review, Research in Social Stratification and Mobility,* and *Qualitative Sociology.*

Richard Swedberg is Professor of Sociology at Cornell University. He has published numerous articles and a dozen of books on economic sociology and social theory, including *Principles of Economic Sociology* (2003), *Max Weber Dictionary* (2005), and *Tocqueville's Political Economy* (2009). He is coeditor of *The Handbook of Economic Sociology* (1994; 2005).

Frederick F. Wherry is Associate Professor of Sociology at the University of Michigan, Ann Arbor. His articles on cultural economic sociology and development have appeared in *Sociological Theory, Ethnic and Racial Studies, The Annals of the American Academy of Political and Social Science,* and *Journal of Consumer Culture.* He is the author of *The Philadelphia Barrio: The Arts, Branding, and Neighborhood Transformation* (2011) and *Global Markets and Local Crafts: Thailand and Costa Rica Compared* (2008).

Introduction

An Inquiry into the Cultural Wealth of Nations

Nina Bandelj
Frederick F. Wherry

THE EVIDENCE HAS BEGUN TO ACCUMULATE. Economic success results from the symbolic resources—collective narratives, reputations, status, and ideas—that nations, regions, and communities have at their disposal. Studies that focus on the material resources within a territory, or the human capital of its population, fail to explain why countries with similar levels of material and human capital endowments find themselves moving at different rates of growth. Some countries are better able to attract foreign direct investment or global tourists compared with their similarly resourced neighbors, and some industries find that the country of origin labels marking their products can make them more attractive (and therefore more economically valuable) in foreign markets. This volume explores the different ways that industries become advantaged (or disadvantaged) in the global marketplace by virtue of their location and by virtue of the meanings encased in place.

Having one's firm "home grown" in Italy differs from having the same type of firm started in Switzerland, especially if the firm is in the high-fashion industry. The opposite might be true for financial consulting. A firm's products and services are wrapped in the narratives that relevant market actors share about the kind of place that anchors the firm and the types of things people in that place are good at doing. Consider too the impact of narratives and reputations on entire regions within a country, whether it be the wine industry of the South African Cape, the tourism service providers of Tuscany, or the microlending projects promoting cultural preservation and local economic development in Mali. How did wine from South Africa enter the global market and compete with more established wine labels from countries such as France and Italy? How has the Tuscan landscape become iconic, and what types of investments and spending does its iconicity make possible? How can small loans be provided to villagers in Mali using locally carved ritual objects as collateral, promoting local economic development and cultural preservation? These phenomena represent what we have coined the cultural wealth of nations—the plentiful supplies of stories, symbols, traditions, reputations, and artifacts that are collectively held and that confer benefits on those able to make legitimate claims to them in advancing their country's prosperity.

The study of the cultural wealth of nations provides a novel approach to understanding economic development and advances a cultural perspective on the economy. We first place our inquiry into both sets of this literature. We proceed to define the cultural wealth of nations and lay out four different theoretical perspectives used to study it. In the second part of the essay we explain how the authors of the ten chapters in this volume approach the study of cultural wealth and summarize their key findings. We conclude with the implications for social scientists trying to study and theorize the wealth and poverty of places comprehensively as well as the implications for economic development practitioners trying to make culture work to the advantage of particular populations.

On Development

How countries advance their prosperity is a perennial question for social science, and the course of history has featured many different approaches. During the early modern period, from the sixteenth to the eighteenth century, it was mercantilism that defined the economic management of European economies, whereby states extolled the protection of domestic industry from foreign competition by imposing tariffs and other barriers to imports while encouraging exports. Belief in mercantilism began to diminish in the late eighteenth century, after Scottish economist Adam Smith launched a powerful critique. In his famous book, *The Wealth of Nations*, published in 1776, Smith railed against the protectionist mercantilist system and argued that the principles of free trade, competition, and choice would spur economic development. Smith argued for the power of free markets where individuals pursue their self-interest, which leads to prosperity for everyone. As Smith wrote, the individual is "led by an invisible hand to promote an end which was no part of his intention . . . By pursuing his own interest he frequently promotes that of the society more effectually than when he really intends to promote it" (Smith [1776] 2000: 345).

Smith's view that the market is the most efficient arbitrator was shared by David Ricardo, who, in *On the Principles of Political Economy and Taxation* (1817), developed the law of comparative advantage to explain why it is profitable for two parties to trade. The core argument is that each can gain by specializing in the good where he or she has relative productivity advantage and then trading that good for others on a free market. Importantly, any kind of state regulation, according to Ricardo, would get in the way of efficient trade and its consequences for economic wealth of nations.

Paying attention to the social and economic change induced by industrialization, the classical sociologists Marx, Durkheim, and Weber could be seen as concerned with economic development. Still, it was only after World War II, at a time of economic reconstruction, the emancipation of colonies, and the beginning of the Cold War, that development became an ideologically explicit project of the international community because the nations of Asia, Africa, and Latin America lagged substantially behind (McMichael 2000). In these regions, politically embedded agrarian structures prevailed, and the challenge was to achieve an industrial transformation. At first, this development project was essentially aimed at universalizing Western development around the world, as envisioned by modernization theorists (Kerr et al. 1960; Rostow 1960). In contrast, neoclassical economists eschewed the gradual development predicated by modernization theory in favor of the sudden and far-reaching implementation of market policies in less developed countries, including the opening of borders to foreign capital, which would increase the overall stock of capital in a country and create positive development spillover effects for the domestic economy (Hymer 1976; Kindleberger 1970; Knickerbocker 1973; Stopford and Wells 1972).

Providing a contrasting explanation, social scientists associated with the dependency (Cardoso and Faletto 1979; Evans 1979; Gereffi 1978, 1983) and the world systems schools (Chase-Dunn and Rubinson 1977; Wallerstein 1974a, 1974b, 2004) argued that military power and economic capital largely explain why some countries have excelled while others stagnated in the global economy and that foreign capital penetration creates inequalities rather than alleviates them. Instead, dependency theorists emphasized the key role of an autonomous bureaucracy with the capacity to formulate and enforce policies of import-substitution industrialization.

Even if eschewing both modernization's natural progression through the same set of development stages for all and the neoclassical power of markets without state intervention, the dependency perspective still focused on the importance of material conditions and endowments for industrialization. In *Dependent Development*, Peter Evans (1979) recognized, but did not focus on, the importance of symbolic resources when he noted that brand-name goods from the First World were preferred to locally produced goods and implied that the symbolic resources that First World firms could rely on made import-substitution strategies less viable in developing economies. An inquiry into the cultural wealth of nations makes it its task to expose how firms located in particular places find themselves at an advantage relative to firms in other places by virtue of the symbolic resources they have at their disposal and the role of state and private actors to manage a country's reputations in a global market.

Indeed, in many low- and middle-income countries today, it is tourism and cultural exports that drive national economic development. International tourism receipts reached US$ 946 billion in 2008 (World Tourism Organization 2010) and have accounted for the largest or second-largest generator of foreign exchange in a number of developing countries. Commodity exports have diversified to include handcrafted and meaningfully charged commodities that most countries failed to record in their official statistics before 2001. Moreover, countries around the world have boosted their investment-attractor services, establishing governmental agencies of trade and investment promotion as well as private sector companies charged with nation branding and marketing a favorable image of the country for the purpose of attracting foreign investment and promoting export demand for the country's products. All in all, low- and middle-income countries have defied the prediction that they would all engage in a race to the bottom offering cheaper prices and larger volumes and canceling out potentially large economic gains for their national economies. Instead, countries have increasingly diversified their exports and added value to that diversification by emphasizing the symbolic qualities of those products—qualities emanating, in part, from the cultural heritage of the people engaged in production, contributing to what we call the cultural wealth of nations. These cultural qualities, their construction and management, and their effects on local, regional, and national economies motivate this volume.

On Culture and Economy

The focus on cultural wealth advances cultural economic sociology. Socio-logical studies of the economy saw a renaissance in the mid-1980s and have since flourished into a burgeoning field known as the new economic sociol-ogy. However, as the pioneering cultural economic sociologist Viviana Zel-izer (2003) commented, economic sociology has had an "uneasy" relationship with culture. Research has either bypassed culture to focus on the struc-tural embeddedness of economic phenomena in networks of social relations (Granovetter 1985) or applied culturalist analyses to "nonstandard" economic topics, such as household or care labor, sexual or informal economies. This has led observers to characterize the cultural perspective on the economy as "a minority perspective" (Swedberg 1997: 168).

Lately, contributions of sociologists who focus on the cultural dimen-sions of economic life have become more prominent (for example, Abolafia 1996; Bandelj 2008a; Beckert 2008; Biernacki 1995; Biggart 1988; Dobbin 1994; Smith 1990; Somers and Block 2005; Spillman 1999, 2010; Velthuis 2005; Wherry 2008b; Zelizer 1979, 1987, 1994, 2005b, 2010). This research has coun-tered assumptions that some economic phenomena are "more cultural" than others and that perhaps the more "standard" economic processes leave little or no room for culture. Nevertheless, this work has mostly endeavored to show how individuals attribute meaning to economic activities they are engaged in—be it buying life insurance (Zelizer 1979), participating in auctions (Smith 1990), trading on Wall Street (Abolafia 1996)—or it has examined the role of economic ideologies (Somers and Block 2005) or national cultural repertoires (Beckert 2008) on economic outcomes. Much less scrutiny has been paid to how cultural understandings, rituals, and symbolic qualities of goods and places affect national development or global economic exchange. True, Max Weber claimed that the Protestant ethic may be the driving force behind the rise of capitalism, but such analyses constrict the definition of culture to very basic categories of religion and values. Instead, our inquiry into the cultural wealth of nations focuses on cultural objects, narratives, symbols, and reputa-tions to examine cultural effects on the economy at the macrolevel of analysis.

Importantly, geographers and anthropologists have also vigorously stud-ied the interactions between culture and economy, adopting what has come to be known as a cultural economy perspective (for recent edited volumes, see Amin and Thrift 2003; Ong and Collier 2004). This perspective has become particularly influential in the economic geography literature, scrutinizing the interface among economy, culture, and spatiality after the cultural turn since the early 1990s (Hudson 2005). Some critics have argued that this scholarship operates with a narrow understanding of culture, overemphasizing consumption as a premier site of cultural economy (Pratt 2004), the economic impact of cultural industries, and the importance of creativity to economic success (du Gay 1997; Hirsch 2000; Lash and Urry 1994; Scott 1999; Singh 2007).

Another strand of research in culture and economy relevant to our cultural wealth inquiry includes studies in cultural and heritage tourism and cultural heritage management (Aoyama 2009; McKercher and du Cros 2002; McMoran 2008; Nuryanti 1996; Turnbridge and Ashworth 1996; Urry 1990). This literature has examined how nations' past, history, and culture, like art and architecture, are represented and showcased in tourism and how these representations shape national identity. One issue this research brings to our attention is that commodification of the past, or of national cultural artifacts, is a contested process (Picard 2008; Summerby-Murray 2002). Cultural representations can serve as an ideological tool. Those who control them shape national identity interpretations, often slanted to exclude the experiences of minorities (Rose 1995). Another issue that tourism literature has been concerned with is the issue of authenticity of representations (Apostolakis 2003; Hughes 1995), debating to what extent what is available to tourists is sanitized, simplified, and bogus (Mitchell 1998; Urry 1990).

We recognize the important work of cultural geographers, anthropologists, and others studying various aspects of cultural heritage, but our focus departs from this research. We acknowledge that cultural representations of places can sometimes be an ideological project, and an intentional effort on the part of the elites, but not necessarily so because cultural commodification often results from the unintended consequences of institutionalized practices (see Kowalski, Chapter 3 in this volume). We are also not concerned with the normative question of commodification of national heritage and whether using cultural wealth for economic development is somehow corruptive of the "essence of places." In our view, identities of places are socially constructed, whereby authenticity is collectively defined. Given this, we follow cultural economic sociology that envisions culture and economy not as two separate spheres but as connected worlds that always intermingle in various ways and not necessarily with corruptive consequences (Bandelj 2008a; Wherry 2008b;

Zelizer 2005b). This coexistence and codetermination is also captured in our core concept, that of cultural wealth, which we now proceed to elaborate.

What Cultural Wealth Is

We suggest a nation's cultural wealth derives from the reputational attributes and cultural products of that nation. On the one hand, when one sees national governments expending resources to market the reputations and symbolic attributes of their countries to attract world tourists and foreign investment, for the sake of national economic development, one bears witness to the creation and maintenance of that nation's cultural wealth. The narratives widely disseminated in the global, English-language press describing the country's major attributes capture these reputations as well. These narratives tell us what the Chinese are good at making, why Brazil is an attractive place to visit, why Italy might be preferred for design but not for financial services, or why anything Swiss is likely to be efficient and on time. One set of symbols and narratives may make a country suitable for the sourcing of cut gemstones; another set of understandings make it a good place for rest and relaxation but not for fine stones, fine art, or tastefully designed (highly priced) furniture.

On the other hand, we also consider a country's cultural wealth to include the number and the significance of its cultural and natural heritage sites, its stock of art and artifacts exhibited in the top international museums of art, and the number of widely recognized international prizes earned by its citizens. Importantly, it would be a mistake to rely solely on existing databases of these artifacts without understanding the politics and logistics of the database construction. Not all country governments are equally competent or motivated to register their stocks of cultural heritage with such organizations as the U.N. Educational, Scientific, and Cultural Organization's (UNESCO's) World Heritage Sites Registry. Also, because one cultural heritage site is not like another and one prizewinner may be nonetheless more highly regarded than another winner, measuring cultural wealth by quantity is not necessarily meaningful, though it goes far in establishing roughly how unequal the distribution of cultural wealth may be (see Centeno, Bandelj, and Wherry, Chapter 1 in this volume). Moreover, stocks of cultural resources may change over time. Monuments, rare objects, and narratives may mature, growing older and more valuable, or they may atrophy as the narratives become dull and less compelling to target audiences. These processes and lives of narratives and symbols can be best captured and understood by an interpretive social science not too insistent on parsimony. Such an approach discovers that any region or nation in the world has latent cultural wealth as the activities its people are engaged in are necessarily imbued with meaning. Still, not all places can reap developmental benefits from their cultural wealth; cultural wealth needs to be activated or mobilized to have potential economic consequences.

The activation process is comprised of symbolic and relational work, and impression management strategies, all of which we could term "social performances of value," that influence how different audiences of observers, opinion makers, producers, and consumers experience and understand cultural wealth. One's willingness to understand certain cultural resources as valuable depends on the elective affinities of the evaluator and preexisting typifications. For instance, some audiences are less suitable for some social performances of value because the religious, ethnic, or regional histories on which the performances are based are either distasteful or uninteresting for the audience mismatched with those performances. On the contrary, individuals (or groups, or firms) with elective affinities to particular cultural performers will be more willing to give these actors the benefit of the doubt and will respond to inconsistencies in their social performances by searching for other reasons why the performance is valid.

Even where audiences and social performances are well matched, a plethora of performances may have a crowding-out effect. Audiences have a limited attention space and scarce resources for purchasing performances and cultural goods. As more cultural suppliers enter the stage, it becomes increasingly difficult for audiences to distinguish one cultural form from another. For instance, rather than distinguishing a Thai from a Burmese style of production, general audiences may only be able to detect that these styles are simply "Asian," missing the distinctiveness that can bring specific advantages (or disadvantages) to Thailand or Burma. Moreover, the narratives of cultural specificity may not be compelling enough to triumph over other narratives. To address this problem, some cultural producers may innovate in style so that their products are inflected with, but not tethered to, original motifs and cultural narratives. These modifications may make the original motifs more salient as a source of contrast or more obscure as memories fade and few originals remain.

Importantly, activation of cultural wealth is not seamless conversion of cultural into economic capital. Determining what "authentically" represents a nation's character or its cultural production is not a straightforward process. People have emotional attachments to particular kinds of understandings, and they tend to want these understandings to be recognized as universally valuable. They react strongly against what they may deem profane interpretations of their place's character because they are human beings whose dignity compels them to decry being debased. Likewise, people feel strong pride in certain characterizations that they deem "authentic." In that sense, meaningful symbols have autonomous power in spurring action as well as in imposing limits on it (Alexander and Smith 2003). In addition, various interest groups have divergent political agendas about what is "authentic" about their nation and how to represent it, potentially in different ways to different audiences, exploiting the multivocality of symbolic and cultural resources (Bakhtin 1981: 291–292). Thus, various actors and/or group representatives stake claims over different possible narrative interpretations, visual symbols, and imagery.

These coexisting tendencies for strategic manipulation and resistance to strategizing about deeply entrenched notions of sacred and profane are evident in increasingly popular nation-branding campaigns (Anholt 2004; Kotler, Jatusripitak, and Maesincee 1997; Potter 2009), which serve to activate the cultural significance of a nation as an attractive place to visit, invest into, or buy from. Even if these campaigns are largely meant as strategic efforts to generate economic profits, they are often accompanied by strong reactions and debates in which the articulation of cultural wealth is contested, not only for political prevail but also in a collective search and the construction of meaning itself.

Finally, the colorful spectrum of people's genuine search for meaning in the construction of commodified culture and their strategic efforts to exploit cultural wealth for economic gain take place in an interconnected global system. This system is characterized both by globally circulating myths (Meyer et al. 1997) and an unequal global division of labor (Frobel, Heinrichs, and Kreye 1980; Wallerstein 1974a, 1974b). The global culture renders certain strategies and narratives more legitimate than others, and the persistent North versus South divide prevents equal access to global markets and curtails opportunities for some nations (or regions) to transform their cultural wealth into economic opportunities. Understanding the placement of any nation in world culture and the world-system makes us aware of macrostructures that often impinge on but sometimes also facilitate cultural wealth articulation in developing countries.

Four Perspectives

This section outlines four perspectives on how to analyze cultural wealth represented in this volume: (1) The political economy perspective emphasizes how traditional understandings of power and economic wealth map onto distributions of cultural wealth, with the former facilitating the latter and the latter reinforcing the former; (2) the global value chain perspective emphasizes how the bulk of economic value is captured at the design and branding phases of production and how industries are helped or hindered in moving up the value chain because of the collective narratives about where they are located and structural constraints, including the reliance on cultural brokers in enacting scripts about location and tradition; (3) the impression management perspective of cultural wealth identifies how collective narratives, information, and place-based images become strategically utilized to construct a coherent and value-enhancing image of a place along with the services and products produced in it; and (4) the cultural sociology perspective insists on the autonomy of culture, emphasizing that culture cannot always be utilized strategically because the myths, narratives, and symbols encasing the commodification of culture become ends in themselves.

The Political Economy Perspective

The political economy perspective stresses that geopolitical power asymmetries are evident in markets for cultural goods. The international division of labor (Centeno and Cohen 2010; Frobel et al. 1980; Gereffi and Korzeniewicz 1994) and the persistent North versus South divide prevent equal access to global markets and curtail opportunities for some nations' (or regions') cultural wealth to become recognized by the rest of the world and converted into economic opportunities. Understanding the placement of any nation in the world-system of international relations (Wallerstein 1974a, 1974b, 2004) highlights the structural constraints that impinge on cultural wealth articulation. Traditional understandings of power and economic wealth map onto distributions of cultural wealth, with the former facilitating the latter and the latter reinforcing the former.

Less concerned with how actors accomplish meaning or generate strategies for impression management of their countries' image abroad, the political economy of cultural wealth traces the countrywide trends in flows of cultural goods to note the stark asymmetry between those places that garner economic benefits from the production and dissemination of cultural goods and those places that don't. This perspective identifies a close relationship between the "value" of culture or cultural artifacts and position in a global world-system. This is consistent with the cultural imperialism arguments, where the already privileged nations, in particular the United States, define what "culture" is globally valuable and export it to the rest of the world.

The Global Value Chain Perspective

Like political economy, the global value chain (GVC) perspective recognizes the division of labor in the global economy but locates it at the level of firms involved in bringing a product from its inception to its end use, that is, throughout a product's value chain. When Gary Gereffi (1999) and his colleagues (Gereffi, Humphrey, and Sturgeon 2005) identified these chains, they honed in on the different stages of assembly and distribution for manufacturers and their various governance structures. Producers involved in the provision of (nonscarce) raw materials and in partial assembly are greatly disadvantaged in the chain; it is the latter stages along the chain that increase the economic rents because they create and control the symbolic value of goods.

The global value chain approach to cultural wealth recognizes the importance of symbolic resources such as designs and brands to increase the profits that firms can capture in the global market and therefore scrutinizes how producers in the developing world can create and control symbolic value to move up the value chain or why they are hindered in doing so. Attention is paid to the collective narratives about places as well as structural conditions, such as the role of intermediaries that act as cultural brokers. This perspective underscores the processes of value creation and value control in global chains of production but also treats cultural artifacts and heritage sites as commodities produced and consumed in the value chain.

The Impression Management Perspective

The impression management approach to the cultural wealth of nations focuses on how cultural attributes of countries have to be strategically managed to generate the kinds of favorable impressions that might attract tourists and investors into the country. This approach adopts Erving Goffman's (1959, 1961) ideas about the presentation of self in everyday life and extends them to teams of actors and directors, including organizations acting on behalf of nations or hired by governments to create the kinds of impressions that would have desirable economic effects, largely via media campaigns. Inherent in this approach is the idea that strategic management of external impressions enables the conversion of symbolic capital into economic capital at a country level, adopting Bourdieu's (1977, 1986) concepts of capital.

This approach privileges the strategic efforts of actors to market their country's cultural wealth and is less concerned with the collective search and construction of meaning. In fact, the cultural resources here are conceptualized as quite malleable; impressions and symbols are considered authentic as long as both the performers and the audience understand them as such. The challenge for the image makers is seen as a need to tap into globally available frames that would resonate as attractive with the global audience, while at the same time making sense for the performers. There is a recognition of the power dynamics in the field of cultural commodification because, unlike individual-level impression management, country-level impression management involves multiple domestic and international actors. These strategic efforts are therefore embedded in domestic cultural politics and shaped by the political history and encounters that the country's official and unofficial representatives have had with other countries' representatives ranked higher in international status.

The Cultural Sociology Perspective

Like the impression management approach, the cultural sociology perspective keeps its focus on individual and group efforts at constructing cultural wealth and its economic consequences. However, this perspective goes much deeper in scrutinizing the collective search and construction of meaning and does not conceive of narratives, symbols, and reputations as mere instrumental resources used to manipulate consumers and importers (Alexander 2003, 2004a). If actors engaged in impression management follow scripts that can be written in various ways, cultural sociology emphasizes that collective narratives overtake the actors and limit the representational goals they seek as well as the sense of plausibility their audiences will have for their performances.

The cultural sociology perspective eschews the strategic intent of capital conversions. Rather, it hones in on the social performances of value that rely on cultural logics marking the sacred from the profane, the modern from the primitive, the developed from the developing, and the orderly from the chaotic. Contrary to the tenets of political economy, the cultural sociology perspective insists on the autonomy of culture, elucidating that construction of commodified culture in the pursuit of prosperity derives from the generation of new meanings or the reinvigoration of old ones, as myths, narratives, symbols, and totems encasing the cultural wealth often become ends in themselves.

Different Theories, Similar Empirical Findings

This volume consolidates chapters that represent, more or less explicitly, these different theoretical approaches to studying cultural wealth and sometimes combine different approaches in a single study. Yet, in the face of this theoretical plurality, the empirical findings converge on the fact that symbolic resources have demonstrable economic effects from one country and continent to the next. We now turn to how the chapters of this volume come together, examining the empirical and theoretical motivations for the volume, the construction of cultural wealth, its conversions into economic wealth, and its deployment in the global value chains.

Part I: Empirical and Theoretical Motivations

The first two chapters provide the empirical and theoretical motivations for studying the wealth of nations. Chapter 1, by Centeno, Bandelj, and Wherry, depicts some empirical trends in the distribution of the cultural wealth of nations to show the dramatic inequalities across these distributions. The location of UNESCO's cultural and natural heritage sites, distribution of top world brands, and flows of different cultural commodities—like art, chocolate, or movies—across the globe demonstrate how some countries are mostly sending and others are mostly receiving highly valued cultural goods. The division of labor in international tourism is also striking, with some destinations distinguished for cultural tourism, or "bells tourism," compared to those being associated with mostly less economically profitable "beaches and bars tourism." In conclusion, the authors reiterate that the world is characterized by a global cultural wealth hierarchy that aligns well with the persistent inequalities within the world-system but doubt that these trends necessarily result from cultural imperialism of the materially dominant Western view. Rather, the authors suggest it would be worthwhile to examine more closely the cultural wealth of nations, to scrutinize the role of institutional practices that balance the cultivation and commodification of culture, to pay attention to the collective accomplishment of meaning that contributes to the durable regeneration of inequalities, and to investigate how (some) places nevertheless defy structural limitations to move up in the hierarchy of cultural wealth.

In Chapter 2, Richard Swedberg provides a theoretical motivation for studying cultural wealth by exploring contrast, complementarity, and continuity in the works of Adam Smith and Pierre Bourdieu. Swedberg argues that Smith's perspectives on economic growth and its social foundations have not been thoroughly understood by economic sociologists. Moreover, by thinking about Adam Smith alongside Pierre Bourdieu, we can see how culture can be conceived in a multitude of ways and how culture needs to become an integral part of economic growth theory. Swedberg's chapter calls on economic sociologists and other social scientists to ask some basic questions about the economy and culture that have thus far been evaded and to think about how Smith's inquiry into the wealth of nations might be reformulated for our time.

Part II: Constructing Cultural Wealth

In Chapter 3, Alexandra Kowalski analyzes UNESCO's World Heritage 1972 Convention as a historical turning point to shed light on the international standards that help countries identify and market their cultural wealth, specifically through practices of heritage preservation. The sequence of decisions and events, as well as the categories of actors involved in the making of what finally became the 1972 Convention, show that "heritage" is constructed and historically contingent not just in its contents but as a practical imperative of symbolic capitalization and accumulation. In light of stark inequalities in cultural wealth among countries portrayed by Centeno, Bandelj, and Wherry in Chapter 1, Kowalski's analysis shows that cultural and knowledge producers (in this case, historians and natural scientists) play a key role in establishing the rules and, perhaps more importantly, the very principle of symbolic accumulation that ultimately maintains the advantage of older state bureaucracies endowed with large cultural administrations. In contrast to explanations of elitism by international organizations, Kowalski points out the unintended consequences of the mechanisms of symbolic speculation through which national policies create cultural value. While the latter are designed by mostly well-intentioned experts and knowledge producers autonomous from political and economic agendas, the practical and institutional norms promoted by these professionals still have strong and systematic negative effects on global cultural equality.

In Chapter 4, Dario Gaggio raises important theoretical questions about how place icons function as symbolic resources, especially given the irony that a landscape's iconic status might render it unfit for (economic) market work, using the case of the Tuscan landscape. In Tuscany, property owners extol the landscape, designated as a World Heritage Site by UNESCO. The iconic status of their landscape attracts tourists, thereby generating rents, but the landscape's symbolic qualities also spark battles over how the landscape's iconic status should be maintained and, consequently, how certain economic activities should be curtailed. A number of individuals and institutions are involved in reconstructing the symbolic value of the landscape (just as Bair shows in Chapter 8 for the case of *Mundo Maya*), but the multitude of actors and institutions involved means that there are some unintended effects on how the landscape will be maintained and evaluated. Gaggio's historical work illustrates how actors both related and unrelated to the tourism industry have made critical decisions affecting the shape of the cultural preservation in Tuscany.

In Chapter 5, Lauren Rivera examines the cultural wealth of stigmatized nations, using the case of tourism in Croatia. Rivera asks how countries with tarnished international reputations mobilize their cultural wealth for economic and political ends. She focuses on Goffman's stigma management strategies and notes how impression management teams use these strategies. In her case study, Croatia's government uses tourism to rebrand the nation's history and culture after the breakup of the former Yugoslavia, eliminating any reference to the Croatian civil war and reimagining it as a Western Mediterranean country, similar to Italy, to enhance its international status and thus international revenues. In this way, Rivera points to an interesting trend of "borrowing" from the cultural wealth of established nations, like Italy, to build a developing country's reputation, something that Regnault (Chapter 7) finds also in Mayotte's elite efforts to emphasize the island's similarities with France.

Part III: Converting Cultural Wealth into Economic Wealth

The chapters in Part III examine how symbolic capital is converted into economic wealth. In Chapter 6, Frederick Wherry and Todd Crosby examine the Culture Bank of Mali. At the Culture Bank, villagers deposit statuettes, objects used in religious rituals, and other cultural objects in exchange for a loan. What makes this bank different from others accepting collateral is that these cultural objects are put on display in the bank's museum, where tourists are charged an entrance fee. Unlike other banks, the object's assessed value does not depend on what it might fetch in an open market but on the amount of verifiable information the loan applicant has about how the object is tradi-tionally used (a narrative that functions as symbolic capital) and where and how it was made. The bank's requirements help keep local cultural narratives alive. What social capital did for the Grameen Bank (see Woolcock 1998), symbolic capital has done for the Culture Bank, utilizing symbolic assets to generate economic capital. The authors also remind us that converting sym-bolic capital into economic capital in developing countries is not a straight-forward process but one that has to incorporate the activities of local people and their understandings of what is important for the cultural and material life of the community.

In Chapter 7, Madina Regnault compares two French territories in the southwest Indian Ocean, Mayotte and Reunion Island, on their success in de-ploying cultural wealth for economic development; Reunion Island is doing much better than Mayotte. Like Rivera in Chapter 5, Regnault focuses on im-pression management at the state level to trace the reasons for this difference. Unlike on Reunion Island, diverse voices exist on Mayotte to push different portrayals of a tradition, leading to little consistent promotion of cultural heritage and financial support for its maintenance and showcasing. Regnault concludes that both private economic actors and public officials on Reunion and Mayotte are well aware that cultural tourism can bring benefits, but proj-ects based on cultural heritage can be successful only when integrated into a system of coordinated public policies that build a consistent image of the island's cultural wealth aligned with local people's expectations.

Part IV: The Cultural Wealth in Global Value Chains

The chapters in Part IV examine how symbolic and cultural resources help firms and regions move up in the global value chains. In Chapter 8, Jenni-fer Bair critically reviews the literature on global value chains to conclude that what has been missing in this important and growing body of work is an analysis of *value* in the value chain. Bair attempts to provide just such analy-sis by examining the *Mundo Maya* project, which spans several countries in Central America and represents a unique cross-national collaborative effort to upgrade the region's tourism from "beaches and bars tourism," to use Cen-teno, Bandelj, and Wherry's (Chapter 1) distinctions, to "bells tourism." *Ruta Maya* follows the traces of the Mayan people across several Central Ameri-can countries, through a region of stunning natural beauty and ecological diversity, dotted with significant archaeological sites attesting to the former presence of a sophisticated pre-Conquest civilization. In 1987, representatives from Mexico, Guatemala, Belize, Honduras, and El Salvador formally endorsed the concept of a multinational tourism project in Mesoamerica along *Ruta Maya*, or Mayan Route, which was to open the way to environmentally oriented tourism, sensitive to the protection of the cultural and historical legacy, resulting in sustainable development of the region and providing jobs and money to help pay for preservation. These valiant and high-flying goals to upgrade the region's "sun, sea, and sand" tourism model typical of Mexico and the Caribbean met with the reality of contentious negotiations, and even conflict, among various stakeholders about how and by whom the region's cultural wealth should be defined and valuated, and how, or even whether, it should be converted into material wealth and utilized for economic development. Bair's analysis points to the politically and socially constructed nature of value and as such has important implications for our understanding of the global value chains dynamics and developmental consequences.

In Chapter 9, Stefano Ponte and Benoit Daviron consider a country's high-quality wines as a mark of cultural wealth that can both yield significant economic benefits and open up struggles for their distribution. But how do countries get into the global wine market? Like Bair in the previous chapter, Ponte and Daviron utilize the framework of global value chain analysis, but their focus is on the ability or inability of producers in the global South to create and control the value embedded in the symbolic quality attributes of a product, which are most often generated and controlled elsewhere in the chain, in the rich countries. Ponte and Daviron use the case of South African wine to show that the industry has upgraded substantially through enhancing not only material but also symbolic value. At the same time, the industry has faced struggles around the appropriation of different kinds of symbolic value, such as trademarks, geographic indications, or fair trade and "empowered" labels, which yield differential profits for various groups of producers. The outcomes of these struggles have resulted in an industry that largely maintains a black–white racial divide. A more general lesson offered by Ponte and Daviron's case study of South African wine is that the process of activating cultural wealth by creating and controlling symbolic value in the South is a demanding process, requiring fairly sophisticated institutions and industry associations, collective action by industry actors, substantial financial investment, and appropriate regulatory support. These are difficult to mobilize, especially in the least-developed countries.

Continuing with a focus on commodity chains of production, in Chapter 10, Mark Graham presents a detailed case study of the Thai silk industry. Graham zeros in on attempts to reconfigure the slowly dying practice of silk production in northeastern Thailand by introducing Internet technologies and e-commerce as a direct way for producers to gain access to the global virtual marketplace. Such development strategies are believed to eliminate the need for intermediaries, which currently capture the bulk of profits in the silk production chains, while Thai producers usually live in poverty. By contrasting chains that have been altered by the Internet (e-commerce) with those that have not, Graham demonstrates that the Internet is rarely being used to successfully disintermediate commodity chains. It is no accident that value within the Thai silk industry is most often created by intermediaries with a detailed knowledge of foreign customer tastes, marketing strategies, and distribution outlets. A myriad of barriers, including physical, linguistic, and cultural ones, as well as lack of technical skill and distance from capital resources, make direct trade between the producer and consumer unlikely. Therefore, for most Thai silk weavers, it is the detailed knowledge of intermediaries who act as cultural brokers, rather than strategies of disintermediation, that will continue to connect them with consumers around the globe and help create the cultural wealth of their nation.

Implications

The Cultural Wealth of Nations specifies the forms that culture takes, the processes involved in their construction, and their deployment by actors and agencies to promote development. The detailed case studies anchor our arguments about how culture matters in actual events, noting how actions do not always progress according to plan because differential interests and/or new goals and understanding about what and how cultural symbols should be defended have real consequences for local, regional, and national economies (Portes 2010). The inquiry into the cultural wealth of nations offers an alternative to standard economic explanations for the wealth and poverty of nations by privileging thick description and historical developments while specifying how affect, narratives, and social performances are not merely the outcomes from the material conditions of existence but are mutually determining of those conditions (Alexander 2003). There are several empirical and theoretical lessons that we can draw from the chapters' findings.

First, any attempt to promote local economic development using symbolic capital should proceed with care. One size will not fit all. Local economic development practitioners tend to see inputs and outputs in the development process much more easily than they see relational processes; however, the failure to account for the meanings imbued in economic interactions will lead to outcomes unintended by policy makers. Wherry and Crosby clearly demonstrate these dangers in Chapter 6 as they describe how early attempts to establish the Culture Bank failed. The conversion of cultural capital into economic capital is not straightforward, nor can attempts to make it more efficient, such as by using new Internet technologies, necessarily work, as Graham concludes in Chapter 10.

Similarly, attempts to find the right buzzwords to promote the positive characteristics of a place and its goods and services may well fall short of the promoters' goals. In Chapter 3, Rivera depicts the rather successful case of Croatia to cover its shameful past and rebrand itself in the eyes of international tourists. But that depended on very consistent efforts on the part of the elites with locals' pragmatic acquiescence, unlike in the case of Mayotte, which Regnault discusses in Chapter 7. For Regnault, cultural tourism promotion is successful only when integrated into a system of coordinated public policies that build a consistent image of a place's cultural wealth, but a system that is also aligned with local people's expectations.

Finally, attempts to move up the global value chain are messier than one might hope. For example, in Chapter 9, Ponte and Daviron use the case of the South African wine industry, which, on the whole, has upgraded substantially by enhancing symbolic value. Nevertheless, the industry has faced struggles around the appropriation of different kinds of symbolic value, such as trademarks, geographic indications, or sustainability (fair trade) labels, which yield differential profits for various groups of producers, maintaining a black–white racial divide. Moreover, as Bair shows in Chapter 8, the politics of representation also become heightened in the coordination of cultural resources that stretch across several nation-state borders with fractured constituencies.

All in all, the contributions to this volume attest to a significant shift in the importance of culture inside actual economies, to utilize cultural wealth, not only education and industrial progress, to advance national prosperity. Similar to the shift to culture inside economies, there has been an important shift lately also in the conceptualization of culture for understanding economic life. While political economic perspectives have always privileged material conditions in determining cultural outcomes, economic sociologists have started to take culture seriously as a force that shapes economic processes, as much as politics and structures do. However, for a long time cultural effects have been considered as part of the social context, keeping the cultural and the economic as two analytically separate domains. Only recently has cultural economic sociology gained new momentum in fighting the separate spheres arguments and emphasizing the constitutive roles of meaning making and economic interests. Our volume showcases theoretical plurality in how to conceive of the relationship between culture and economy. Still, amid this plurality resonates an understanding that deploying culture for economic purposes does not corrupt some "true cultural essence" and that central to this process of cultural commodification is careful attention to the meaning making of actors involved in economic efforts. It is the task of future research to advance this cultural economic sociology at the macrolevel of analysis and spell out further its critical repercussions for understanding the wealth of nations.

Empirical and Theoretical Motivations

1 The Political Economy of Cultural Wealth

Miguel A. Centeno
Nina Bandelj
Frederick F. Wherry

Men of all the quarters of the globe, who have perished over the Ages, you have not lived solely to manure the earth with your ashes, so that at the end of time your posterity should be made happy by European culture. The very thought of a superior European culture is a blatant insult on the majesty of Nature.
—J. G. Herder

THE RELATIONSHIP BETWEEN CULTURE AND THE ECONOMY—including its effects on economic development—has a long academic history and has been the subject of considerable study and debate in the past few years. We are still asking which shapes which. Is it, to use Marx's words, "the consciousness of men [*sic*] that determines their being" or, on the contrary, "their social being [involved in relations of production] that determines their consciousness" (Marx [1859] 1978: 4)? Does cultural wealth make economic capital accumulation more likely, or does economic accumulation provide the means for making the wealthy appear more attractive than the working classes?

We can conventionally date the start of such discussions to Weber's thesis in *The Protestant Ethic and the Spirit of Capitalism* (Weber [1905] 2002). Weber downplays the relations of production and the conflict between the propertied and the propertyless classes when he explains the rise of modern capitalism. Instead, Weber emphasizes the Calvinist ethic and worldview that led people to become dedicated to work and to engage in trade and investment. Although he is not the first to do so, Weber is credited with linking how people think about the world to how they act on its economies. Later analyses of the same ilk include the work of modernization theorists in the 1950s and 1960s (Apter 1967; Bellah 1958; Levy 1962) and arguments about how a civilization's culture accounts, or not, for its industriousness and potentially leads to the conflicts between nations (Huntington 1996). For instance, David Landes has argued that the "rise of the West" was intimately linked to the particular cultural characteristics (attitudes toward science, thrift, and industriousness) of the societies of Western Europe. It is these cultural advantages, proposes Landes, along with a hospitable climate and a more competitive political system, that explain why there is more economic wealth in the West and more poverty elsewhere (Landes 1998). Alejandro Portes and Patricia Landolt (2000) have critiqued this line of thinking for its circular reasoning: Industrious nations are hypothesized to do industrious things. Avoiding the truism requires a close engagement with how we define culture, what its material and ideational sources are, and how culture as a predictor is not merely a restatement of the cultural, social, and economic outcomes it is presumed to cause.

Immanuel Wallerstein (1990) launches a critique against cultural universalism from the political economy perspective. Wallerstein posits that the world system has existed for centuries and that the struggles for control over scarce resources have shaped the present-day advantages and disadvantages that countries experience in the global economy. For Wallerstein, culture is camouflage: The tactic of "creating a concept of culture as the justification of the inequities of the system, as the attempt to keep them unchanging in a world which is ceaselessly threatened by change . . . therefore the very construction of culture becomes a battleground" (1990: 39). Universalist claims of cultural values and absolutes hide particularistic facts, and this occurs both globally and locally (where the particular "us" is turned into a universalistic "us" to disguise inequality). Because there is a hierarchy of states and a hierarchy within states, the ideology of universalism serves as a palliative and a deception. Wallerstein notes how such cultural arguments can be used to justify both outcomes that may result more from historical legacies as well as those resulting from current-day attitudes toward work, investment, and savings. The discourse on culture functions to "blame the victim" by assigning to the global losers a culturally generated "original sin." Thus, the development discourse wraps the world in universalistic legitimacy and then ascribes a particular position to failure in meeting universalistic criteria.

Like Wallerstein, Pierre Bourdieu (1984, 1993a) is cognizant of the power hierarchies but provides an understanding of the links between the economic and cultural at the individual level and sheds light on how understandings of what is "universally" valuable set in. Bourdieu argues that the tastes people have for different types of cultural performances and products depend on the material and social conditions of their existence. The possession of economic capital (money, assets), but mostly cultural capital (educational background and ease with and knowledge of the higher arts), enables an individual to understand what will be generally regarded as high versus low culture, what will be worthy of widespread recognition, and what will deem disdain. But aesthetic tastes do not hover above humankind, in the intellectual stratosphere where only the chosen may travel; rather these tastes are grown during periods of struggle, and these struggles over taste happen among groups of people with accumulations of economic and cultural capital. As understandings about what is "universally" valuable set in, the struggles that made these understandings congeal are effaced.

While acknowledging the agency of the dominant in writing the rules for what is universally valuable and therefore worthy of deference from the dominated, Bourdieu also situates these struggles and the dispositions of the dominant and the dominated in fields where the varying accumulations of cultural and economic capital (along with other forms of capital) shape the dispositions that actors have for revering or politely rejecting an aesthetic form such as design styles, artworks, and musical expressions. The actors themselves are unaware that their dispositions are shaped by the objective conditions of their existence and that the accumulations of different forms and quantities of capital makes them more disposed toward some forms of culture but not others.

Not only are individuals unaware of where their tastes come from, but they are also in denial about how their tastes for particular cultural forms or their respect for a specific aesthetic might lead to economic profits. Bourdieu argues that, for individuals to profit financially from culture, they often disavow their economic motivations, even to themselves, to keep on course their performance of the desire for and protection of culture in its "authentic" form. Culture cloaks power as both the dominant and the dominated deny that their concerns for culture have economic (or even political) implications, thereby rendering the existing hierarchies of inequality more stable by making them seem to be a reflection of the natural order of things. Who should go against nature and expect to win? It is by virtue of sincere belief and taken-for-granted denials that culture may do its work.

In justifying hierarchies of inequality, Saul Bellow cavalierly remarked: "Who is the Tolstoy of the Zulus? The Proust of the Papuans? I'd be glad to read him."[1] Bellow implied a global division of talent akin to social Darwinism's survival of the fittest. The most common reaction to such a claim may be best referred to as cultural relativism. Such a perspective denies the possibility of an absolute scale of cultural value. There is no "best" novel (nor is the novel necessarily the "highest" literary form). Cultures and cultural products need to be understood in their social and historical contexts. From this perspective, Jane Austen is not necessarily one of the leading depicters of the condition of female subjugation and emancipation, but a chronicler of the manners and concerns of Regency Britain. These novels are no more entitled to belong to a universal canon than the oral epic tales of Shaka Zulu's conquests.[2]

Interestingly, the two positions, universalism and relativism, can use the same references to argue their point. Arguing for their universal value, one side can point to the apparent global reach of Shakespeare, Mozart, and Michelangelo to defend the supremacy of a particular cultural tradition. The other perspective can similarly point to these artists and emphasize that it is no accident that they are so highly regarded because they are all representatives of the Western culture that militarily conquered and dominated the world. Had tribes from the southwest Pacific Ocean conquered and dominated the world, the argument goes, the Proust of the Papuans, in the words of Saul Bellow, would have gained more global prominence and regard than Proust (of the French) and those similarly deemed estimable.

This debate about the universality or relativity of culture is important for the discussions of the cultural wealth of nations. How should one judge the relative cultural wealth of parts of the world and its origins? Can we speak of a cultural wealth begetting economic development, or is it more accurate to say that the worth of culture is, at least partly, determined by the amount of money and gunboats behind it?

A critical first step in resolving this debate without falling into an ideological abyss is to make the phenomena as concrete as possible. For the purposes of this chapter, let's define *cultural wealth* as the value added derived from the intangible qualities of products and services emanating in part from the perceived cultural heritage of the people engaged in their production. To what extent is the market value of a cultural item simply a reflection of the political and economic position of the place from which it originates? Conversely, can local cultural products from less powerful nations achieve some success in the global cultural market and then reflect some of this glory on their national origins, thereby making it arguably easier for the next cultural export from their country? Similarly, global disdain for particular cultures can make it extremely difficult for its products in the marketplace even if their designs and production techniques closely resemble those of products from elsewhere that command higher prices and that enjoy widespread recognition as valuable

(Wherry 2007). This leads us to ask about the historical conditions in which products find themselves esteemed and why this esteem is conferred in some time periods but not others (although the products have existed across time).

It is vital to understand that such a series of questions goes beyond the simple issue of "Americanization" or commoditization of global culture, as the advocates of cultural imperialism propose. Nor is this an argument for hybridity (Pieterse 1994) and the "localization" of the global (Ritzer 2003). What we need to understand is the relationship between the "value" of culture or cultural artifacts and a position in a global "world-system" (loosely understood). In short, what is the relationship between global political economy and global cultural wealth? While our ambition is not to provide a definite answer to this question, we want to motivate such an inquiry for future research by posing parallel questions, such as: Is there a global class system? Is there a global "cultural" class system? How does it manifest itself? We take up these questions by scrutinizing, first, the hierarchies in global cultural production and, second, in global tourism.

The Culture of Global Class

Is there a global class system? By class system we mean three things. First, does the distribution of global wealth demonstrate dramatic gulfs between regions, and does this level of inequality merit the label of a "class system," whatever the mechanisms of its creation and maintenance? Second, does a nation-state's position within the global hierarchy of cultural wealth enable or disable potential sources of income? That is, does the nation-state's position in the global pyramid determine access to cultural production capacities? Third, does one's position in the global hierarchy help define expected cultural consumption patterns?

As to the first, there is little doubt that the world is divided between regional haves and have-nots. Ignoring for the moment internal distributions of income, the group of richest nations representing roughly one-sixth of the world's population currently produce and consume three-fourths of global production (Figure 1.1). At the very top we have the twenty-five wealthiest economies, which consist almost exclusively of countries in northwest Europe and its predominantly white colonial offshoots in North America and Oceania. The global wealth hierarchy is even more skewed. One estimate is that North America accounts for 34 percent of the world's wealth, Europe 30 percent, the Asia-Pacific region 24 percent, and the rest of the world

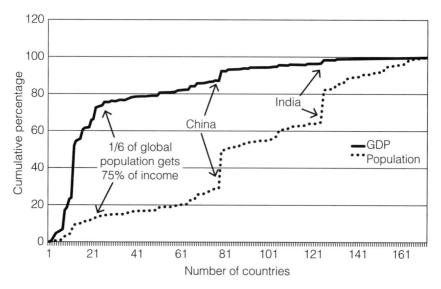

Figure 1.1 Global income distribution (by country).
SOURCE: World Bank (2007).

12 percent. The top five countries (the United States, Japan, Germany, Italy, and the United Kingdom) account for two-thirds of the world's wealthiest individuals (Davies et al. 2006). Even more striking than differences between nation-states is the (estimated) ethnic and racial distribution of global plenty as shown in Figure 1.2. The global poorest consist overwhelmingly of Africans and South Asians, while the vast majority of the global rich are of European descent (Dikhanov 2005).

Similar distinctions among the different parts of the world may be observed in less precise measures such as the implicit value of an individual human life. Note that the accidental death of a group of European descendants somewhere in the globe will merit much more global media attention than the equivalent number of Africans or Asians. For example, Google counts comparing coverage of the lost Air France jet in route to Paris and a Yemenia flight that crashed in Comoros within days of each other indicate that immediately after the crash the Air France flight disaster received at least four times the news coverage of the Yemenia one. News from places such as Bangladesh or the Philippines appears to be merited only if more than a hundred people die in particularly tragic circumstances. It seems unimaginable that the news media would pay scant attention to 2 million violent deaths occurring over a decade in Europe or North America, yet the news hardly

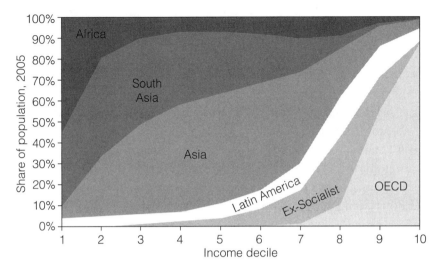

Figure 1.2 Global income distribution (by region).
SOURCE: Dikhanov (2005).

considered this magnitude of violent death remarkable for the eastern Congo. Similar distinctions would appear to apply to the application of human rights in different parts of the world. Take, for example, this fictional interchange from *Our Man in Havana* between the protagonist Wormold and the Batista-era police captain:

"Did you torture him?"

Captain Segura laughed. "No. He doesn't belong to the torturable class."

"I didn't know there were class-distinctions in torture."

"Dear Mr Wormold, surely you realize there are people who expect to be tortured and others who would be outraged by the idea. One never tortures except by a kind of mutual agreement." (Greene [1958] 1970: 164)

It would appear that the world remains divided, in the words of Graham Greene's Captain Segura, between "the torturable" and "the nontorturable." In other words, people from different parts of the world obtain different types of status, according some with more rights but others with more obligations, making some of them more remarkable, more easily seen, and more worthy of emulation. These differences in status have material and bodily consequences.

The major question is whether this inequity is autoreplicating and durable (Tilly 1999). Does position in the global order shape the economic opportunities of these societies? The notion of the "new international division of labor," a result of the global industrial shift whereby, in search of low cost, manufacturing is relocated from the developed Western countries to developing countries in Asia and Latin America, is explicitly predicated on some workers receiving significantly less pay than others and receiving less governmental environmental and safety protection (Centeno and Cohen 2010; Frobel, Heinrichs, and Kreye 1980; Gereffi and Korzeniewicz 1994). The global South–North migration is another manifestation of such distinctions: Citizenship in a privileged northern country can practically assure that many of life's disagreeable tasks will be done by those with less coveted national identities, emigrating from the South; therefore, one could argue that there is a substantial premium for already being wealthy, leading the hierarchy of cultural production to resemble the global economic hierarchy.

Possessing economic wealth makes generating cultural wealth more likely, and cultural wealth itself acts as a resource from attracting and generating economic wealth; yet the creation of cultural wealth is not a straightforward process. Studies of cultural imperialism suggest that the dominant class consciously and deliberately marshals its ideological and cultural resources (including its instruments of physical and symbolic violence) to maintain its dominant positions within its own nation-states and across entire regions of the world; however, some forms of symbolic domination result from institutionalized practices and/or historical accident. Paying attention to these practices, historical contingencies, and the agency of cultural entrepreneurs who use collective narratives and symbols to move up in the global hierarchy helps us understand how imperialistic control can be weakened or (with good timing) overcome.

The struggles for dominance in different aesthetic, political, and market fields have gone on for centuries and become submerged in present-day evaluations of cultural works. The supposed universalism of the "flat" global marketplace hides within it an implicit and deterministic Western bias. It may be true that "anyone can enjoy" a Coca-Cola or *The Magic Flute* and that such products somehow tap into a thoroughly cultural appreciation within all of humankind; yet, functionalist arguments notwithstanding ("It's not imperialistic, it is simply the best"), the global hierarchy of cultural value is a product of historical forces that may have little to do with the intrinsic value of objects. The consequences of this go beyond the definitions of the canon for Literature 101 and help define the paths to development of many societies.

Geographical Hierarchy in Cultural Production

A society's pathway to development is related to its stocks of world heritage, and these stocks are unevenly distributed across the globe. The U.N. agency's program for the preservation of "World Heritage Sites," as Figure 1.3 pointedly shows, leaves no doubt as to where the "world heritage" seems to be located. Over half of the nearly 1,000 sites currently protected by UNESCO may be found in Europe or North America, while only seventy-six sites are located in Africa. Perhaps more tellingly, while nearly 90 percent of the European and North American sites are human-made (and thus "cultural"), a third of those outside these regions are "natural" (more indicative of geological luck than any cultural value). A glance at the interactive map provided by UNESCO makes the global distribution of heritage value quite clear.[3]

It may appear that this West-centric recognition of cultural value across the globe results from a powerful elite faction using their own standards of

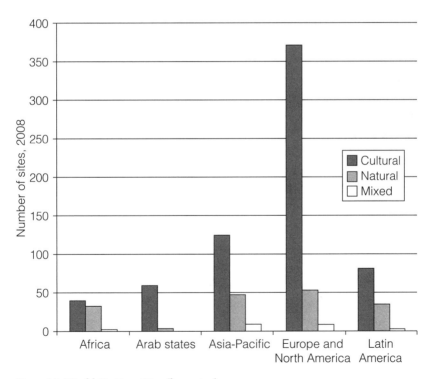

Figure 1.3 World Heritage Sites (by region).
SOURCE: UNESCO (2011).

culture to dominate the cultural symbols of the subaltern, as per cultural imperialism theory. However, as Alexandra Kowalski (Chapter 3 in this volume) demonstrates, the cultural and natural understandings of World Heritage emerged among separate organizational clusters and grew in parallel over an eight-year period before being merged into the World Heritage system we now know and thus result more from institutionalized practice than elite intentions. Just as Kowalski demonstrates how historically contingent the construction of the World Heritage system was, she suggests that changing such a system would require the participation of a large number of actors and institutions and would likely have outcomes that its reformers do not intend. Still, in their effort to protect and conserve places recognized as having universal value, the architects of the World Heritage system have made visible and public at the international level how cultural wealth is distributed globally.

Similar geographical inequities may be found in any supposed repository of global knowledge or culture. Whether in lists of "100 Best" art pieces (films, books, paintings) or in more scholarly enterprises, the Eurocentric bias of global cultural hierarchies has survived decades of assault with remarkable aplomb. Of perhaps greater concern for students of development, we may find a similar hierarchy in a broad array of consumables. On the higher value end, the countries who enjoy a reputation for fashion or industrial design are not only few but also concentrated among the cultural "usual suspects." French high fashion, Japanese technology, Swedish industrial design, or British aristocratic styles are universally recognizable. Arguably, the economy that has enjoyed the most privileged position in this regard is Italy, whose reputation in all areas of design has survived many a manufacturing disaster. Let us not forget that reputations are not merely about "bragging rights" but that they help determine the commercial possibilities available to a society. Products from countries with high reputations enter the cultural wealth market more easily and are sold with much greater ease.

This is evidenced in the lists of top global brands, which shows a strong domination by the United States and Europe. Global brands, such as Coca-Cola, Google, Nokia, and Toyota, are trademarks that, in and of themselves, establish the value of a product and allow sellers to command relatively high prices. As Figure 1.4 shows, of the 100 global brands measured by Interbrand for *Business Week* magazine in 2010, fifty originate in the United States, forty come from the West European countries, eight from Japan, two

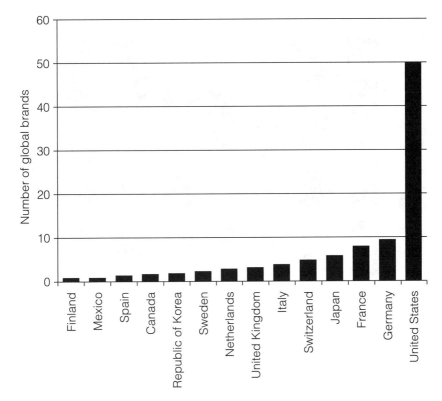

Figure 1.4 Global distribution of brands (2010).
SOURCE: Interbrand (2010).

from South Korea, and one (Corona) from Mexico (Interbrand 2010). Only three of 100 top global brands come from non-Western countries (excluding Japan).

Consider the advantages that such domination provides for export-oriented industries. The fact that global manufacturing exports remain dominated by these same countries may have a great deal to do with the real added value of these country's products but also with the countries' much more amorphous reputations. Indeed, such domination is quite apparent in export sectors where one might expect that reputational effects would be highest. Global trade in areas such as medicines, perfume, musical instruments, and art, for example, is characterized by the dominance of developed countries accounting for roughly 90 percent of the global volume (Figure 1.5). In a time period with greater standardization of production processes and more means

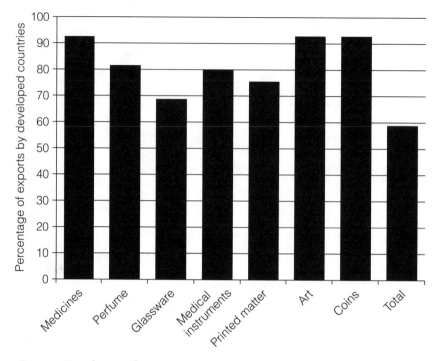

Figure 1.5 Distribution of prestige exports (2007).
SOURCE: Elaborated from Comtrade (2011)

to verify quality, it would seem that the country of origin should matter less for the production of many of these goods. On the other hand, it could be argued that there is a cumulative advantage to producing goods where they have long been produced because the expertise is there along with the appropriate suppliers and downstream production services. However, this line of argument does not address why these places became primary production sites in the first place and why other potential production sites find it so difficult to capture more market share.

We can see a similar pattern if we analyze the composition in the world trade of cocoa (a raw commodity) and the chocolate produced from it. Cocoa and chocolate can serve as a good test case: The origin of the former is fairly irrelevant, while that of the latter can account for a surprising amount of its value, as the literature on global value chains substantiates. Just imagine the reputation and thus appeal of Belgian chocolate versus chocolates from Burkina Faso, for instance. Indeed, developed countries account for more

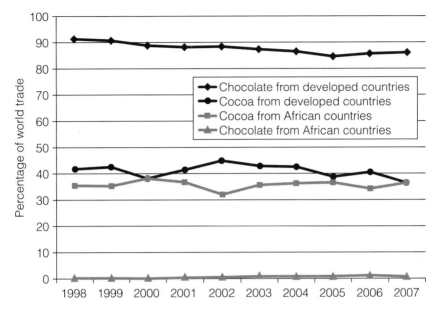

Figure 1.6 Distribution of global chocolate trade (2007).
SOURCE: Elaborated from Comtrade (2011)

than 85 percent of global trade in chocolates but only about a third of that in cocoa (and much of that is actually a reshipment of imported goods). African countries, on the other hand, account for about a third of all cocoa exports but a miniscule share of chocolate sales (Figure 1.6). A similar pattern characterizes global commerce in tobacco. Developed countries account for roughly 20 percent of global trade in tobacco but 65 percent of the trade in cigarettes. For the developing world, the ratio is reversed. In both of these cases, the very significant value-added premium that comes from processing the raw material and then packaging and marketing the finished product tends to be concentrated in the already wealthy countries.

How about recent developments in creating and selling authentically "Third World" products (often under the banner of social justice)? Do they undermine the apparently rigid global hierarchy? Based on the data of fair trade products sales, these (still) have only a marginal effect. According to the World Trade Organization (WTO), the 2008 sales of fair trade products, while growing significantly from the previous year, amounted to a meager US$4 billion compared to world merchandise exports, which were valued at

US$10 trillion in 2005 (WTO 2010). Many efforts at promoting Third World products still betray underlying assumptions. The category of "world music," for example, may be a valuable addition through which greater variety is made available to consumers, but it retains an almost colonial air of cultural segregation.

Indeed, media imperialism scholars have argued that the United States lies at the core of the design and production of popular culture items such as music, movies, and TV (for review see Crane 2002). For example, the various *Crime Scene Investigation (CSI)* programs are syndicated to 200 markets, making *CSI* the most watched drama show in the world in 2010 (TV by the Numbers 2010). Even when noncore countries are not purchasing the actual product, they nonetheless are influenced by the product's concepts. Copies of shows such as *Survivor* or *Who Wants to Be a Millionaire* or *American Idol* become replicated across the world, seemingly with only an inflection of the local.[4] A notable exception in cultural production, especially in movies, is India, pronounced as the most prolific movie-making country in 2005, with more than 1,000 feature films produced in that year, compared to 700 in the United States. However, the top ten grossing films in 2005 were all English-language films, earning almost $6 billion, with $3.5 billion coming from non-U.S. audiences (*Screen Digest* 2006).

This media domination partly reflects the deep hegemony of European languages (and English in particular). There are exceptions, such as the "national" languages of Hindi and Mandarin, but in general if two people from different cultures meet, they are most likely to converse in a European language they have both learned in school. This gives these languages (and again especially English) and their cultural products a remarkable advantage as they can be treated as "universal" or "value neutral" when in fact they very much represent a particular geopolitical time and space.

Even when they are in the background, these languages dominate. The flow of translations, for example, indicates the overwhelming centrality of works in English in the network of global literature. Literature originally published in English and French (whether now published in Bengali or Finnish) helps to define the very notion of literary merit. The Bengali or Finnish authors meeting at PEN seminar in Dakar may celebrate their global cosmopolitanism through their shared reading histories. Will they notice that these largely exclude the books of the other and largely consist of translations of the "classics"?

Because English-language books are at the center of the global production, Johan Heilbron examines the structure of English translations that make books from other cultural backgrounds more widely available to the English-speaking and book-prize-conferring public. Heilbron depicts book translations as belonging to an international system of linked producers and consumers with contexts of production and contexts of reception amenable to sociological investigation. He writes: "Instead of conceiving the cultural realm as merely derivative of global economic structures, it is more fruitful to view transnational cultural exchange as a relatively autonomous sphere, as an arena with economic, political, and symbolic dimensions" (Heilbron 1999: 432). There is a hierarchy with a core, a semiperiphery, and a periphery. Language groups can move between positions over time; however, it is a long-term process. One need only think of the rise of the English language and the decline of the French as a case in point. Different language groups occupy various positions within a structured hierarchy. Their structural position of the language group may be territorially tied to a specific country, or it may transcend national boundaries. English, Spanish, and French, for example, stretch across vast territories. The power of the language groups to reproduce themselves through book translations rests on the inequality in the resonance of these languages and what they represent within the cultural world system.

The politicoeconomic domination by European languages and cultures is made manifest in higher education. While many American students may study abroad for a semester or two in order to improve language skills or simply "encounter the other," flows of students to the United States are much more significant (Figure 1.7). It appears that to study in the United States (and less so, in Europe) is to achieve a special legitimacy. One indication of this is the overwhelming representation of graduates of American universities in the government cabinets of many Latin American, African, East European, and Asian countries. This diffusion of knowledge boosts America's reputation in the global hierarchy.

Global Tourism: Bells, Beaches, Bars, and Nation Branding

A global hierarchy also seems to define the tourism industry, which deserves special attention because, according to the U.N. World Tourism Organization, tourism expenditures amounted to US$ 946 billion in 2008 with 920,000,000 international tourists on the move that year (World Tourism Organization 2010).[5]

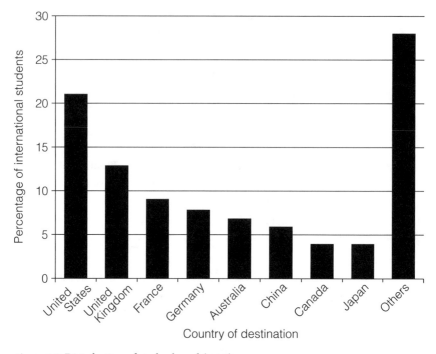

Figure 1.7 Distribution of study abroad (2008).
SOURCE: Institute of International Education (2009)

A look at a simple distribution of world travelers reveals that the developed countries remain the leading destinations for holiday travel (Figure 1.8). Latin America (excluding Mexico), Africa, and South Asia receive a small fraction of tourists and their dollars (roughly 10 percent of the respective global totals). Leading tourist destinations include France, Spain, the United States, China, Italy, and the United Kingdom. International passenger revenue in the United States came across the Atlantic (46 percent, overwhelmingly from Europe), from Latin America (25 percent), and from Asia and Oceania (29 percent). In Europe, international revenue came from North America (35 percent), from other parts of the continent (25 percent), from South America (6 percent), from Asia (21 percent), and from the Middle East and Africa (12.5 percent). In Latin America, intraregional revenue for passengers accounted for 34 percent of the total, while 40 percent came from North America and 20 percent from Europe.

A distinction should also be made between the volume of international tourists flying to different regions of the world and the kinds of those tourists.

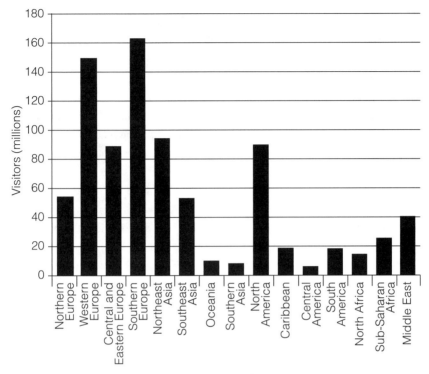

Figure 1.8 Distribution of tourism by region (2008).
SOURCE: U.N. World Tourism Organization (2011).

Here we refer to three type of tourism associated with the various parts of the world: bells, beaches, and bars. By "bells" we mean cultural tourism (and cultural heritage sites). Tourists enter cathedrals with their clanging bells and visit museums that their peers consider "must-see" sights. The "beaches" designation refers to the seaside and natural attractions known for rest, relaxation, and/or debauchery. By "bars" we recognize that some "party places" will be by the seaside (an intermingling of a beach and bar form of tourism), but other sites of interests will derive their value solely from the entertainment industries they provide. Evidence would indicate that the developmental effects of the beaches and bars tourism are not as significant as the bells kind. Thus, a challenge for countries trying to leverage their economic wealth from global tourism is to market themselves as "bells" destinations. In the next section, we consider Thailand's efforts in this direction.

Rebranding a Country's Image: The Case of Thailand

Attracting wealthier tourists willing to purchase local products and staying in domestically owned hotels generates significantly more revenue than receiving young visitors who stay at international chains or hostels and whose only interest in local products may be of the illegal (or the "low-brow") sort. One need only look at Thailand's efforts to move away from the bars (images of brothels and debauchery) and toward bells (highlighting its temples and cultural resources) and upscale beaches, signaled by the descriptions of spas and tree-house luxury hotels being depicted in *The New York Times*.

As the U.S. military established bases in Thailand during the conflicts in Vietnam and in Indochina, Thailand's reputation flourished as a perfect getaway for rest, relaxation, and commercial sex. Indeed, the U.S. military treaty with Thailand designated it as an official site for U.S. soldiers to enjoy "rest and recreation" in the 1960s and 1970s (Enloe 1989; Nuttavuthisit 2007; Truong 1990). When these soldiers returned home, they carried with them fantastic tales of the beaches of Pattaya and the brothels of Bangkok mixed with the wonders of temples, palaces, and exotic marketplaces. Therefore, it should come as no surprise that the majority of tourists to Thailand are single men or that weekend flights from more repressive countries such as Singapore are full of men taking a weekend escape to Bangkok, some dressed in their designer jeans and tightly fitting tops, wheeling a carry-on sufficient for the task at hand. The nightlife does not equal commercial sex, but the trade is such that newspaper editorials have lamented that Thailand gets too much press for sex and nightlife but not enough for its history, food, temples, culture, and natural beauty.

According to marketing specialist Krittinee Nuttavuthisit, working on the Branding Thailand Project,[6] the commercial sex trade has emerged as a blot on the nation's image in recent consumer surveys. Nuttavuthisit (2007) highlights some of these negative perceptions based on thirty in-depth interviews in the United States and on 120 online surveys. Some of the online questions include "What are the first words that come to mind when thinking of Thailand?" and "Which three words describe Thai products?" Among the responses to these queries, commercial sex work, the poor, and poverty stood on the negative side of the ledger, and the exoticism of the country as well as the friendliness of its people stood on the positive side. Nuttavuthisit argues that people who have never been to Thailand had bad impressions of the country based on television programs and magazine articles about Thailand's commercial sex trade and child prostitution. The Thai government's survey of registered sex workers numbered nearly 74,000 persons, but NGO estimates place the number at 300,000 in the 2009 Human Rights Report of the United States Department of State (U.S. Department of State 2009). With reports in *The Economist* stating "throw a stone in Bangkok, and the chances are you will hit a gambler or a brothel goer" ("Bookies and Pimps," 2003), as well as depictions of the sex industry in a Christina Aguilera music video and in the movie "Bridget Jones: The Edge of Reason" (Nuttavuthisit 2007), such negative perceptions present themselves as easily recognizable and quickly associated characteristics of Thailand. The *Longman Dictionary of English Language and Culture* (1993) once referred to Bangkok as "The capital of Thailand, a place often associated with prostitution" (Nuttavuthisit 2007: 25).

It is difficult to rebrand a country when the authors of the new message about what Thailand has to offer have to contend with other legitimate sources of information that offer contradictory messages (see Rivera, Chapter 5 in this volume), yet there are material and cultural reasons why the Thais want to rebrand their country. The government expects higher tourist revenues to come from the types of travelers who want to stay in luxury hotels, visit temples, and look for high-end fashion and furniture. Nearly a tenth of the country's labor force works in the travel and tourism sector, which generates up to 7 percent of the country's gross domestic product (GDP), exceeds all other sectors in export earnings and represents the largest contribution to GDP compared with other countries in the region. These material considerations aside, the Thais have an emotional attachment to their homeland (as most people do) and do not want their innocent daughters presumed lacking in moral propriety or the "value" of their entertainment and tourism sites limited to beer halls, beaches, and brothels. The Thais also want to be recognized as having universally valuable cultural contributions because they are human beings whose dignity compels them to decry being debased.

This highlights the limits of understanding nation branding as simply strategic action of impression manipulation. Symbols representing Thailand or any other country cannot be utilized in any way that marketers please. According to Jeffrey Alexander and Philip Smith (1993), meaningful symbols have autonomous power in spurring action as well as in imposing limits on it. Hence, even if a country such as Thailand could specialize in being an entertainment venue of bars, beaches, and brothels and could profit mightily from it, it is likely that political coalitions would mobilize against such an economic specialization and that many of the members of the coalition would not have an economic stake in the effort.

The challenge of other developing countries is not to re-create their international reputations but to initially position themselves on the map of global tourist destinations, to find their tourist niche, by nationwide impression management campaigns featured in the global press and via international marketing. One such country is Slovenia, which has pronounced tourism to be one of its most important economic areas for development.

Positioning a Country on the Global Tourism Map: The Case of Slovenia

In the strategy for Slovenia's national economic development written in 2001 as part of the country's accession efforts to the European Union (EU), tourism development has been identified as a strategic development direction, although the country has been receiving only about 0.3 percent of European tourists. Observers have long lamented that this is due to the low recognition of the country in the eyes of the world. Indeed, Slovenia is a rather young state, established in 1991 after the fall of communism and the breakup of the former Yugoslavia that has never before in history had state sovereignty. Moreover, its name makes it easily confused with Slovakia (the republic of former Czechoslovakia) and Slavonia (the region in former Yugoslavia). Its national flag is almost identical to the Slovakian one, except of the details of the coat of arms, and features stripes of red, blue, and white, which are very common on many of the European flags.

However, systematic efforts to increase the country's visibility on a global map and to market it as a tourist destination to the global, not only regional, audiences began after the country acceded to the European Union and was preparing for the EU presidency, beginning in January 2008. As part of these efforts, in the spring of 2005, the government established a state agency, the Sector for Promotion and International Cooperation, under the auspices of the Ministry of Culture of the Republic of Slovenia and charged the Slovenian Tourist Office (STO) with a creation of a crucial marketing tool—a CNN spot to be viewed by global travelers.

But what makes for a representation of a country in thirty seconds? What is its "essence"? Or better yet, what kind of an "essence" would be attractive to a global citizen? The actual spot featured mostly the natural beauties of the country, including the sea, the vineyards, Lipizzaner horses, fields, rivers, the karst caves, and mountains, interspersed with images of outdoor activities like sailing, horseback riding, golfing, and skiing. In light of our bells/beaches/bars typology, these images were appealing to the beaches/nature type of tourism. However, there were also some appeals to the architecture and arts of the capital city of Ljubljana and the medieval coastal city of Piran, clearly suggesting that the country possesses some bells as well. Indeed, the spot was criticized for trying to portray too much, going after bells, beaches, and bars all at once, under the slogan "Slovenia—Diversity to Discover." The spot was also changed in the last minute because the Minister of Foreign Affairs found the image displayed at the end of the spot (four little flowers that used to be the logo of the STO) inappropriate as a symbol representing a country.

After the CNN spot aired, and considering the controversy it generated, the government officials in July 2006 decided it was time to yet again rebrand the country's image, to find a new logo and a new slogan, to increase the country's recognizability. This time they considered a public call for proposals to be the most democratic and effective way of finding the country's essence. Many entries arrived for this public competition and the chosen slogan was *I Feel Slovenia*, with the segment *love* in S-*love*-nia written in bold, as in "I Feel Love." The creators of the slogan explained: "We borrowed the slogan I Feel Love from pop music, because it is widely recognizable and popularized across the globe. It is known all over the world . . . Thanks to Donna Summer, the slogan is so simple that it needs no explanation, and speaks for itself. That was the intention" (reported in Hočevar 2006). Yet again, the public and the professional design community issued public protests with the content and the selection process, calling the selected slogan "pathetic" and "ad hoc" (Marn 2006), but *I Feel Slovenia* was accepted as an official slogan by the National Assembly at a special session in 2007. It remains to be seen what the effects will be of this slogan on Slovenia's recognizability in the world. But as a commentator at a recent public discussion on Slovenian National Television about strategies to increase recognizability of Slovenian brands suggested, it is probably not wise to revamp a country's image every few years (Tajnikar 2010).

In brief, the cases of Thailand and Slovenia show that whether it is to re-create the existing impressions of global tourists or to create new ones that attract, these countries, as any other world's country in the contemporary world culture (Meyer et al. 1997), engage in nation branding. The process can be understood by applying Goffman's (1959) dramaturgy and impression management at the country level. One country's cultural and symbolic resources are multivocal and therefore can be appropriated variously by the internal and external audiences. There are also front stage and back stage impressions. The impression management teams employed by countries (and often coming from international advertising agencies) are charged with striking a tenuous balance between local "authenticity" and global "recognizability" and with instilling confidence in the chosen country representations. The domestic and international audiences react to these marketing efforts because of their own convictions of what is appropriate and right about a country's culture, not always with economic stakes in mind. Therefore, even if these impression management efforts may seem very strategic, we find that nation branding may be best understood as a social performance, elevating meaning, rituals, and symbols as explanations for action, rather than strategic action of impressions manipulation.

The attempts to negotiate place are not merely concerns with status position but also a keen (though sometimes unrecognized) effort to establish the character of place and the externally recognizable qualities of a nation's people. The portrayal of market actors as using symbols strategically for status display or to maintain dominance ignores the importance of symbols and meanings for motivating action and for making sense of why a country should be proud that it is known for how well its people make a particular product, develop particular forms of designs, or continue to provide access to artworks and places that are universally valued (for example, Alexander 2003; Wherry 2008b).

Still, in the spirit of our political economy of cultural wealth discussion, it is undeniable that countries are engaging in such social performances and positioning themselves not on a flat global map but within a global hierarchy, recognizing that there are places below, at, and above them in status. The impression management efforts of countries are attempts at finding a global tourist niche as they are efforts to negotiate their own "place" in the hierarchy vis-à-vis other places.

Conclusion

In *Rise of the Creative Class* (2002), Richard Florida presents reams of data marking the new geography of creativity, well-being, and wealth in cities and regions of the United States. Similarly, we have presented the geographic distributions of cultural production and tourism flows around the world. We have argued that some world regions and countries beget economic benefits as a consequence of having creative and cultural attributes. The existence of UNESCO's World Heritage List implies that nation-states possess particular sites of universal value in terms of their cultural or their natural heritage, yet scrutinizing the origins of cultural and natural heritage sites included in UNESCO's list reveals a great inequality in the distribution of these sites with core countries richly blessed in cultural heritage but all countries (core and peripherally) nearly equal in their endowments of natural heritage.

Evidence from the geographical distribution of the world's top brands, the export of high value-added commodities, and the global tourist destinations that we presented in this chapter point to significant Western dominance and mark the global hierarchy of cultural wealth. Is this hierarchy attesting to cultural imperialism? Moreover, is it epiphenomenal to real material divisions in the world-system in which the core powerful states exert their influence over the poor peripheral countries?

The purpose of the present chapter was not to provide definite answers to these questions but rather to map the geographical distribution in production and consumption of (some) cultural goods to motivate the inquiry into the origins and consequences of the cultural wealth of nations. Nevertheless, we want to provide some concluding remarks to suggest a corrective to the political economy of the cultural wealth of nations that takes inequality across countries as support for cultural imperialism and gives causal priority to the material conditions of life.

We think it overstated to assert that the distribution trends we presented result from the imperialism of the dominant Western view, as we lack evidence of elite intentions behind these efforts. Rather, in our view, the cultural world-system constitutes a historically situated life of things, places, and ideas, and the biography of commodities (Kopytoff 1986) circulating within it manifest regenerating life cycles along with reincarnations of the dead. This cultural system is solidified through institutional practices that rely on a delicate balance between the cultivation of culture and the commodification of symbols representing that culture. From this standpoint, collective emotions, meaningful narratives, and the accomplishment of meaning through marketing and consumption are not dismissed as secondary to the "real action" of material exchange but are central to understanding how the material realities, and inequalities, of the global marketplace durably regenerate themselves over time (Alexander 2003). The task of the inquiry into the cultural wealth of nations rests on scrutinizing how social actors from particular places collectively accomplish social performances in producing cultural wealth with an eye toward how nations can move up in the hierarchy of cultural wealth.

2 Bringing Together the Ideas of Adam Smith and Pierre Bourdieu

Richard Swedberg

ECONOMIC SOCIOLOGY, GENERALLY SPEAKING, lacks a growth theory; and economics has a growth theory that is much too narrow for its task. Economic sociologists, apart from Marx, never seem to have been very interested in investigating what causes the growth of the economy, but much more in showing—against the economists—that social factors affect the way that the economy works. Economists, in their turn, have operated with such a limited view of what makes people and society act the way they do that they have failed to develop an effective growth theory. We still do not understand why certain nations take off, and others do not, according to someone like Paul Krugman (2004).

An inquiry into the cultural wealth of nations seems a fruitful step in this direction. But what exactly does the expression of "the cultural wealth of nations" mean? I think that one can answer this question in several ways. The answer I have chosen to settle on is that it points, following Adam Smith, to a theory that has as its goal to explain "the wealth of nations." And it does so, I also would argue, following Bourdieu, by looking not only at traditional economic factors but also at social and cultural ones.

This chapter rescues Adam Smith's discussion of economic growth from the one-dimensional depictions of economic self-interest and the invisible hand to demonstrate that Smith took into account the different moral judgments of buyers and recognized that a firm had to understand how generalized others characterize the firm's attributes. The chapters in this volume detail the symbolic, nonmaterial attributes encasing a firm's commodities, and this particular chapter argues that attending to the symbolic and moral dimensions of commodities is a sensible extension of Adam Smith's thought.

The ideas of Smith need to be paired with those of Pierre Bourdieu for a fuller understanding of interest and motivation in the marketplace. If buyers differ in their economic ethos, and these differences explain how the purchase of different categories of goods is (or is not) justified, we can better understand why the demand for one country's goods may be greater than another, holding the material conditions of production and distribution constant. In other words, there are nonmaterial constrains on development, and they perpetuate material inequalities. This chapter delves into the ways that Smith and Bourdieu complement one another and the ways that they differ so that the theoretical motivations for a cultural wealth of nations may be more fully understood.

The Many Sides of Adam Smith and Pierre Bourdieu

For an audience of social scientists it is not necessary to prove that Bourdieu is much too often cast as the sociologist who invented the three concepts of field, habitus, and capitals and then applied them to pretty much everything, from art to science. The equivalent stereotypical image of Adam Smith is as an advocate of free trade and the notion of the invisible hand. According to an authority such as Kenneth Arrow, "The profoundest observation of Smith [is] that the [economic] system works behind the backs of the participants; the 'directing' hand is 'invisible'" (Rothschild 2001:116). Arrow is also of the opinion that this is "surely . . . the most important contribution [of] economic thought" to our understanding of social processes. A historian of economic thought, writing on the invisible hand for *The Journal of Economic Perspectives*, sums it up in a similar vein: "Adam Smith's famous simile comparing the market system to an invisible hand continues to convey the essential message of Anglo-American political economy" (Persky 1989: 195).

Both of these interpretations impose themselves on us, as it were; and it is hard to talk about either Adam Smith or Pierre Bourdieu without addressing them. One can also say that they are characterized by a certain coercion as well as exteriority and that they therefore fulfill the two criteria of what constitutes a social fact, according to Durkheim. Social facts, to recall, consist among other things of "ways of thinking" (Durkheim [1895] 1964: 4–5).

Now, if we are going to join the intellectual powers of Adam Smith to those of Pierre Bourdieu—which is the purpose of this volume—we must somehow go beyond these one-sided and stereotypical interpretations. While Durkheim tells us what social facts are and how to explain them, however, he has less to say about how to dissolve them and (as in our case) how to recast the ideas of a thinker in a fresh way. This is nonetheless what we will have to do. I will try my hand at this in a systematic way a bit later in this chapter. Before that, I simply want to illustrate the point that there exist other Adam Smiths and Pierre Bourdieus than the Man of the Invisible Hand and the Man of Field-Habitus-Capitals.

Some Other Sides of Adam Smith, as Seen by Sociologists

Sociologists have as a rule seen different sides of Adam Smith than have the economists. According to economic historian Keith Tribe (1999: 613), economists largely embraced the first two books of *The Wealth of Nations* with its discussions of production, distribution, value, productive labor, and unproductive labor. They largely ignored Book III's and V's discussions of the role that government appropriately plays in the economy. And economists largely ignored Smith's other writings (such as the *The Lectures on Rhetoric* or *The Theory of Moral Sentiments*), which cannot be reduced to propositions for studying contemporary neoliberal issues. Even if some sharp criticism can also be found in the work of the sociologists, on the whole, their ambition has been to add to Adam Smith rather than show where he goes wrong. Sociologists seek out those writings of Adam Smith's hidden away in the metaphorical closet. This allows the Adam Smith of the sociologists to have a broad view of the economy, one that includes institutions and references to society at large. The invisible hand is not very much commented on because the Smith of the sociologists is a critical analyst of economy and society.

To this general summary of how sociologists have viewed Adam Smith, it should be added that many of the major sociologists have read his work and also commented on it. This is definitely the case with *The Wealth of Nations* but less so for *The Theory of Moral Sentiments*. And while many of the central areas in what we may term Adam Smith's economic sociology have been mapped out, a full-scale study of this side of his work has never been produced (but see, for example, Reisman 1976).

Auguste Comte, to start from the very beginning, once suggested that the chair in political economy at Collège de France should be abolished and replaced by one that was more suitable to his own interests (Lepenies 1988:17). As is clear from this anecdote, Comte held economists in low regard—with the exception for Adam Smith, whose work he admired. Emile Durkheim had a similar opinion: Sociology should replace the ideological and unscientific science of economics—but Adam Smith was well worth reading and had made major contributions to social science.

Indeed, as a young academic, Durkheim lectured on *The Theory of Moral Sentiments* in the early 1880s. He agreed with Smith that "a moral law based on self-interest" would "obviously" be a foolhardy project, but he also criticized Smith for overestimating the role of moral sentiments (Durkheim 2004: 237). The latter, Durkheim explained, could never constitute the point of departure for an analysis of morality. Moral sentiments were the result, not the cause, of "the moral law" (Durkheim 2004: 237–239).

But it is of course in Durkheim's main dissertation, *The Division of Labor in Society* (1893), that his most famous discussion of Adam Smith's ideas is to be found. The whole work is centered around Smith's notion of division of labor, as elaborated in *The Wealth of Nations*. While Smith, in Durkheim's opinion, had been "the first to attempt to establish a theory [of the division of labor]" and also had "coined the term," he had not gone far enough (Durkheim [1893] 1984:1). The division of labor exists not only in "economic life"; it is also "a law of nature" and "a moral rule," according to Durkheim ([1893] 1984: 2–3).

Durkheim was especially fascinated by what he viewed as the moral dimension of the division of labor, and this topic inspired some of the best sociology he ever produced. The main purpose of the division of labor, he argued, was not economic but moral. Modern society was marred by "abnormal forms of the division of labor," which produced "anomie." But with the help of so-called corporations, the cracks and holes in the social structure could be filled in, as it were, with moral texture and society thereby restored to life.

Moreover, the German-speaking social scientists read and appreciated Adam Smith. References to *The Wealth of Nations* can be found in many of Marx's works, from *The Economic and Philosophical Manuscripts of 1844* to *Capital* from 1867. Marx argued that Adam Smith belonged to the period when bourgeois economic thought was still progressive. He was also impressed enough by the theory of division of labor to suggest that the idea of a "technical division of labor" (in, say, a factory) should be complemented by the notion of a "social division of labor" (in, say, society at large; for example, see Tucker 1978: 394).

But Marx was also sharply critical of Adam Smith's work. For one thing, he disliked the use that Smith made of isolated hunters and fishers in his account of the economic past; "Robinsonades," as he called them (Tucker 1978:

222). He also blasted Smith for suggesting that the goal of the economy was consumption and not the accumulation of capital. This was "absurd" and an example of "a fundamentally perverted analysis" (Marx [1867] 1906: 647).

Weber, of course, had read Adam Smith. *The Wealth of Nations* was, for example, on the massive reading list that Weber had compiled for his students in economics in the 1890s (Weber [1898] 1990:3). In one of his early writings, Weber also made clear what apparently was not so clear to everyone at the time in Germany, namely that Adam Smith did *not* advocate that self-interest should guide the individual in his or her life (Weber [1903–1906] 1975: 83, 229). Like Marx and Durkheim, Weber was also fascinated by Smith's idea of division of labor; to the technical and social divisions of labor that that Marx had operated with, he added another, called "the economic division of labor" (Weber [1922] 1978: 114–140). On the whole, however, Adam Smith does not figure very much in Weber's work; and in *Economy and Society* one can find only one explicit reference to his work (Weber [1922] 1978: 819).

A reference to Smith appears only once also in another seminal work in economic sociology from this period, namely Georg Simmel's *Philosophy of Money*. Simmel provides a minor discussion of Adam Smith, arguing that this British economist realized that at a certain level of economic development money begins to operate as an instrument rather than as something that is valuable in itself, such as gold or silver (Simmel [1907] 1978: 173–174). What is remarkable about this reference is not so much what Simmel says about Adam Smith and his theory of money but that he mentions the name of Adam Smith at all. Simmel was not like Weber, who furiously peppered his texts with references and loved to add long and labyrinthine footnotes. Only two authors of economic works are cited in the more than 500 pages of *The Philosophy of Money*—and Adam Smith is one of them (Simmel [1907] 1978: 173–74, 524).

All in all, European sociological classics provided limited discussions of Smith's work. The only work written by a sociologist that is exclusively devoted to Adam Smith was, as it turns out, authored by one of the founders of U.S. sociology. This is *Adam Smith and Modern Sociology* (1907), written by Albion Small of the University of Chicago.

Small was the first sociologist to cast Adam Smith as a moral philosopher and to argue that his economic analysis was an integral part of his moral philosophy. This, it deserves to be emphasized, is the interpretation that today is generally accepted among scholars (for example, Tribe 1999). Where Albion

Small stands alone, in contrast, is in his opinion that sociology is the successor in modern society of moral philosophy. *Adam Smith and Modern Sociology* ends with the following sentence, set in italics by Small for stronger effect:

> *Modern sociology is virtually an attempt to take up the larger program of social analysis and interpretation which was implicit in Adam Smith's moral philosophy, but which was suppressed for a century by prevailing interest in the technique of the production of wealth.* (Small 1907: 238)

The last words in this quotation also summarize Small's critique of the economists and how these, in his view, had mishandled the heritage of Adam Smith. What especially upset him was that they had essentially transformed Adam Smith's concern with moral issues into a technical issue of economic reasoning. While Smith had argued that increased consumption of the common human, and increased revenue of the sovereign, were the two major goals of the economy, the economists pushed these to the side and replaced them with a goal of their own: the growth of capital. To quote a sentence by Small that is as much to the point today as when it was written a hundred years ago: "In other words, the classical political economy tended toward abandonment of the attempt to interpret life as a moral problem, and substituted an attempt to interpret life in terms of the technique of economic production" (Small 1907: 200).

In the generations of sociologists that came after the classics but before modern sociology—that is, between something like 1920 and 1980—few sociologists were concerned with Adam Smith. Two important exceptions exist, which need to be discussed. They are Joseph Schumpeter and Karl Polanyi, two of the most creative minds in economic sociology.[1]

Schumpeter was the first person to expressly refer to Adam Smith's "economic sociology," but he did not make a study of Smith's contribution in this respect. The reason for this is not clear but probably has to do with Schumpeter's low opinion of Adam Smith:

> His very limitations made for success. Had he been more brilliant, he would not have been taken so seriously. Had he dug more deeply, had he unearthed more recondite truth, had he used difficult and ingenious methods, he would not have been understood. But he had no such ambitions; in fact, he disliked whatever went beyond plain common sense. He never moved above the head of the dullest readers. (Schumpeter 1954: 185)

In his famous book on entrepreneurship, *The Theory of Economic Development* (1934), Schumpeter writes: "Division of labor, the origin of private property inland, increasing control over nature, economic freedom, and legal security—these are the most important elements constituting the 'economic sociology' of Adam Smith" (Schumpeter 1934: 60). To this statement he then adds, by way of an explanation why he considers them sociological: "They clearly relate to the social framework of the economic course of events, not to any immanent spontaneity of the latter."

In *History of Economic Analysis*, written many years later, Schumpeter mentions two other aspects of Adam Smith's economic sociology: its egalitarian dimension and its historical dimension. He writes in his usual playful (and elitist) manner about Adam Smith's democratic attitude:

> A judiciously diluted Rousseanism is also evident in the equalitarian tendency of his economic sociology. Human beings seemed to him to be much alike by nature, all reacting in the same simple ways to very simple stimuli, differences being due mainly to different training and different environments. (Schumpeter 1954: 186)

Schumpeter also says that Book III in *The Wealth of Nations* (which is devoted to the history of trade and early civilizations) could have constituted "an excellent starting point of a historical sociology of economic life that was never written" (Schumpeter 1954: 187).

Karl Polanyi was, as we know, very well read in the history of economic thought, and this naturally included *The Wealth of Nations*. In *The Great Transformation* (1944) he argues that it was Adam Smith who inspired the creation of the infamous *homo economicus* through his notion of man's "propensity to barter, truck and exchange one thing for another" (Polanyi [1944] 1957: 43). To this rather surprising remark—surprising because John Stuart Mill is usually seen as the person who created the fiction of Economic Man—Smith adds the interesting comment that this construct has had a very negative impact on the research on precapitalist societies. Polanyi also criticized Smith's opinion that the division of labor had been caused by this propensity to barter, truck, and exchange. In fact, he noted, the existence of division of labor in society is linked to a number of other phenomena, such as gender relations and geographical conditions.

But even if Polanyi was critical of some aspects of Adam Smith's work, his general view was favorable. When he sorted those who had contributed to the development of economic thought into those who were "societal" and those who were "economistic," he placed Adam Smith among the former. Polanyi based this opinion on the fact that Adam Smith dealt with the labor market as well as the division of labor in "institutional terms" and, more generally, that Smith regarded "economic life [as] only an aspect of national life" (Polanyi [1947] 1971: 128).

"Reference to the 'hidden hand,'" Polanyi added, "has been exaggerated out of all proportion" (Polanyi [1947] 1971: 128). In reality, Adam Smith had argued the very opposite of the thesis that the pursuit of self-interest leads to wealth for all: "Adam Smith wished to discourage the idea that the self-interest of the merchant naturally benefited the community" (Polanyi {1947] 1971: 128).

Today's economic sociologists have not shown very much interest in Adam Smith, and, as I earlier mentioned, the economic sociology of his works still remains to be written. In carrying out this task, however, there exist some contemporary works that can be of assistance (see, for example, Hill 2007; Lie 1993; Singer 2004,). For instance, Jack Barbalet's (2005) article suggests that *The Theory of Moral Sentiments* contains a sophisticated social psychology. Smith's ideas about "the impartial spectator," Barbalet argues, are very similar to those of Cooley about the looking-glass self. However, Barbalet's article does not touch on the economic aspects of *The Theory of Moral Sentiments* and how this work is linked to *The Wealth of Nations*. To do so is important in order to counter the old economists' argument about the inconsistency whereby humans are portrayed as self-seeking egoists in *The Wealth of Nations* and as sentimental altruists in *The Theory of Moral Sentiments* (for example, Tribe 1999: 613, 622).

Today's economic sociologists have not been overly interested in *The Wealth of Nations* either, even if a reference here and there can be found to this work. The most comprehensive attempt that I know of to grapple with the whole book has been made by Giovanni Arrighi. In his volume *Adam Smith in Beijing* (2007) there is a chapter entitled "The Historical Sociology of Adam Smith," in which the author, on point after point, attempts to undo the neoliberal view of Adam Smith (Arrighi 2007: 40–68). Arrighi, however, does not discuss *The Theory of Moral Sentiments*, nor does he try to place Adam Smith in the tradition of economic sociology.

Another Side of Pierre Bourdieu

It is possible to go through the interpretations of Pierre Bourdieu that have been made by sociologists, in a similar way that I have done for Adam Smith and in this way show that his work is much more complex and interesting than the formula field-habitus-capitals would lead us to believe. There exists ample material to use for an exercise of this type because Bourdieu's work has been much discussed in contemporary sociology, as exemplified by a recent article in *Annual Review of Sociology* on the theme of "Bourdieu in American Sociology, 1980–2004" (Sallaz and Zavisca 2007).

I have, however, decided *not* to follow this route, mainly because I think it would not be very interesting for the reader to be shown in this way that Bourdieu is much richer than his stereotype. What I have decided to do instead is to give an account of a study that will make this very point. It will do so because it was written *before* Bourdieu had developed his three key concepts. It will also do so because it is an unknown study and therefore has not had the time to be given a stereotypical interpretation.

The study I have in mind is one that Bourdieu worked on in the early 1960s and that was never published. It is called *The Bank and Its Customers: Elements for a Sociology of Credit*, and it was produced by Pierre Bourdieu together with Luc Boltanski and Jean-Claude Chamboredon (Bourdieu, Boltanski and Chamboredon 1963). The study resulted in a manuscript of some 200 pages, which I some years ago was lucky enough to get a copy of at Bourdieu's Center in Paris (minus the statistical appendices). Because this study is one of the best analyses in economic sociology that I have ever read, it also deserves to be known for other reasons than the ones I just mentioned.

The empirical material for the study is qualitative as well as quantitative. Bourdieu and his coauthors conducted a small survey, together with interviews, of the customers of a bank in the city of Lille ("Compagnie Bancaire"). In these and other ways the authors carefully document how the clients of the bank respond with great anxiety to the fact that they have to approach a bank and try to arrange for a loan. This anxiety is caused by the fact that getting credit is very important to them and also that they know next to nothing about loans and credit. Most of them think, for example, that a fair rate of interest would be something like 5 percent.

The customers, it turns out, do not really understand what credit and similar economic terms mean, and the reason for this is that they have never been taught this kind of everyday economic knowledge. Schools do not teach it, and neither do the universities. What people do know about credit, the authors show through their survey, also depends on what social group they belong to. Income, education, and general culture all play a role for the kind of practical economic knowledge that a person has.

But Bourdieu and his coauthors do not only present the reader with an early and pioneering study in what today is known as "financial education." They also argue that it is absolutely necessary to realize that people do not view the economy as something objective but as deeply infused with values and morality. Two very different types of ethos exist in French society: what the authors call "savings morality" and "credit morality." The former is dominant and generally regarded as legitimate. The norms that are associated with this type of ethos tell people that they should save before they buy something and that they should be ascetic and not enjoy something before they own it. Credit morality, in contrast, is a hedonistic type of morality and has little legitimacy.

There exists one important exception to the savings morality in people's mind, and that is when you take a loan for housing. Housing, the authors point out, has a number of qualities that make it exempt from the savings morality. It represents a major purchase; it is durable; and it is a necessity, not a luxury or something frivolous.

The authors also argue that one may also want to view the exception that housing represents in terms of the historical transition from a "traditional ethos" to a "capitalist ethos." In a society with a traditional ethos, only savings are to be used, and credit is viewed as a sin. In a fully developed capitalist society, in contrast, credit is used in a systematic and rational way for productive investments. People's decision to use credit for housing, and for a small number of items for personal consumption, indicates that French society is currently somewhere in the phase of transition to a fully capitalist society.

At the end of *The Bank and Its Clients*, Bourdieu and his coauthors sum up the sociological approach to economic topics by contrasting it to economics. Economists, they argue, make the assumption that economic constraints translate directly into specific types of actions. *Homo economicus* always reacts in the same way to the same stimulus. Sociologists, in contrast, have found that economic constraint is mediated by people's economic ethos. Economic behavior is influenced by the understanding that people have of their economic actions, and this understanding includes values and morality.

Adam Smith and Pierre Bourdieu on Interests, Market, and Firms

If my argument so far in this essay works in the way it is intended to do, the reader should by now feel that the social facts of "Adam Smith" and "Pierre

Bourdieu" do not give an adequate picture of what can be found in the works of these two authors. In the rest of this chapter I will continue with my attempt at undoing these social facts—but with one addition. This is—following the theme of this volume—that I will also try to bring Adam Smith and Bourdieu a bit closer to each other and finally confront both of them with the theme of the cultural wealth of nations.

The latter is a difficult task for a number of reasons, not least the time gap between Adam Smith and Bourdieu. Adam Smith (1723–1790) was born in Kircaldy, Scotland, and his father was a civil servant. His career was as a moral philosopher with a deep interest in economic and governmental matters. According to his major biographer, Ian Ross, he was somewhat withdrawn and notoriously absentminded, falling into trances in suitable and unsuitable places (Ross 1995). He published only two works during his lifetime—*The Theory of Moral Sentiments* (1759) and *The Wealth of Nations* (1776)—which he carefully added to throughout his life. Before he died, he gave instructions that his unpublished writings should be burned, including a full manuscript on law and government.

The life and circumstances of Pierre Bourdieu (1930–2002) are, in contrast, as follows. Bourdieu was born in the small village of Denguin in the South of France, the son of a postal worker. From early on, he tells us in his brief "self-analysis," he felt anguished and in opposition to his surroundings (Bourdieu 2007). Originally a student of philosophy, Bourdieu soon decided to make a transition to social anthropology and eventually to sociology. In 1964 he began teaching in Paris, where he remained for the rest of his life. His first studies were devoted to the difficult situation of the Algerian people during French colonialism, while his later production was exclusively devoted to various aspects of French society. If Adam Smith's production was minimal, that of Bourdieu was maximal; by his death he had authored some twenty volumes.

Again, given the difference between Adam Smith and Bourdieu, is there some way of bringing their work and ideas together? I think there is, and this is to present and confront their views on the same subject. By proceeding in this way, I will try to show that their views can begin to react to each other and also to start to mingle with one another in the mind of the reader. They will do this, I suggest, mainly because of three different processes. The first is by *complementarity*—when the views of our two authors turn out to complement each other. The second is by *contrast*—when their ideas are so different that they illuminate each other. And the third is by *continuity*—when their ideas follow each other historically and, in this way, link up to each other in a time sequel.

An Example of Complementarity: Smith and Bourdieu on the Role of Interests

The first issue on which I will compare the views of Adam Smith and Bourdieu is that of *interest*. This concept is central to the analysis in *The Wealth of Nations*, as we know from the famous phrase that we do not owe our dinner to the benevolence of the brewer, the baker, and the butcher but to their self-interest. By the simplifiers of Adam Smith, this is then directly linked to his notion of the invisible hand. Everybody, by following their self-interest, the argument goes, helps to advance the general interest of society.

Bourdieu does not seem to have been very interested in Adam Smith; the only time that he even mentions his name is, to my mind, in an interview in which he attacks the way that Adam Smith uses the concept of interest.[2] "Adam Smith's notion of self-interest," the reader is told, "[is] an a-historical, natural, universal interest, which is in fact simply the unconscious universalization of the interest engendered and presupposed by the capitalist economy" (Bourdieu 1993b: 18).

While granting Bourdieu's critique, it should immediately be pointed out that the idea of self-interest, automatically leading to an increase in society's general welfare, is contradicted in a number of places in *The Wealth of Nations*. One amusing example of this can be found in Smith's analysis of university professors and their interest in giving good lectures. If the professors are paid a flat salary by the university, their inclination will be to lecture "in as careless and slovenly manner" as possible (Smith [1776] 2000: 821). If they, in contrast, are paid with fees by the students (as half of Adam Smith's own income was at the University of Glasgow), the professors will do a better job (Smith [1776] 2000: 820).

While this example has been mentioned only to amuse the reader (and make him or her guess if I am paid to write this chapter or if it is part of my regular duties), I also want to cite another example that illustrates the same point, in a more serious manner, namely that Adam Smith did not assume that self-interest automatically leads to a rise in general welfare. What I have in mind is Smith's important argument that modern society consists of three groups or "orders," which are all linked to each other through their types of "revenue" (Smith [1776] 2000: 285–288). These are the people living off land, the people living off wages, and the people living off profit.

To each group answered what would later come to be called a factor of production: land, labor, and capital ("stock"). Each group had its own interest, and this interest could either "promote or obstruct" the general interest (Smith [1776] 2000: 286). Furthermore, several factors affected the way that the interest of an order and the general interest were linked to each other. For one thing, for someone to promote the general interest he or she had to have "a tolerable knowledge of that interest" (Smith [1776] 2000: 286). Owners of land, according to Smith, were deficient in this regard. There was also the fact that the person had to be able to understand the general interest, and the average worker was typically "incapable either of comprehending that [general] interest, or of understanding its connexion with his own" (Smith [1776] 2000: 286).

This lack of knowledge and understanding had a different impact on the development of the general welfare, depending on the group or order where it originated. For various reasons, which Smith carefully explains, their impact was minor when landowners and workers were involved. It was, in contrast, different when it came to the owners of capital. "Merchants and master manufacturers" also belonged to "an order of men whose interest is never exactly the same as that of the public, who have generally an interest to deceive and even oppress the public, and who accordingly have, upon many occasions, both deceived and oppressed it" (Smith [1776] 2000: 288).

If we now switch from Adam Smith to Bourdieu, it should first of all be pointed out that while Smith is famous for his use of the concept of interest, this is not the case with Bourdieu. A careful reading of his work, however, shows that the notion of interest plays a key role also in his work. One may even argue that interest constitutes the fourth key concept in Bourdieu's arsenal—and that it is as important as field, habitus, and capitals.

The concept of interest has a rich history with which Bourdieu was familiar. If one were to single out which works and people influenced Bourdieu the most, one would have to make a special mention of Weber and his sociology of religion. Weber, among other things, made a famous distinction between ideal and material interests that can also be found in Bourdieu.

Bourdieu's first contribution to the concept of interest is related to Weber's point. The economists, in his view, had unduly restricted the concept of interest to material interest and then insisted that no other interests existed in society outside of the economy. In Bourdieu's view, this was totally wrong. Each and every area of society had its own type of interests, or, to be more precise, each field had its own set of interests. There was a general "economy" to all of society, which must not be confused with its "'economic' economy" (see, for example, Bourdieu 1977: 183; 2005: 6).

Bourdieu's attempt to define what constitutes an interest is related to what he terms "the game." "*Interest*," as he put, it, "is 'to be there,' to participate, to admit that the game is worth playing and that the stakes created in and through the fact are worth pursuing; it is to recognize the game and to recognize its stakes" (Bourdieu 1998b: 77; cf. Bourdieu 1990; Bourdieu and Wacquant 1992: 115–117). The opposite of interest, which Bourdieu also calls "*illusio*," is indifference or "*ataraxia*." If you do not feel caught up in something, you have no interest in it.

A further contribution by Bourdieu to the analysis of interest, and one that sets him apart from Adam Smith, is his insistence that interests are not somehow biologically given or universal in character. "Far from being an anthropological invariant, interest is a *historical arbitrary*" (Bourdieu and Wacquant 1992: 116). Or, more precisely: Interests are always social constructions. "Anthropology and comparative history," Bourdieu notes, "show that the properly social magic of institutions can constitute just about anything as an interest" (Bourdieu and Wacquant 1992: 117).

Bourdieu's fourth important contribution to the analysis of interest has to do with his insistence that it is part of a conceptual pair: *interest-disinterest*. Because one area of society is seen as being totally dominated by (economic) interest, many other areas (as well as precapitalist society as a whole) came to be seen as dominated by *disinterest* (for example, Bourdieu 1993a, 1998b). In, say, the field of high culture, people are proud to announce that they are *not* interested in economic matters. To Bourdieu, this means that the real interest in this field, which is noneconomic in nature, is allowed to remain hidden and to drive the activities of people in secret and unrecognized ways.

The ideas of Adam Smith and Bourdieu on interest can be called complementary. Smith has a more subtle and effective interest analysis than he is usually given credit for, especially by those who identify him with the notion of an invisible hand. But it is also true, as Bourdieu points out, that Smith believed that interest is ultimately something given and eternal. Especially through his insistence that interests are constructed socially, Bourdieu adds to Smith's ideas and complements them.

An Example of Contrast: Smith and Bourdieu on the Role of the Market

While the ideas by Adam Smith and Bourdieu on the concept of interest can be said to be complementary, their ideas on the market are diametrically opposed. While Adam Smith was basically friendly to the idea of the market and saw it as part of what leads to the wealth of the nations, Bourdieu regarded the market as a dangerous threat to the well-being of the population. There is also a biological aspect to Adam Smith's ideas about the market that is lacking in Bourdieu.

Adam Smith is usually associated with the free market ideology and seen as one of its most important advocates, nearly a libertarian. But Smith was no libertarian; he carefully outlined the duties of the state in *The Wealth of Nations*. More important, he viewed the economy as having two major goals: to provide for the well-being of the population and to supply the state with an income sufficient to its tasks. Or, in his own famous formulation: "Political economy [sic] . . . proposes two distinct objects: first, to provide a plentiful revenue or subsistence for the people, or, more properly to enable them to provide such a revenue or subsistence for themselves; and, secondly, to supply the state or commonwealth with a revenue sufficient for the public services" (Smith [1776] 2000: 455).

The market in modern vocabulary is an ambiguous word and has, besides its ideological overtones, at least two meanings: as a marketplace and as a mechanism for the efficient coordination of economic activities. As to the former topic, Adam Smith has little to say. There exist no detailed descriptions of marketplaces and their institutional features in *The Wealth of Nations*. All that can be found are basically references to "the market price," by which Adam Smith meant "the actual price" as opposed to "the average" or "the natural price" (for example, Smith [1776] 2000: 62–63).

There is, however, as earlier mentioned, a biological dimension to Adam Smith's ideas about the market. This has to do with his statement that there exists "a certain propensity in human nature . . . the propensity to truck, barter, and exchange one thing for another" (Smith [1776] 2000: 14). Only humans have this propensity, Smith makes clear; to prove his point, he adds, "Nobody ever saw a dog make a fair and deliberate exchange of one bone for another with another dog" (Smith [1776] 2000: 14).

As to the market as a coordination mechanism, this is where the invisible hand comes in. But Adam Smith, it would appear, meant something quite different with this metaphor than what modern economists mean by the efficient coordination of the economic system. He also, as is often pointed out, used the term "invisible hand" only three times in all of his production—once in his "History of Astronomy" (1795 [1980]), once in *The Theory of Moral Sentiments* (1759), and once in *The Wealth of Nations* (1776; for example, Rothschild 2001:116).

The reason Smith used this metaphor at all seems to have had much to do with his fascination with the way that complex things operate, be they live bodies or mechanical devices. But to Smith these were not what we today call "emergent phenomena"; someone, as he saw things, had at one point or another deliberately created the mechanism in question. In some cases it was "the wisdom of man," as exemplified by the watch (Smith 1759 [1976]: 168–169). In other cases, it was "the wisdom of God," as in the example of human bodies and, it would appear, the economy (Smith 1759 [1976]: 168–169).

While Adam Smith, to repeat, was essentially positive to the market because it did play a role in creating the wealth of nations, Bourdieu was always very critical of it. In his first studies, he emphasized the negative role of capitalism in Algeria. And from the early 1980s and onwards, he spent quite a bit of his energy fighting neoliberalism, which he viewed as a dangerous threat to the welfare state (for example, Bourdieu 1998a).

While Bourdieu's ideas on what one may call market ideology are well known, sociologists seem to be less aware that he also developed a sociological theory of the way that the market operates. In his programmatic statement on economic sociology, "Principles of an Economic Anthropology," Bourdieu gives a description of what constitutes a market that comes close to a definition:

> What is called the market is the totality of relations of exchange between competing agents, direct interactions that depend, as Simmel has it, on an "indirect conflict" or, in other words, on the socially constructed structure of the relations of force to which the different agents engaged in the field contribute to varying degrees through the modifications they mange to impose upon it, by drawing, particularly, on the state power they are able to control and guide. (Bourdieu 2005: 204)

Bourdieu, in other words, does not think that repeated acts of exchange are enough to produce a market; the structure of the field also plays an important role in what happens. The market, as he says, "is a two-way relation that is always in fact a three-way relation, between the two agents [the buyer and the seller] and the social space within which they are located" (Bourdieu 2005: 148).

From Bourdieu's perspective, Harrison White's model of markets is seriously deficient because it looks only at the way that actors signal to one another and leaves out all structural considerations (White 1981). The same argument is leveled at Max Weber, who defined a market as the result of the way that sellers and buyers first compete with each other and then enter into exchange with each other (Weber [1922] 1978: 82–85, 635–640).

One consequence of Bourdieu's argument is that prices are not set at the intersection of demand and supply. What decides the price are instead the forces of the field. Or, in Bourdieu's own formulation: "It is not prices that determine everything, but everything that determines prices" (Bourdieu 2005: 197).

By disregarding the impact of the field, the analyst also often buys into the myth that a contract in the market is something that is freely entered into by two equal partners. Drawing on his research on Algeria, Bourdieu writes: "The Kabyle people have a name for this kind of contract, which gives the dominated the right to be eaten by the dominant; they speak of a contract between a lion and a donkey" (Bourdieu 2008: 378).

What does not come out very clearly in Bourdieu's definition of the market—which was just cited as the "totality of relations" and the "socially constructed relations of force" (Bourdieu 2005: 204)—is how strongly he emphasizes that demand and supply have to be socially constructed. They do not simply exist, as the economists assume; they are instead the result of long and laborious processes in society. While this may sound abstract and a bit diffuse, the way that Bourdieu describes the coming into being of demand and supply in his empirical studies quickly dispels that impression.

One of these empirical studies, which is at the center of *The Social Structures of the Economy* (2005), deals with the production and sale of one-family houses in the late 1980s in France (Bourdieu 2005). Bourdieu begins by carefully outlining the habitus of the different types of buyers. In analyzing the way that demand is socially constructed, he is also careful to emphasize that a house represents much more than a financial undertaking. People do not invest only their money into their houses but also time, work, and emotions. The house is the place where a family is going to live for a long time, and it is packed with social and symbolic significance.

The field of the producers of one-family houses is also carefully outlined. People in France, Bourdieu shows, want houses that are unique and authentic, something that the construction companies are well aware of. Small firms can easily provide houses of this type, but this is more difficult for huge, industrial type of firms.

This is where advertisement comes into the picture. Small firms are typically local and do not need to advertise. The industrial type of firm, on the other hand, has to do this, and it typically fills its ads with symbols that are linked to the dreams of the buyers. Advertisement, in brief, plays a crucial role in the social construction of the supply.

And so does the state. *Social Structures* contains a detailed description of how the French state initiated a housing policy in the 1970s that had as a goal to facilitate for individuals to get loans to buy houses. This approach, Bourdieu points out, also meant that social housing was pushed back, and it represented in this respect the historical beginning of neoliberal politics in France (cf. Bourdieu 2008: 198).

Not until far into the book, and after first having carefully shown how demand and supply are socially constructed, does Bourdieu bring the two together and show what happens when they meet. On the one hand, there is the buyer, who is full of the hope of having a house that answers to his or her dreams—but who is also full of anxiety about how to go about this. On the other hand, there is the sales agent of the construction company, eager to make a sale, but who also has to make sure that the buyer qualifies for a bank loan.

As the sales agent knows, most people dream of a house that is far from what they can afford. If they are to end up with a house at all, they typically have to choose something that is quite different from their original vision. The sales agents, in short, have to convince the buyers to settle for less and to engage in what Bourdieu describes as "a work of mourning" (Bourdieu 2005: 171).

In the case of the market, Adam Smith and Bourdieu turn out to have very different views. One is fundamentally positive to the existence of markets and their capacity to add to the wealth of nations, while the other is deeply critical. The contrast between the two positions, however, also helps to illuminate the position that is taken by the other. We see, for example, how Bourdieu supplies some of the mechanisms that are lacking in Adam Smith's theory, while Adam Smith is more interested than Bourdieu in the macroeffects of the market.

An Example of Continuity: Smith and Bourdieu on the Role of the Firm

While Adam Smith's ideas about self-interest and the market are part of the construction of "Adam Smith" as an ideological social fact, this is not the case with what he has to say about the firm. This, however, does not mean that attempts have not been made to turn his opinion also on this topic into ideology. In one of the most important scholarly articles that helped to launch the laissez-faire conception of the modern firm, Adam Smith is used to supply some justification of the argument.

The article is "Theory of the Firm: Managerial Behavior, Agency Costs and Ownership Structure" by Michael Jensen and William Meckling (1976). It is an important article because it helped to introduce an agency approach to executive compensation and became as such part of the very successful movement to unleash executive pay. The Adam Smith quotation that opens the article reads as follows:

> The directors of such [joint-stock] companies, however, being the managers rather of other people's money than of their own, it cannot be well expected, that they should watch over it with the same anxious vigilance with which the partners in a private copartnery frequently watch over their own. Like a stewards of a rich man, they are apt to consider attention to small matters as not for their master's honour, and very easily give themselves a dispensation from having it. Negligence and profusion, therefore, must always prevail, more or less, in the management of the affairs of such a company. (Smith [1776] 2000: 800, quoted in Jensen and Meckling 1976: 305)

This quote comes from a passage in *The Wealth of Nations* that deals with one of the many types of economic organizations that are discussed in this work. All of these organizations were structured in very different ways from the modern firm of today; it is therefore misleading to draw close parallels between the eighteenth-century "firm" and the modern firm. If we could use the ideas of Adam Smith and Bourdieu as a contrast, in the case of the market, and to complement each other, in the case of interest, when it comes to the firm, all we can do is to show that there exists a historical continuity between the two. Adam Smith and Bourdieu indeed address the same topic—capitalist economic organizations—but with 200 years of important development in between.

Adam Smith discusses five different types of economic organizations in *The Wealth of Nations* that all have something in common with the modern firm: "corporations," "co-partneries," "exclusive companies," "regulated companies," and "joint-stock companies" (Smith [1776] 2000: 142–164, 681–693, 781–818). Corporations were typically legal-administrative units, such as cities, but also included guilds. *Co-partnery* was the English name for a type of simple organization that merchants had entered into everywhere for hundreds of years, in which the parties were responsible with their whole fortunes for the debts. Restricted companies were companies of merchants, who had monopoly on some kind of trade. In regulated companies, each of the participating merchants had to invest a certain sum, but they could trade on their own. Also, in joint-stock companies individual investments had to be made, but individual trade was not allowed.

Corporations, insofar as they were economic organizations, were on the way out in Adam Smith's time. The most important example of a restricted company in the late 1700s was the East India Company, which Adam Smith was very interested in (Smith [1776] 2000: 681–693, 806–814). His judgment was that the East India Company had stunted the growth of India, reduced its population, and bred a culture of corruption.

Adam Smith also discusses the regulated company and especially the joint-stock company. The former he saw as less interesting and similar to guilds. The joint-stock company, in contrast, is discussed in considerable detail. Drawing on different forms of empirical evidence, including an analysis of some fifty joint-stock companies, Smith concluded that in most cases this type of company was unsuitable for its tasks. The reason for this was that, unless a joint-stock company had a monopoly, it would have to buy and sell in two very competitive markets—in the homeland as well as in the colonies—something that was very difficult and took much vigilance. Unless the traders were also the owners, which they were not in a joint-stock company, they would not have an incentive to be extra vigilant.

According to Smith, there existed a few exceptions to this argument. Four types of activities lent themselves very well to the form of the joint-stock corporation, even in the absence of a monopoly. These were banking, insurance, and management of a canal or the water supply of a city. In these cases there existed stable and well-known "routines" for how to make money, and this is what made them different (Smith [1776] 2000: 815).

What Adam Smith has to say about corporations or the firm is interesting today mainly from a historical perspective. It is also clear that when we make the jump in this essay from *The Wealth of Nations*, written in the late 1700s, to Bourdieu's works, written in the late 1900s, we end up in a very different type of universe.

Bourdieu's most important statement about the modern firm and the role that it plays in the economy is to be found in his programmatic chapter "Principles of an Economic Anthropology," found in *The Social Structures of the Economy* (Bourdieu 2005: 193–222). The economy, it is here argued, can be conceptualized as an economic field; the key actors in this field are firms.

The structure of the economic field is, as in any field, determined by the volume and structure of capitals. There are, first of all, the usual types of capital: social capital, cultural capital, symbolic capital, and financial capital. Symbolic capital, for example, has to do with such things as "goodwill" and "brand name" when it is part of the economic field. There also are some types of capital that are specific to the economic field, such as commercial capital and technological capital. The former includes a firm's science and technology resources and the latter such items as distribution network, marketing resources, and sales power.

The firms that make up the economic field all fight with each other, even if the struggle is not always direct ("indirect struggle" [Bourdieu 2005: 204]). Some firms are dominant and decide how things are to be done, while firms with little power have to go along. Huge firms are typically powerful, and small firms often find some special niche. Medium-sized firms, in contrast, often have to do what the huge firms decide.

Despite the emphasis on choice and freedom for the firms in the economic field ("strategy"), the field nonetheless constitutes a stable social configuration and is resistant to change. Small firms rarely challenge dominant firms with success. When change does occur, it is often the result of forces outside the field—in the form of some new technology, some demographic change or an invasion from another nation or field. A redefinition of the boundaries can also lead to changes in the field; the same may happen if some firm is able to mobilize the state for its purposes.[3]

Individual firms constitute fields in their turn, according to Bourdieu. This means that what matters to a firm is primarily its structure, not the individuals who are part of it. The field of the firm is embedded in the field of the economy, Bourdieu specifies, but it also has its own relative autonomy. The key actors in the firms are the owners and the managers; their systems of dispositions (habitus) are crucial for the understanding of who will decide the strategy of the firm.

From this brief presentation of the analysis of "the firm" that can be found in the works of Adam Smith and Bourdieu, respectively, it should be clear that they have little in common. One theorizes the very beginning of an economic form and the other the same form 200 years later. Adam Smith basically attempted to understand the beginnings of the Industrial Revolution, when the industrial form of capitalism was just beginning to take shape, while Bourdieu was concerned with a very advanced form of industrial capitalism.

Concluding Remarks: Toward a Cultural Wealth of Nations

So far in this chapter I have tried to attack the existing images of Adam Smith and Bourdieu or their transformation from live thinkers into social facts and ideological and scholarly icons. I have done this in two ways: by giving detailed accounts of their analyses and by comparing the two on three points, and in this way—by contrast, by complementarity, and by continuity—breathe some life into the perception of their analyses.

All of this has been a necessary exercise, I feel, to grapple with a difficult topic such as the cultural wealth of nations. The three examples I have chosen—interests, the market, and the firm—are all necessary components of such a theory of the cultural wealth of nations. You cannot construct such a theory, I would argue, without taking interests, the market, and the firm into account.

To theorize the cultural wealth of nations fully is to develop a growth theory. Bourdieu never developed such a theory; he was much more interested in what causes inequality than what makes the economy grow. Adam Smith, and economists more generally, tend to push issues of inequality to the side in favor of explaining economic growth or decline. Consequently, there exist good reasons for trying to bring Bourdieu and Adam Smith together, especially where the symbolic sources of growth are also the perpetuators of material inequality and where two seemingly unrelated issues ("economic" issues of growth and "social" issues of inequality) become mutually important for explaining one another. In other words, material *and* symbolic inequalities (what this volume calls the cultural wealth of nations) explain growth.

What would such a growth theory look like—a growth theory that is social and that also puts inequality on the agenda? This is a question that needs a very long answer, not only a different chapter. Still, I hope that I have accomplished at least two things in this present chapter: I have raised this important question and indicated two excellent points of departure for beginning an enterprise of this type—the ideas of Adam Smith, on the one hand, and of Pierre Bourdieu, on the other.

Constructing Cultural Wealth

3 When Cultural Capitalization Became Global Practice

The 1972 World Heritage Convention

Alexandra Kowalski

WHAT IS CULTURAL WEALTH, and how do national policies produce it? This chapter answers these questions by analyzing a turning point in the history of contemporary policies of heritage conservation—the genesis of UNESCO's 1972 World Heritage Convention. The convention provides the process whereby historic or natural sites are recognized as having "outstanding universal value." It establishes the principle for a list of World Heritage (WH) sites and spells out procedures through which state parties commit to preserve their historic heritage.

The impact of the convention has been significant. The promise of financial returns to the governments and economies that secured acquisition of the WH label (Yang 2000) caused the norm to become effectively global in the decades that followed. It is global in three distinct senses. First, virtually all states are now participants. While rich countries seek the label as part of concerted policies to control tourism, developing countries use it to jump-start or develop their tourist economies. Second, UNESCO's policy tools homogenized criteria for the selection, care, and exploitation of heritage across the world (Smith 2006, Rowlands and DeJong 2007). Third, the convention marked the emergence of an international policy of heritage conservation and, in its wake, of a stratified world system of cultural accumulation in which developed countries benefit from 60 percent of WH designations. The distributional imbalance reflects the global power structure in general and the North–South divide more particularly—although, we will see, the pathways of power are more complex than the correlation might suggest. The international agreement was thus a major turning point in the global history of cultural policy.

Drawing on the theory and methods of "eventful sociology" outlined by William Sewell (1996) and pursued in a variety of forms by contemporary historical sociologists (Adams et al. 2005), this chapter analyzes the adoption of the convention as an event, that is, as a transformative sequence of inter-actions and encounters. (Abbott 2001, Abrams 1983) It shows evidence of the impact of contingent geopolitical strategies on the creation of a WH system as well as of a transnational mobilization of conservation professionals. The decisive role of experts and, through them, of relatively autonomous scien-tific practices in designing and institutionalizing the WH system suggest that cultural production should be made central to the social theory of "cultural wealth" and to empirical examinations of instances of its (unequal) produc-tion. This chapter offers the concept of "cultural capitalization" as a means to account for the role of knowledge producers in creating rules of symbolic value production and cultural value itself.

Genesis of the World Heritage Convention (1964–1972)

The Convention Concerning the Protection of the World Cultural and Natu-ral Heritage was adopted by the General Conference of UNESCO on Novem-ber 16, 1972. The document itself was produced over a period of about twenty years, in a long process that owes to a variety of factors, including a number of contingent encounters and short-term strategic calculations. The official nar-rative of this genesis featured in UNESCO publications gives full credit to René Maheu, UNESCO's director general between 1961 and 1974 (UNESCO 1990). This account provides a conveniently single point of origin: an indi-vidual, representative of some symbolic consensus within UNESCO. The role of Maheu and of UNESCO should, however, be understood in context. As I demonstrate in the following pages, the convention resulted in fact from the complex and contested convergence of two distinct and relatively autonomous projects. One of these projects, owing to the cultural services of UNESCO, defined World Heritage as a collection of historic sites; the other, elaborated successively by environmentalists in the U.S. government and by activists from the International Union for the Conservation of Nature (IUCN), defined World Heritage primarily as a set of natural sites.

The US-IUCN Environmentalist Project: Trust and Register

The earliest and clearest organizational blueprint for what ended up becom-ing the Convention on World Heritage came not from UNESCO but from a national initiative of the U.S. National Park Service. As part of a series of events taking place during the "Year of International Cooperation" decreed by the Johnson administration in 1964, a "Conference on International Cooperation" was organized in 1965. The National Park Service coordinated the conference section on National Resources, Conservation and Development, where the project of a World Heritage Trust "for the identification, establishment and management of the world's most superb natural and scenic areas and historic sites" was proposed and discussed (Train 1972).

The conference reflected a turn in world politics and U.S. foreign policy. The geopolitical blocks of the Cold War were eroding under the impact of decolonization. In 1955 the Bandoeng conference united Third World countries in a movement of "nonaligned" nations with interests distinct from the two Cold War blocs. After 1962 the movement multiplied into several regional alliances with distinct or divergent agendas. American foreign policy adapted to the emergence and diversification of this movement by making the forms of its power more diverse, favoring at times developmentalist strategies over direct intervention.

The Committee on National Resources, Conservation and Development was composed of conservation experts and activists. Two prominent environmentalists were more particularly involved: Joseph Fischer, president of the NGO Resources for the Future, and Russell E. Train, founder and chairman of the African Wildlife Foundation (1961–1969), vice president of the World Wildlife Foundation (1961–1969), and at the time the newly elected president of the Conservation Foundation (1965–1969). The committee was assembled and coordinated by officers of the National Park Service, the agency that had implemented the conservation of designated natural and historic sites in the United States since 1916 (Train 1972). The committee imagined the World Heritage Trust as a support system to the conservation of natural and historic sites in poor countries through the contributions of rich countries. The main mechanism for the allocation of the trust funds was a "register of world heritage sites," assembled and managed by a competent board of directors. The "Register" was the name of the record of landmarks kept by the National Park Service ("register of historic places"). The notion of "trust" belonged to the language of Anglo-American philanthropy and referred to the voluntary nature of contributions that this fund would solicit.

The project was not immediately taken up by the administration, but the election of Richard Nixon in 1969 put it back on the U.S. foreign policy

agenda. The Vietnam War had become a global spectacle of total technological warfare waged on both humans and nature. The United States was frequently portrayed as the ultimate environmental villain, and this portrayal
further damaged its international reputation (Lewis 1985). The new administration, at pains to pacify both domestic and foreign liberals, made environmental policy a priority. In 1969 Russell Train was named undersecretary of
the Department of the Interior before he became, a year later, chairman of
the Council on Environmental Quality (CEQ) in charge of elaborating new
policy frameworks. In December 1970 the CEQ gave birth to the Environmental Protection Agency (EPA), and Russell Train became its administrator.
Through Train, the trust project had gained an advocate at the center of the
American political system.

In September 1971 international delegations met to prepare the U.N.
Conference on the Human Environment (known today as the Conference of
Stockholm), which was to take place in the fall of 1972, and Train headed the
American delegation. He seized the occasion to bring to the table a version of
his 1965 proposal of a world heritage trust. Unexpectedly, the U.S. proposal
was joined by two similar proposals with distinct origins. One was the Stockholm committee's own project for a "World Heritage Foundation," solicited in
February 1971, drafted by the IUCN and the Food and Agriculture Organization (Batisse and Bolla 2003: 19–20), and introduced by Fischer in April in the
form of a draft convention. Because of Fischer's involvement in the 1965 U.S.
Trust project, this proposal was largely based on the latter. The other proposal
was a "Convention on World Heritage" drafted by UNESCO experts on culture and sent to the Stockholm committee in the summer of 1971. The latter
convention was scheduled for submission to the General Conference in the
autumn of 1972. Where did this proposal come from?

UNESCO's Cultural Project: Fund and List

After the creation of UNESCO and of the International Council of Museums
(ICOM) in 1946, relevant parties in the international community debated
the possibility of establishing "an international fund to subsidize the maintenance and restoration work of monuments and sites" (Titchen 1995: 40). The
idea surfaced and was rejected twice over the following twenty years, due to
the opposition of several national delegations from both the North and the
South (in particular the United States, India, and Syria). For the U.S. government, the fund meant an obligation to finance projects that could not be easily

controlled and geared toward meeting American foreign policy interests. For developing countries, it meant a possible intrusion of Western powers into their internal affairs. By 1964 the consensus was that the preservation of ancient sites should remain out of the bounds of UNESCO's competence and that "each state ought to ensure the preservation of its monuments at the national level" (Titchen 1995: 46).

The historians and architects who served as administrators or advisors at UNESCO were the principal advocates for the fund. Director General Maheu was supportive of the project but lacked political backing. Starting in 1964, however, the situation changed in two ways. Inside UNESCO, culture professionals became more mobilized and organized. In the broader political world, public opinion became more receptive to the idea that "heritage" was "in danger."

Around 1964, the international community of art historians and archeologists mobilized around international preservation issues. This mobilization was the outcome of both long-term and immediate factors. The long-term factor was the progressive institutionalization of this community through international declarations and organizations since the 1930s. The 1931 Charter of Athens asserted the need to protect ancient architecture and marked the symbolic beginnings of international cultural cooperation in the field of heritage preservation (Titchen 1995). By placing the charter under the patronage of the League of Nations, professionals of historic conservation (historians of art and architecture, architects, and archeologists) took their claims out of the national institutions that had bred them since the nineteenth century onto the international scene (Choay [1991] 2001).

In 1964 this same community of professionals produced another document, the Venice Charter for the Conservation and Restoration of Monuments and Sites, signed by representatives of eighteen countries that thereby committed to tend to their historic monuments through adequate legislative and administrative procedures. The nongovernmental professional organization International Council on Monuments and Sites (ICOMOS), the cultural equivalent of IUCN, formed in the wake of the charter to serve as a pool of experts for the international community, especially through UNESCO. In practice, ICOMOS functions as a sort of union of historic conservation professionals (historians, archeologists, and other professionals of culture) representing their interests on the international scene. ICOMOS supplied the drafters of the UNESCO convention.

This professional mobilization was helped by contemporary events as well. International outrage erupted over the affair of the Aswan Dam in Egypt. When Gamal Abdel Nasser became president of Egypt, he touted his mission to be the modernization of the country. A standard trope of modernization was the building of a dam and the provision of mass electrification. As the Nasser administration began planning the dam's construction in 1959, concerns emerged over the fate of the country's cultural heritage. The planned dam would flood parts of the Nubian lands and its temples. The archeological community and the global world of educated literati stood in shock. In the West the story was widely publicized and covered by the press. The temples of Philae and Abu Simbel had been fetishes of Western tourism and archeology since the nineteenth century. Both Egyptian and Sudanese governments petitioned UNESCO for help in saving the historic sites threatened by the dam. Rene Maheu launched a long and broad fund-raising and media campaign resulting in the collection of $80 million. The money allowed extensive archeological surveys of the area as well as the reconstruction of fourteen temples, stone by stone, on a mount hovering over the valley, where they still stand today. The operation did not benefit the Egyptian tourist industry only, however. The Kennedy administration received an important compensation for its support through the "gift" of one of the temples by the Egyptian state—the Temple of Dendur, rebuilt in the Metropolitan Museum in 1967.

Because similar campaigns were happening in Venice and Florence and because the attempt to salvage the Philae and Abu Simbel temples were successful and widely talked about, the question of a permanent fund for the protection of cultural heritage became an obvious priority for UNESCO. The Nubian episode had provided the cosmopolitan middle-class and the international community of culture professionals with a model for promoting and developing an international policy of historic conservation. The professionals' hope for a more systematic and more binding arrangement took the form of the Venice Charter. Meanwhile, Maheu's campaigns had created not only public support in the North but also demand from the South.

The General Conference, in its fourteenth session of 1966, finally granted the director general the role of "coordinat[ing] and secur[ing] the international adoption of appropriate principles of scientific, technical and legal criteria for the protection of cultural property, monuments and sites" (Francioni 2008: 24). The fund project was back on tracks. Experts met in February 1968 to elaborate the principles of cooperation. Thirteen countries (the United

States, five Western European countries, three countries from the Eastern bloc, two from Asia, one from the Middle East, and one from Africa) were represented together with international nongovernmental organizations, including ICOMOS. The U.S. project of a World Heritage Trust (developed in 1965) was introduced at that point as a possible template for coordination (Titchen 1995). The expert group was expanded considerably to include more national representatives before it gathered again in 1969 and concluded with recommendations in July 1970.

The UNESCO group recommended that the list be established through a system of petitions for international aid from national states rather than from a supranational administrative or scientific body. The goal was to avoid legal and political conflicts between national regulations and international decisions—a concern that had dampened support for the fund. Experts insisted that the list should be highly selective and "spectacular" in order to secure the kind of international public support that had been manifested during the Nubian and Venetian campaigns. At the same time, the list should demonstrate its universality by representing the world's geographic and cultural diversity. Natural sites were excluded from the list. Finally, the group recommended that the policy be framed in the form of a binding convention between state parties rather than as a voluntary trust (Titchen 1995: 59–60). In October 1970 the General Conference of UNESCO decided that the expert group would finalize a draft convention by April 1972. The work of cultural experts remained confidential until the General Conference of 1970 (Batisse and Bolla 2003: 16). The Science Department of UNESCO then became aware of it and brought this information to the organizing meetings of the Stockholm conference at the beginning of 1971.

UNESCO Meets the U.S. Delegation: Merging Projects

The memoirs written by two UNESCO officials about the 1970–1972 period (Batisse and Bolla 2003) provide clear evidence of the tensions and power struggles that emerged when all parties involved attempted to preserve control of their respective project. UNESCO, whose views were represented by Maheu, was generally worried that the conference would impinge on its own environmentalist territory. The cultural services division of UNESCO, staffed by Europeans trained in a humanist culture that saw culture and the natural environment as mutually exclusive entities, were expressly insensitive to environmental issues. Going in the opposite direction, the IUCN radicalized its positions by reducing culture in its draft to a nonentity in an attempt to preserve the specificity of its proposal. This put an end to the already shaky support of the American delegation, intent on keeping nature and culture joined in one project, causing its temporary withdrawal from the negotiation. As to the Food and Agriculture Organization (FAO), it considered the environment its own domain over and above UNESCO.

By mid-1971 both IUCN and the cultural offices of UNESCO were favoring the option of two separate conventions. This introduced a divergence of interests between the cultural services of UNESCO and UNESCO as a whole. The objective risk was for the organization to end up with two competing agreements that would undermine the symbolic effect of each of them. Even worse, it could lose one of the projects to either the FAO or to a new, independent trust. The organization could not ignore the strong environmentalist momentum. All participants were generally at risk of ruining a project that they had spent years elaborating. The only reasonable path for UNESCO was to overcome its cultural staff's reticence, enter a negotiation with the Stockholm Preparatory Committee, argue that its convention could easily integrate natural sites, appear open to the IUCN and FAO initiatives, and thus become the sole stewards of the only World Heritage Convention in the world.

To this end, the UNESCO administration gave jurisdiction over both negotiations and any future draft of the convention to its science department. Equally devoted to their organization and to their environmentally inclined discipline, the scientific staff put their professional networks in the Stockholm circles in the service of mediation. On the Stockholm side, the preparatory committee thought that no effective legal agreement could be reached without or outside of UNESCO and took the matter out of the hands of a working group too inclined to support IUCN and the FAO. On both sides, thus, the upper administrative echelons dominated expert factions.

The final denouement was only made possible by the return of the U.S. delegation, however. After being overshadowed by the IUCN initiative for many months, the delegation decided to act on two types of commitments: the U.S. government's commitment to the model of a voluntary "trust" and the American environmentalist community's commitment to the joint protection of nature and culture under one institutional umbrella. When the preparatory committee requested to see UNESCO's draft convention (summer 1971), the U.S. delegation produced its own unsolicited draft convention in prevision of the new round of negotiations that was likely to open. Over the heads of the Stockholm organizers, they sent it directly to UNESCO (Batisse and Bolla 2003: 29–30, 74–75). The U.S. draft came with a request. Because UNESCO would probably be the organizational base from which future versions of the agreement would be discussed, they were asked to consider the American project and to merge it into one with their own. UNESCO representatives were invited to Washington to discuss the merger. They welcomed a chance to demonstrate their organization's capacity and complete willingness to protect nature in order to gain the support of Washington. Washington, for its part, advocated again for a voluntary trust model. UNESCO officers, while demonstrating their competence and openness, managed to postpone further discussion of financial issues to the moment of the next General Conference. Washington supported the shift of the discussions from Stockholm to UNESCO.

Between April and July 1972, UNESCO's expert group met again and conjoined the cultural and the environmentalist projects, somewhat tuning down the cultural focus of their document. The project was featured in Stockholm and stamped with the conference's seal of approval in the summer of 1972. Beyond the substantive point of including nature, the document only minimally accommodated most U.S. requests. The "World Heritage Trust" became a fund for "heritage in danger." With the overwhelming support of experts from developing countries, the model of voluntary contributions, which was favored by the United States and Germany and gave powerful donors political control over the uses of the funds, was abandoned.

The concept of a register of sites established from above was transformed into a list to be made through a bottom-up application process. Besides the list of world heritage in danger, a longer list of world heritage tout court gave access to the purely symbolic reward of a label and served as a mechanism of enticement for state members to flesh out and update their national institutions. The WH list became the centerpiece of the final convention through a long Article 11, which imparted on state members the obligation of establishing national registers, through nationwide surveys to be completed according to international scientific standards. Article 11 confided the board function, mentioned in U.S. documents, to a World Heritage Committee in charge of designations and of fund allocations. The WH Committee was a device advocated by legal experts from developing countries that mitigated the power of IUCN and ICOMOS through the buffer of an independent bureaucracy.

The WH Convention was endorsed by the General Assembly in November 1972, after more debate about the sources and budget of the fund, and signed by 120 member states (Francioni 2008). In a speech to the U.S. Senate in 1973, President Nixon explained the functions of the new WH Convention as follows:

> [It creates] international machinery for the identification and protection of natural and cultural areas of outstanding universal value which constitute the common heritage of mankind. For this purpose, the Convention establishes a World Heritage Committee to develop and maintain lists of areas of outstanding importance and a World Heritage Fund to provide international assistance for the protection and conservation of these areas. While the Convention places basic reliance on the resources and efforts of the States within whose territory these natural and cultural sites are located, it would also provide means of assisting States which have insufficient resources or expertise in the protection of areas for the benefit of all mankind. (Quoted in Titchen 1995: 70)

The first applications reached the committee in 1974, and the convention actually came into effect in December 1975. The first meeting of the committee took place in 1977. The first round of twelve designations was published in 1978. The number of state parties to the convention today is 186, and the average number of places being designated as WH sites is around twenty-seven yearly. By 2009 the general list included 890 sites—689 cultural, 176 natural, and 25 mixed properties distributed across 148 countries.

Explaining the Convention: Mechanisms of Cultural Capitalization

As several contributions in this volume point out, the creation of value on the markets of what is conventionally called "cultural goods" (*biens culturels, beni culturali*), is the outcome of complex processes of strategic and symbolic interaction. The production of cultural value follows communicative and strategic paths—sometimes straight, sometimes meandering—that make sense only in light of the historical events that make the concerns of some groups resonate with a larger public. While the eventful genesis of the WH convention confirms the significance of global economic and political power relations in the cultural field, it suggests the crucial importance of temporality in affecting the specific outcomes of these relations. It also highlights the essential role of relatively autonomous cultural bureaucrats and other cultural policy actors in initiating and shaping the mode of value production for World Heritage Sites.

By "mode of value production" I mean the set of rules and resources (Sewell 1992) that, without necessarily determining specific courses of action, have a lasting and structuring impact on value-producing practices. Before identifying significant aspects of this autonomous structure of practice and its effects on WH designations, let us analyze the constitutive impact of historical contingency on power struggles.

Historical Contingency and Power

The convention came out of an encounter between two distinct movements that grew autonomously from each other for a period of about eight years. One was environmental; the other, cultural. These movements found support in two distinct sets of organizations: environmentalist agencies (the U.S. National Park Service and IUCN) supported by some Western governments (U.S. and Scandinavian) and a mobilized international community of cultural experts and academics organized through ICOMOS, supported by an international organization (UNESCO) and by a growing clientele of Third World governments.

The cultural project met the opposition of both First and Third World players for about two decades within UNESCO (1946 until the mid-1960s). As demonstrated by the failure to implement the U.S. Park Service project in 1965, the latter did not receive political support before 1969, the year of Nixon's arrival to power with an environmentalist and ideological agenda to improve the country's political standing on the international scene. Various constituencies of U.N. members became keener to support the World Heritage project after the latter was accepted by developing countries with regional power, such as Egypt or Syria. Establishing the World Heritage system was thus largely dependent on the contingent transformation of political or geopolitical interests and on their dialogical convergence. Without changes in the global geopolitical conjuncture, and without the success of UNESCO's Nubian experiment, these interests might not have been realized.

The contingency of geopolitical strategies is certainly relative to a broader political-economic structure of interests, as suggested by the important role played by the U.S. in the negotiation. Persistent, stark and growing distributional inequalities across the North and South also point in this direction (Smith 2006; Zouain 1997). On the current list, 40 percent of sites are located in Europe and 20 percent in North America, securing a comfortable 60 percent for the developed world (against 50 percent in 1996). This leaves a declining 10 percent to both Africa and the Middle East, a declining 15 percent to Asia, and a slightly better performance for Latin America, which now totals 15 percent of WH designations. In spite of greater numbers of applications and designations in Africa and the Middle East, skyrocketing numbers of applications from Northern countries, especially from Europe, have delivered the lion's share of designations to the already advantaged.

This correlation between political-economic power and WH designations makes it tempting to explain the convention in functionalist terms, by reference to the interests of powerful nation-states involved in its creation and operation. The present analysis suggests, however, that the causation process is more convoluted than the correlation suggests and its outcome, largely unintentional, cannot be conceived as an explanation. The convention was perceived *at a certain point* as an instrument of domination by the U.S. government but not so consistently before and even after that point. The support of the U.S. government was secured only through a contingent negotiation process in which other actors sometimes prevailed. While being drafted, the convention became an emergent site on which the global power structure was not simply played out but also fiercely challenged. In fact, the United States and other rich countries failed to impose the procedures that most mattered to them. The mandatory fund and voluntary application process, two crucial features obtained by Third World actors with the support of UNESCO professionals, in particular, meant that major funders lost direct control over both list and fund.

The convention, besides, was precisely *not* crafted as an instrument of power. It was imagined by professionals of culture, environmentalists, and scientists as a pragmatic redistributive device to protect objects of symbolic and scientific interest in countries deprived of adequate infrastructure. As in any developmentalist project, perhaps, good intentions were subverted by the interplay of contingent strategies and power struggles. The core element of the redistributive system originally imagined by scientists and activists—the fund—remained throughout the negotiation one of the most problematic issues. Its budget in the end amounted to a few million dollars reserved for extreme cases of "heritage in danger" in poor countries. When compared to the amount raised by Maheu during the Nubian campaign, the paucity of the fund appears to owe mostly to successful resistance on the part of powerful U.N. members to fund projects on which they had no direct control.

Transformed into a mandatory fund, the "trust" became relatively marginal in the final version of the convention—the "heritage in danger" label to which it is attached serves primarily today to warn neglectful states of the possibility of label withdrawal. The normative tool (the list) was thus de-coupled from its redistributive counterpart (the fund) and became a purely symbolic marker of cultural value. The move was supported by Third World countries concerned about their own sovereignty and/or local influence. We know how time and usage transformed this symbolic measure into the most effective mechanism of cultural wealth production afforded to member states by the convention. In the 1980s the label appeared to confer prestige on sites that could be then more easily promoted on the international tourist market, securing considerable economic dividends to these sites' national custodians. By the mid-1990s, the number and increasingly diverse origins of applications made the label one of the most solid cultural institutions in the world.

The original system of direct redistribution was thus superseded by a more liberal alternative based on symbolic enticement and voluntary applications. Usage proved this system to be structurally biased in favor of wealthy countries with the infrastructure required to turn natural and cultural resources into eligible World Heritage sites and labeled sites into development poles. While it squares particularly well with today's neoliberal order, the system-specific structure remains an unintended product of relatively contingent strategies.

Practice as Structure: Cultural Capitalization

The eventful genesis of the WH system makes it clear that the concept for the convention, with its two pillars of the fund and the list, originated primarily from the symbolic interests of mobilized communities of environmentalists, scientists, and cultural experts. These communities bore the project with persistence over almost two decades, in part independently from each other, and over and against lasting political hostility, until their efforts finally caught the wind of changing political strategies. The commitment of some individual figures to the scientists' and humanists' cause, such as UNESCO Director General Rene Maheu, himself an academic by training, or environmentalist turned upper-rank administrative officer Russell Train, afforded lasting institutional support to this collective mobilization and ultimately permitted to resolve disciplinary differences and organizational conflicts within the movement.

The decisive role of experts in initiating, supporting, and shaping the convention stands as a reminder that cultural wealth in modern, highly differentiated polities tends to be produced by relatively autonomous cultural producers (Bourdieu 1993a). It is, therefore, more likely to be generated through the mediation of this field rather than directly by either contingent encounters or political and economic systems. What was then the specific role of cultural producers in creating the WH system as a means of production of cultural value? What are the *rules and resources* structuring the field and the practice of contemporary conservancy and, through it, the production of cultural wealth by national and international institutions?

Two groups composed of distinct professionals (IUCN natural scientists and ICOMOS humanities scholars) conceived of similar conservationist projects in the same time period of about four years (1964–1968), without apparent mutual influence and in spite of missing political support. And while some intense competition between agencies representing distinct disciplines threatened to divide the convention in to several, less powerful projects, their ultimate convergence and merging in the spring of 1972 was fast and uneventful. Key to the relatively easy merge was the formal similarity between the documents and the profound agreement between the parties involved in their merging about the meaning of "heritage" and the means of its conservation. Heritage was a material resource and a capital to be managed and augmented. Its conservation required selective knowledge accumulation through lists allowing for "rational" intervention on physical sites and objects.

Lists are part of a well-established bureaucratic-scientific "tool kit" (Swidler 1986) in both natural and historic conservancy. Since the early modern period, nature and culture have been preserved through the selective accumulation of valued material objects in a designated location (museum, park, library, archive, glass box, cabinet, site), allowing for their display, study, and leisurely contemplation by scholars, artists, or ordinary citizens (Bennett 1995; Duncan and Wallach 1980; Pomian [1987] 1990; Prior 2002). This process of physical accumulation and care is systematically accompanied by accumulation of a more symbolic type. Objects and their attributes are listed in visual and textual form through annotated lists, illustrated catalogues, and other inventories of collections. Whether by means of glass boxes, or of a paper inventory, or of an electronic database, contemporary conservancy relies on such characteristic apparatus of lists (Eco 2009; Herrero 2010). It is this structure of conditions for cultural accumulation that experts from IUCN, ICOMOS, and the National Park Service implemented when designing their convention scheme.

The diverse names of register, record, or list stand for thick and complex sets of formal procedures through which distinctions, in the sense of categories that are at once cognitive and evaluative (Bourdieu 1984), are created to discriminate among the numerous candidate sites. These procedures justify, in a rationalist mode, for example, the selective allocation of symbolic (listing) and financial (funding) resources. In the case of the WH system, the promoters of each candidate site make a thick historical argument to ensure that their site fulfils at least one of the ten criteria of "outstanding universal value." Its representativeness or rarity has to be assessed through a technical discussion of the findings of preliminary surveys of national or regional resources. The WH list is itself also a collection of factual and normative descriptions of sites.

Cultural wealth may thus be defined as an objective capital of symbolic goods that is managed through cumulative practices of documentary and physical conservation. Heritage acquires the value of a symbolic resource by being surveyed, recorded, and preserved. The logic of practice that endows it with symbolic value also provides the means of its conversion into economic value because symbolic valuation happens through a process of objectification that makes a site amenable to physical manipulation and thereby amenable to commodification. The totality of these practices is the mode of value production that I call "cultural capitalization."

This sociological definition of cultural wealth production sheds new light on the generative mechanisms that govern the contemporary political economy of cultural goods. Listing a World Heritage Site in accordance with the convention's procedures presupposes practices of cultural capitalization not just at the international level but also at the national level. Completing the kind of preliminary survey required by the scientific standards of the convention requires an apparatus of cognitive production and value creation that includes universities, disciplines, and scholars with minimal international recognition; a cultural and/or environmental bureaucracy employing scholars as experts or training its own experts; governmental and nongovernmental organizations employing cultural and/or environmental specialists; and a framework of laws prescribing conservation as a capacity of the state and the collective duty of the nation.

This system of extraction of symbolic value understandably gives a structural advantage to ancient, large, and well-trained cultural and environmental administrations. With a history reaching back to the eighteenth or nineteenth century, European and North American organizations can commit a substantive workforce to the costly field and archival research required to support comparative arguments. Experts in the North also rely on an ancient and externally recognized pool of previously accumulated knowledge and skills. The aggravation of distributional inequalities since the early 1990s, explained by the explosion of applications from Europe, where state decentralization has multiplied political centers, demonstrates the impact of this state-structural factor. UNESCO's failure to correct inequalities through technical assistance and methodological reform over the past twenty years also shows that the unequal distribution of global cultural wealth is solidly rooted in the historical trajectories of states.

Since the early 1980s, indeed, the UNESCO administration has been aware of the biases that threaten the legitimacy of its list. Every new set of operational guidelines has addressed the problem. Universality was defined in operational ways, as geographic and quantitative representativeness, to allow for better control of biases and representations. In 1999 the "global approach" doctrine reiterated the methodological necessity of conducting preliminary national surveys (drawing up tentative lists) to better control the representativeness of the WH list. Preliminary technical assistance to poor countries was improved to entice and help them develop these surveys as well as strong applications. The categories of legitimate heritage defined by UNESCO have long privileged "cultural" over "natural" sites; religious over secular monuments; architectural and material vestiges over expressive and intangible productions—in brief, objects that Western science is well trained to identify, study, and single out, over others. In the early 1990s experts started elaborating new categories, introducing, for example, the notion of cultural landscape (1992) to better capture types of heritage that traditional art-historical approaches tended to ignore. The 2003 convention for the protection of intangible heritage pursued the same end.

If the WH system has maintained and even increased Eurocentrism in the list, it is thus not for a lack of critical understandings about how value is socially constructed (Taylor 2009) but due rather to the structural selectivity of cultural capitalization itself. The mode of production of cultural capital is predicated on states' capacity for symbolic accumulation, that is, on the solid apparatus of experts and institutions that only dominant states have. Experts and, through them, the expert-based designation process involuntarily reinforce the structural biases of this system when they insist, as they tend to do, on fixing its flaws through such devices as the "tentative list" and the extensive "national surveys" of cultural resources.

Conclusion

The drafting and adoption of the 1972 convention was part of a process of formation of a global field of heritage preservation, itself the outcome of the professionalization and bureaucratization of the scientific field at the international level. This process made material culture convertible into a resource to be managed and accumulated by procedural means—legal, technical, and bureaucratic. More than a pleasant metaphor, and beyond any form of economistic reductionism, the notion of cultural wealth is a literal descriptor for what is a historically entrenched social fact—the speculative relationship to the symbolic in contemporary society.

The genesis of the World Heritage system shows that knowledge producers played a decisive role in shaping some key mechanisms of symbolic speculation through which national policies create cultural value. The benefits of taking full account of this role are multiple. For social theory, examinations of the mode of cultural wealth production contribute to a more nuanced and complete explanation of the symbolic inequalities in the world system of states and of their correlation with economic inequalities. From an empirical point of view, the finding opens new research questions—for example, about the role of national and international experts in the design and implementation of specific projects of economic development through cultural capitalization (such as the regional *Ruta Maya* program analyzed by Jennifer Bair in Chapter 8 of this volume). Finally, from a critical perspective, awareness of the relatively autonomous role of cultural producers in creating new forms of symbolic inequality or in entrenching old ones, reroutes our cultural critiques toward more relevant targets. The WH administration, for example, cannot be said to mystify the unequal distribution of heritage designations if it has actually been struggling with the problem of distributional inequality for decades and if its original mission was to function as a redistributive mechanism. The question is rather why redistribution failed and what part the WH system played, as an autonomous system of value production, in this failure. Examining practices of cultural capitalization helps us better understand symbolic and correlated material inequalities around the world.

4 Selling Beauty

Tuscany's Rural Landscape since 1945

Dario Gaggio

IN THE COURSE OF THE LAST FEW DECADES, rural Tuscany has come to enjoy global iconic status. One only needs to turn the TV on or take a walk in any shopping mall in North America or northern Europe to witness an abundance of diverse references to Tuscan life. Countless middlebrow novels, memoirs, movies, and television shows celebrate the homey pleasures or piquant adventures to be experienced "under the Tuscan sun." Few chain restaurants resist the temptation to add the adjective "Tuscan" to their chicken pesto sandwiches or bean soups, often accompanying these linguistic references with pictures of farmhouses and cypress trees. These linguistic and visual signs conjure up notions of harmonious beauty in historically unique settings, unspoiled by the tensions of modernity. But Tuscany and the sensorial constructs associated with it are not only icons; they are also brands. The Tuscan chicken pesto sandwich will sell more easily or for a higher price than a generic, supposedly less original and authentic, product. This chapter deals with the association and tension between the cypress tree and the dollar sign (that is, between symbolic representation and economic value) and with the ways in which this tension relates to Tuscany as an actual social and historical formation.

Tuscany possesses remarkable cultural wealth, in the sense that the representations of its landscape and history have served as a form of capital, convertible into economic wealth and social prestige. How Tuscany accumulated its cultural wealth, however, provides a cautionary tale for governments or private sector actors attempting to generate cultural wealth out of thin air. Cultural wealth accumulation has not been a linear process in Tuscany, nor has it been uncontroversial to decide what aspects of the Tuscan landscape and heritage would come to be seen as desirable. Policy decisions made for completely different goals have had important, but unintended, effects on Tuscany's cultural wealth. Moreover, the involvement of many uncontrolled, and uncontrollable, actors has meant that there was no single institution that could dictate the features of the Tuscan landscape and the management of its representations. This was especially the case in the three decades after the end of World War II, before the landscape came to be deemed to possess universal value. This lack of singular control meant that the objects and images that became "typical" for the area emerged in the course of interactions among the various actors. Some of these emergent images have become iconic and are therefore obvious candidates for branding.

In this chapter I will first provide a theoretical discussion of the relationships between symbolic and economic value when applied to landscape representations and practices. In particular, I will focus on the tensions between iconicity and branding, making the case that it is the potential conflict between the two that is most productive of value and that the historical processes through which societies navigate this tension are often fraught with contentious negotiations and contingencies. Landscape, a public good whose images can be nonetheless appropriated and marketed for a variety of purposes, is an ideal terrain to investigate the processes through which societies convert symbolic value into economic wealth. I will then show how for several decades after the end of World War II rural Tuscany became the stage for a variety of competing development projects, aimed at stemming the area's depopulation and marginalization. In this phase, the valorization of the landscape was only one of several strategies to be proposed and certainly not the one most widely shared among rural Tuscans and their political leaders. It was only in the late 1970s that a complex and largely unintended convergence of local and extralocal processes made landscape conservation and valorization a hegemonic option for Tuscany's future. I locate this shift in specific institutional venues, especially the newly empowered regional government, and illustrate how valorization was predicated on specific policies targeting areas as diverse as the regulation of housing supply and particular forms of rural tourism. It was the relative failure of many of the modernization strategies envisaged in the immediate postwar decades that made landscape valorization a successful path to relative prosperity in more recent decades. This focus on landscape conservation and valorization, however, remains contentious to this day, and the rent that accrues to Tuscany's accumulated cultural wealth depends on delicate and often tenuous political compromises among a variety of actors, who keep interpreting Tuscany's rural landscape and heritage in quite different ways.

Iconicity, Branding, and Landscape

Scholars have only recently begun to explore the notion of iconicity from a social perspective, in the wake of the spatial and visual turns taken by several disciplines (Burke 2001; Ethington and Schwartz 2006). In this context, an icon is a particular kind of aesthetically (usually visually) appreciated symbol. But icons are particular kinds of symbols that develop from two kinds of tensions. First, icons need to be repeated and reproduced without losing their distinctiveness. In other words, icons must be widely legible by a collectivity without losing their aura. Second, icons originate from the tension between representation and presence, to use the language introduced by art historian Hans Belting (1994). In other words, icons are symbols "impressed with" the power of the real thing. An icon of Christ was supposed to be impressed with Christ's true features. Remember Saint Veronica, who offered Jesus a piece of cloth on his way to Golgotha and received the impression of his features in return. It can be argued that modern icons still receive their power and salience through their connection with the "true image" or the authentic narrative to which they refer. In sum, an image becomes an icon when it comes to possess symbolic value, and such value is bestowed on the image through its association and connection to a shared narrative of authenticity. An image of the Tuscan hills, for example, becomes iconic when it is believed to be the aesthetic reflection of an idyllic life style dating back to premodern times: The idyllic character of this life style is believed to have produced and preserved the beauty of the landscape.

The icon's symbolic value may be converted into economic value through a process of branding. A successful brand is a sign that is capable of commanding a rent (that is, extra value) in the market. Of course not all brands are iconic, although most brand promoters pursue a variety of strategies to increase the iconicity of their brands (that is, their association with images or narratives of authenticity), for example by placing their branded products in movies or television shows (Holt 2004) or in actual social settings in operations of "social marketing" (Lury 2005: 191). Conversely, many icons never become brands. Some icons indeed exist in seemingly irreconcilable opposition to branding and commercial value. This is the case, for example, with many religious and political icons, whose auras rely on being perceived as above the realm of the market. The sacredness of these icons stems precisely from their seeming distance and/or overt hostility to commercial considerations, and entire institutional apparatuses are built with the purpose of keeping God and Mammon strictly apart. The Catholic Church, for example, pursues a variety of strategies to avoid the commercial exploitation of images of the Virgin or the saints.

When the branding of an icon is successful, the outcome is the creation of an iconic brand. In the case of successful iconic brands, the interaction of the two tensions on which iconicity relies (distinctiveness versus repetition, and presence versus representation) gives rise to a third one, sacredness versus commodification. In other words, an iconic brand is a symbol that perpetuates without pose the tension between the narrative of authenticity that produces the icon's symbolic value and the commercial strategy that undergirds branding and produces economic value. As Celia Lury maintains, a successful brand is a set of heterogeneous relations between products that must preserve its coherence over time. Unlike price, which organizes economic exchange through mere representation and quantitative equivalence, "the brand comprises (some of) the world itself" (Lury 2004: 4). Therefore, iconic brands rely on a delicate balance that is quite vulnerable. The iconic brand, for example, can be marketed so heavily as to suffer from overexposure, producing too much reproduction and too little distinctiveness. Even worse, the narrative of authenticity to which the iconic brand refers may lose its credibility, in which case the image becomes a representation without presence and ceases to be an iconic brand altogether. In such cases, consumers may come to believe that the iconic brand has sold out, in the worst possible sense of the expression. So far, Tuscany has been remarkably successful in avoiding these pitfalls, and I will explore the historically rooted reasons for this success in the rest of this chapter.

All iconic brands are vulnerable and unstable, but the emergence of geographically defined iconic brands is a particularly delicate process: Places are complex categories, and the management of their meanings is often outside of any one actor's control because such meanings are mediated in a myriad ways and subject to unpredictable events (Ward 1998). Such vulnerability goes a long way toward explaining why the iconic branding of places is such a profitable activity and why these profits are often relatively widely shared: Precisely because of their vulnerability, iconic places are quite rare, and their branding is seldom the preserve of a few powerful actors.

Tourism is of course the industry most interested in the promotion of iconic places, but many other activities (local crafts, the production and marketing of foods, and even cultural productions such as cinema and literature) rely on their value-producing aura. Following Dean MacCanell (1976), I argue that tourists generally visit Tuscany in a search for authenticity, defined as an experience of coherence and totality, contrasted with the fractured and relatively meaningless character of the tourist's perception of modernity. Like in a modern form of pilgrimage, MacCanell maintains, the tourist collects such experiences of authenticity in the ongoing attempt to make herself whole. But I also argue that in rural Tuscany the local population actively participated in the construction of authenticity, searching for meaning and coherence with even more determination than the tourists. I argue that such participation was crucial to the successful production of Tuscany as an internationally recognized iconic place. This emphasis on the relational character of authenticity, as well as on its heterogeneous dimensions, dovetails with much recent sociological reflection. Following Frederick Wherry, for example, authenticity should not be understood as residing in a product but in the social conditions of its production (Wherry 2006: 24). In a similar vein, the quest for authenticity, however unattainable, organizes highly diverse social actors around specific performances and expectations (Grazian 2003). In the Tuscan case, this search for coherence, which structured the interactions between locals and tourists, has reinvented the landscape as a legible system of signs. Legibility, however, relied on a drastic process of selection and simplification, which entailed the erasure of the narratives that did not fit the newly marketable image of Tuscany as symbolically represented in its landscape.

Landscape is one of the most debated and controversial concepts in human geography and a term widely used in many other disciplines (Wylie 2007). In the scholarly literature the term *landscape* appears in a broad variety of ways, sometimes figuratively, to denote subjective perceptions or representations that illustrate the sensibilities of individuals or collectivities (Steedman 1984), and other times literally, as the stage on which action unfolds and the shared spatial structure that allows social change to "take place" and that is transformed in the process (Braudel 1972). Not all senses of landscape are representational, but to become iconic a landscape needs to be widely represented and recognized. Any represented landscape suggests particular "ways of seeing" (Cosgrove 1984) and "structures of feeling" (Williams 1977) belonging to its author and intended audience, but it simultaneously entertains specific relations (whether imagined or real) with the material territory to which it refers. Landscape representations are also crucial to the formation of national identity, although this process of selection was more controversial in Italy than in other European countries (Agnew 2002).

Even though any landscape representation is always a reified snapshot of something inevitably more complex and dynamic, in an iconic image of a landscape this process of reification is somehow masked or suspended, so that the onlooker can "believe" in it. Not unlike the icon of Christ, the photograph of the Tuscan hills is believed to be the depiction of something authentic—of a coherent civilization or of a particular relationship between an artist and his or her physical surroundings. Thus, an iconic landscape must be legible as a system of signs produced by a coherent civilization and/or by an inspired artist, and it must be endowed with the sacred aura capable of transmitting an experience of wholeness. A branded iconic landscape is born of the careful marketing of this experience. In reinventing and marketing the landscape, rural Tuscans have come to redefine themselves.

The Crisis of Sharecropping and the Rural Exodus

If particular images of the Tuscan landscape are to be imagined as depictions of an authentic civilization, what kind of civilization forged the historical landscape of the Tuscan hills? As a first approximation, the Tuscan rural landscape can be said to be the product of the historic sharecropping system (*mezzadria*), a form of land tenure once pervasive in the hilly areas of north-central Italy (Giorgetti 1974; Sereni 1997). Classical *mezzadria* was imagined for centuries as a partnership between a landlord, who provided most of the capital necessary for agriculture, and the head of a peasant family, who contributed his labor and that of his relatives. Peasants lived in scattered farms of varying size, often in relatively large multigenerational or extended families. Sharecroppers were to divide the revenue of their toil with the landowner: Usually half of it stayed with the peasants (who consumed most of it), and half went to the landlord (who sold it to pay his middlemen and buy the many things that urban life offered). Most large-scale Tuscan landowners did not participate directly in the management of their farms, for which they hired middlemen (the *fattori*). In the larger estates, the landlord had a villa, where he spent some pleasant times hunting and entertaining (the so-called *villeggiatura*). In proximity to the villa stood the *fattoria*, where the produce was collected and stored, the wine and oil were produced, and the accounting books, which documented who owed what to whom, were kept. Sharecropping created a landscape of scattered farmhouses placed in the middle of manicured mixed cultivations, including wheat, vines, olive trees, fruit trees, fodder, and all the products the peasant family needed for subsistence (and the landlord for his conveniently diversified, and therefore safe, rent). This layer of rural settlement and cultivations, which developed over several centuries starting in the late Middle Ages, lay over an older early medieval layer of castles, which morphed into hilltop villages where craftspeople, day laborers, and the local middle class lived.

The sharecropping system entered its irreversible crisis during the Nazi-Fascist occupation of 1943–1944 and in the aftermath of World War II (Mori 1986). Tuscan sharecroppers aided the activities of the insurgents (the partisans) during the Resistance, and rural Tuscany was the site of several retaliatory massacres of civilians carried out by the German occupiers and their Italian collaborators. The legacy of the Resistance, however flexible and contested, forged a strong and long-lasting bond between most Tuscan peasants (both sharecroppers and day laborers) and the political organizations of the Left, above all the Communist Party and the organizations affiliated with it (Orlandini and Venturini 1980). These experiences, coupled with the expectations of the returning soldiers, created a climate of social tension that many observers characterized as prerevolutionary. The four years between Liberation in the summer of 1944 and the failed assassination attempt on Communist leader Palmiro Togliatti in July 1948 constituted the most volatile period, but the landowning classes faced the possibility of full-blown insurrections well into the 1950s. These conflicts ensured that the Tuscan countryside would no longer appear as a silent and marginal space, as it had for centuries before 1900, or as an area to be paternalistically managed from above, as had been the case under Fascism. Rather, after 1945 rural Tuscany seemed to matter on its own terms for the first time in its long history, as a front in the Cold War that was being fought at the national and international levels and as a space defiant of the increasingly conservative trends prevailing at the national level.

After the war, the Italian Communists no longer focused exclusively on the virtues of land collectivization, as they had done for decades, but their political message was anything but coherent and univocal, wavering between the defense of small-scale ownership against allegedly monopolistic landlords and the promotion of cooperatives as a stage toward more radical scenarios.

Some historians have persuasively argued that the main appeal of the Marxist forces in rural Tuscany was not strictly ideological but rather broadly social and cultural (Ballini, Lotti, and Rossi 1991). For the first time, national political forces did not descend on the land with simple hegemonic goals but organically integrated with local societies, letting a new political class deeply rooted in the territory emerge from within the peasants themselves. For the first time, for example, peasants and the sons (sometimes even the daughters) of peasants became mayors and local administrators of towns across the region. Whatever else they might have been standing for, the Communists seemed to be willing to let the peasants speak for themselves, and in front of an audience that crossed national and even international boundaries (Bonifazi 1979). This perception of spontaneous autonomy and organic integration between political and civil society should be taken with a grain of salt, but as a myth it proved resilient and inspiring at the local level. If myths of harmony and class collaboration had sentenced Tuscan peasants to silence and irrelevance for centuries, now struggle and class insubordination would finally force the powers that be to listen and realize that ordinary peasants could no longer be ignored.

The sharecroppers were not so much defeated as defused—by the stalling strategies of the landlords, who refused to invest in their farms; by the national government, dominated by the conservative Christian Democrats, who offered incentives to individual peasants to open mortgages and become small-scale farmers without a comprehensive land reform; and by the industrialization of several areas of Tuscany itself, also favored by the availability of cheap labor. Starting in the mid-1950s, Tuscan sharecroppers began to leave their farms behind, in what contemporaries called, with Biblical language, the rural exodus. Tuscan agriculture shed two-thirds of its workforce from the early 1950s to the early 1970s. Even though Tuscan peasants, especially the younger ones, left the farms in droves, they typically did not go very far. Between 1955 and 1960, for example, 437,000 people changed commune of residence without leaving Tuscany, while 155,000 arrived from other regions, in the presence of very modest emigration flows. Moreover, most migrants did not move to Florence, the regional capital, transforming it into a large city like Milan or Rome; the Tuscan city that grew the most in the 1950s and 1960s was the textile center of Prato, followed by Grosseto, Tuscany's southernmost provincial capital (L'Abate 1964). These data help explain why the exodus combined the genuine trauma of displacement with the development of new kinds of ties between town and country. Former peasants radically changed their lifestyle, but they could almost see their places of origin from their apartment windows.

Not coincidentally, the areas that are now the most iconic were affected by depopulation particularly hard. The southern half of the Chianti, just north of Siena, had lost more than half of its population by the early 1980s. The same is true of the Orcia valley, south of Siena, since 2004 one of UNESCO's World Heritage Sites because of its landscape. Depopulation had an enormous impact on the land. The system of mixed cultivations typical of *mezzadria*, which relied on vast amounts of (largely unpaid) manual labor, began to disappear. It is now virtually extinct. Uncultivated land expanded, as the legibility of the territory declined accordingly. Many mixed vineyards fell into complete disrepair. Houses, terraced fields, and entire villages followed the same destiny.[1] In sum, by the late 1960s, this had become a landscape of ruins, a monument to the powers of attraction of urban modernity—in a sense, the exact opposite of what Tuscany stands for today.

No space embodied these contradictions more poignantly than the share-croppers' houses. Starting shortly after Liberation, Tuscan peasants began to protest their living conditions, drawing attention to the pitiful state of the buildings in which they lived.[2] The landlords balked at making major (and sometimes even minor) investments at such politically and economically uncertain times, and this unwillingness or inability to invest led of course to a general deterioration of the housing stock. Tuscan peasants began to compare their living conditions to those of other social classes, finding their traditional living arrangements increasingly inadequate. They clamored to have their houses supplied with electricity and running water (40 percent of rural houses still lacked electricity a decade after the end of the war). They also complained about the lack of separation between themselves and their animals, especially the cattle that were often housed downstairs from their bedrooms, as along with their noxious but useful bodily products. Especially in the more isolated areas, many of these houses were abandoned without any restructuring attempt. Approximately 20 percent of the dwellings in the province of Siena were uninhabited in 1981, but if we exclude the three largest and most urbanized communes (Siena, Poggibonsi, and Colle), the percentage of abandoned dwellings increases to a whopping 33 percent.[3]

Dreams and Nightmares of Modernization

The seemingly incessant spread of these ruins elicited a variety of contradictory responses. A few Leftist leaders, who viewed scattered settlement as incompatible with a dignified life, went as far as to recommend the razing of the old houses and their replacement with rural villages, which could have stopped or at least slowed down the exodus by providing farmers with easy access to the amenities of modernity (schools, hospitals, shops, cinemas, and so on). More commonly, the local Communists argued for land tenure reforms that would have put peasant families in the position of receiving public subsidies for the restructuring of the houses where they resided.[4] But the response that was to become the most consequential in the long run was the aestheticization of these buildings, now viewed as monuments to a dying way of life that had shaped the *bel paesaggio* of Tuscany. A small army of amateur photographers belonging to the urban upper-middle classes began to roam the Tuscan countryside, documenting the architectural and landscape values of a territory that, on the face of it, looked increasingly valueless (Biffoli 1966; Gori-Montanelli 1978). Unlike the pictures ethnographers and reformers took earlier in the century, which lingered on the sun-parched necks of laboring peasant men or on the nimble fingers of home-spinning farm girls, the photographs of these postwar amateurs were eerily devoid of people, even when they depicted farmhouses that were still inhabited. Their main enemy was not the abandonment of these buildings but their utilitarian restructuring. In a 1961 article sent by one of these photographers to the bulletin of Italia Nostra, the main national organization for landscape and cultural preservation, readers are invited to compare two pictures of the same Chianti farmhouse, taken one year apart (Gori-Montanelli 1961). The author extols the house in the earlier image for the elegance and purity of its architectural proportions. The later photograph, which depicts the result of the restructuring carried out by the sharecropper after his purchase of the building, was meant to fill the reader with horror: Gone was the tower, gone was the gated courtyard, and the windows were now double in size!

If some urban viewers were horrified by the aesthetics of modernization, it was the emptiness itself that filled with dread many rural political leaders, who confronted constantly dwindling constituencies. This rural elite of peasant extraction kept dreaming of agricultural modernization well into the early 1970s. They dreamt of a kind of agricultural modernization capable of stemming the exodus while providing the extant rural dwellers with competitive income levels. They welcomed mechanization and the use of artificial fertilizers, but they viewed them in function of a demographic stabilization that never happened.[5] The recapitalization of Tuscan agriculture could not but take place through a massive increase in value added and labor productivity. In short, it took decades for local leaders to realize, and regretfully accept, that a truly modernized agriculture could not support tens of thousands of peasant farmers. Indeed, for economic as well as political reasons, investments in agriculture took off only after the exodus was well under way. In the early 1960s funds came first from the national government through its two "Green" five-year plans (*Piani Verdi*). These national plans were then combined with European subsidies through the 1960s until they merged into the European Community–controlled European Agricultural Guidance and Guarantee Fund (EAGGF) in the early 1970s. Of the 18 billion lire allocated by the two Green Plans in the province of Siena in the course of the 1960s, almost 60 percent was spent to foster mechanization, 23 percent for mostly large-scale projects of agricultural restructuring (especially irrigation), and 5 percent each to implement vine monocropping and support animal husbandry (especially cattle raising). In the face of depopulation, the earlier government's commitment to creating a new class of small independent farmers had abated. Tiny amounts were reserved for small-scale farmers or were meant to spread small-scale landownership.[6] Overall, European subsidies confirmed and strengthened these guidelines through the 1970s and 1980s.

The spatial consequences of this process of recapitalization were momentous. All over Tuscany, but especially in the most renowned areas such as the Chianti, the dying mixed vineyards typical of sharecropping agriculture, where rows of vines stood interspersed with fields under rotation and other trees, were replaced with specialized ones, implanted on American roots resistant to phylloxera (Figure 4.1). On a smaller scale, olive tree cultivation was also restructured in the wake of the devastating cold blast of February 1956, with specialized olive groves being installed on the best-exposed hillsides (Fiorentini and Massa 1979). In other microregions, such as the Orcia valley, where wine production had never been a major specialty, the landscape of *mezzadria* was replaced by vast wheat fields, also duly subsidized by the European Community. In the Chianti many terraced hills were bulldozed over for tractor use, while in the Orcia valley and in other areas of southern Tuscany many of the eerie mounds of clay typical of the region were dynamited

Figure 4.1 Landscape in the Florentine Chianti with the landlord's villa and the sharecropping family's house in close proximity. Wikipedia Commons/Simone Benelli.

out of existence. But this process of spatial specialization coexisted with even grander projects based on the vision of turning the Tuscan hills into green pastures for intensive cattle raising. Several dams were built or half built, and some 12,000 small hillside lakes were dug at the state's expense in hope of obviating to the severe summer droughts typical of the Mediterranean climate.[7] Today most of these lakes have been abandoned, converted into fishing ponds, or are used for the irrigation of vineyards and olive groves. The signs of these aborted visions, as well as those of highly capitalized specialized agriculture, mark the difference between today's landscape and the traditional landscape of *mezzadria*, now relegated to tiny plots cultivated by Sunday farmers.

In sum, the Tuscan countryside circa 1970 was the object of many contradictory and often disoriented gazes. A burgeoning "conservationist" movement coexisted with modernizing visions predicated on radical territorial transformations. But these modernizing projects were themselves quite diverse and based on different degrees of acceptance of depopulation and commercial specialization. Productivist impulses, which for instance imagined the Tuscan hills as a possible site of massive irrigation projects and intensive animal farming, coexisted with more targeted (and realistic) plans to capitalize on the region's "natural" vocation for high-quality and high-value-added agriculture. The political economy of winemaking stands out in this regard. Large-scale Tuscan winemakers, led by Baron Ricasoli and a handful of other forward-looking landlords of aristocratic descent, were at the vanguard of a national movement for the protection of wine brands and quality.

By the 1960s, wine legislation already had a long and troubled history in Italy (Borrione 1999). It was well known that much wine that was marketed as Chianti, for example, had never even seen the hills of central Tuscany, to the chagrin of Ricasoli and the "authentic" Chianti producers. Italian large-scale traders (as opposed to producers) were particularly hostile to regulation, used as they were to traveling the peninsula hunting for deals and cultivating their contacts to then sell wine under many well-established denominations in absolute freedom and according to different tastes and income levels. But plenty of low- to mid-quality producers also depended on this kind of flexibility. If Americans expected their Italian red wine to be named Chianti, have some predictable general features, and be priced reasonably, why should such demand go unmet, Ricasoli's opponents argued, especially because the Chianti region, devastated by the phylloxera epidemic and rocked by political strife, could not even produce enough wine to satisfy it?[8]

In the end, only the momentum created by European integration managed to break the stalemate between the proponents and opponents of regulation. By the early 1960s it had become apparent that the impending establishment of an integrated market for wine called for a degree of regulatory coordination across national borders. The French producers and traders, no longer able to protect their market with tariffs, put considerable pressure on their government to demand stricter controls over the quality and provenance of Italian wine. The idea that Italian winemakers could play by laxer rules than their French counterparts was indeed a hard sell, and the French government was in the position to make the European Community's agricultural funds dependent on Italy's willingness to conform. Even the Communist opposition in the Italian Parliament had to accept the iron logic of these arguments. The result of these pressures was a 1963 law on *denominazione d'origine*, which linked provenance, brand, and quality on the French model of the *appellation d'origine* (Guy 2003); established a public record in which vineyards had be registered; and instituted a powerful national committee of wine experts to settle disputes and set standards. What is particularly important in light of this chapter's focus is that the law established a system of manufactured scarcity, setting maximum yields per hectare and making the conversion of land into vineyards a relatively cumbersome process, especially after its early stages of implementation. Thus, Chianti, which was already the iconic Italian wine around the world but suffered from a reputation crisis, could gradually reinvent itself as a veritable iconic brand capable of commanding increasing rent levels. This logic of socially and politically manufactured scarcity, as we will see, was applied to other venues as well, ultimately reinventing the "landscape" as a whole.

The Tuscan Landscape as Touristic Resource

If "modern" agriculture was one of the uses of emptiness, the other, of course, was tourism. But it would be a mistake to assume that rural Tuscans in the postwar decades understood tourism as a "natural" vocation of their territory and a likely (or even desirable) path to economic prosperity. In the late 1950s and early 1960s Tuscan provincial governments used a variety of loans and grants for the construction of new roads and the paving of existing ones. Like in the rest of Italy, these activities, coupled with the spread of automobility, literally opened new vistas and spawned new imaginings. A journalist sent in 1956 to Mount Luco, one of the highest points in the Sienese portion of the Chianti, to cover the construction of a new road and the installation of a powerful TV antenna, did not even think of criticizing the aesthetic dimension of this decision. Rather, with the antenna firmly behind, he was startled by the beauty of the landscape lying in front of him. But in the same breath he proceeded to doubt that tourism could count for much in the foreseeable future:

> People [in the Chianti] hope that it will be possible for landscape lovers to discover this charming corner: an enterprising little man has already built a small bar and restaurant in the area, dreaming to become a pioneer. Obviously no one among those who are seriously concerned with the many pressing problems of this region is betting on tourism as the ace in the hole. To the contrary, tourism is at most regarded as a deuce. But people think that, if someone started to visit the Chianti, a myth would crumble: that of the supposed wealth to be found in this decayed corner of Paradise.[9]

This quotation reveals more than a deep skepticism toward the power of intangibles, such as landscape beauty, to effect lasting economic changes. The journalist also conveyed a commonsense approach to landscape that needed to be overcome before the Tuscan countryside could assume iconic status. For the journalist landscape was a view from somewhere, a specific vista from "a charming corner," rather than a symbol or a civilizational sign that could be filled with projections and meanings.

Even though Article 9 of the Italian Constitution, promulgated in 1948, expressly stated that the new republic "protect[ed] the landscape and the artistic and cultural patrimony of the Nation," the conception of landscape as the coherent expression of a historic civilization—that is, as patrimony—was anything but hegemonic until the 1980s. Once again, it was in specific conservationist circles among the enlightened urban bourgeoisie that this notion began to take ground (Dalisi 1964). According to this sensibility, the landscape was beautiful, and therefore worth protecting, when it was legible as a system of signs that mirrored a specific socionatural configuration. This systemic legibility was of course extremely vulnerable, for it relied on a cultural construction of coherence that was at best elusive. A beautiful landscape was something transmitted from the past and that present generations had to treasure for it to remain "true to itself." Therefore, this conception of landscape relied on a view from nowhere; it was a mythical construction that developed in a collectively negotiated temporality that in turn directed and educated the observers' gazes. This (and not that) was what a Tuscan rural landscape ought to look like! But where should the line between coherence and incongruity be drawn? Some observers argued, for example, that the pervasive and blatantly novel presence of vine monocropping, with its reliance on cement poles, had already ruined the landscape of the Chianti region (Gianfrate 1988). But others noticed that many depictions of Tuscan medieval landscapes, starting with Ambrogio Lorenzetti's *Allegory of Good and Bad Government*, included what looked like specialized vineyards (Moretti 1988). And indeed, in the late 1990s cement poles were banned and replaced with more credibly medieval-looking wooden ones. The patrimony had to be invented and legitimated before it could be conserved (Barrère 2005).

It is exceedingly difficult to locate with any precision the time and venues when this admittedly peculiar understanding of landscape, destined to become very familiar, came to be appropriated and reinterpreted by the people of rural Tuscany. But I can point to two relevant processes—one more political and the other more social in character—that reached maturity in the course of the 1970s. On a political level, in 1970 several government functions, including territorial planning, were devolved to regional governments. Now the territorial future of Tuscany would be largely decided in Florence, rather than in Rome. The 1970s and early 1980s also signaled the height of popularity for Tuscany's Communist Party, a political force that despite its electoral success had failed to lead the transformation of rural society in a coherent direction during the season of struggles and that by the 1970s suffered from something of an identity crisis. Now, strong with solid pluralities in the regional government, Tuscan Communists would try to make up for that failure. Not only was the Communist Party especially strong in the countryside of central and southern Tuscany, where it often garnered the absolute majority of votes; the Tuscan countryside was also where the Resistance had been fought and where the Party had come of age and laid roots after two decades of persecution and dictatorship. The long-standing emotional bond between the Communist regional political elite and rural Tuscany was increasingly tinged with nostalgia.

Before this partially novel political backdrop, a variety of contradictory social processes were at work in the Tuscan countryside. The most important of these trends was the arrival of a partially new kind of tourism. Florence and Siena had been on the international tourism map since its origins, dating back to the aristocratic Grand Tour, but that kind of tourism was an urban, or at most suburban, affair. Upper-class foreign tourists created colonies of art connoisseurs who aimed to relive and retrieve the glories of the Renaissance in front of audiences of their peers. Therefore, they needed to live in proximity with each other and near the objects of their appreciation—the museums, basilicas, and palazzi that could quench their thirst for beauty, not to mention the art dealers who catered to them (Roeck 2009). The villas of the richest among them overlooked the city (usually Florence) both in a physical and metaphorical sense. For them the countryside was at best a notion to contemplate from afar and compare with artistic renditions, rather than a space to be in contact with. The new residential tourists of the postwar period, aided by road and even highway construction that made the countryside easily accessible for the first time, descended from northern Europe (and to a lesser extent from urban Italy) and began to buy not only the landowners' villas but also the farmhouses abandoned by the sharecroppers, now barely worth the mortar that kept them together, and to "restore" them. These restorations were carried out not with an eye to the needs of modern farming but with an appreciation for these buildings' exquisitely outdated features. It was their lack of utilitarian value that marked them as worthy of preservation. Thus, these tourists' sensibilities dovetailed with those of the urban conservationists who had been photographing these buildings for years.

The Chianti began to receive a significant influx of foreigners only in the early 1960s and the rest of rural Tuscany even later. These people fell in love with the emptiness—both literal and metaphorical—around them, which allowed them not only to buy property but also to project onto the landscape their aspirations and anxieties. Many of these residential tourists were upper-middle-class British citizens, whose increasing presence and visibility warranted the coinage of a new toponym, Chiantishire (Flower 1979). They also formed something of a colony, kept together by emulation and competition, but their objects of desire were no longer the Renaissance artifacts of their urban forebears, now permanently out of reach to all but the wealthiest, but barns converted into libraries, pigsties rehabbed as sitting rooms, and of course the wines and cheeses that some of them helped to produce and all of them tasted and commented on. What drew them to central Tuscany was, besides each other, the landscape, now firmly understood as the product and symbol of a mythical civilization and way of life. A 1968 article in the *New York Herald Tribune* noted that "[the Chianti] was so protected from the usual tourist track that the present landscape can still be recognized in the 12th and 13th century paintings of the Sienese primitives."[10]

These early, rather genteel, residential tourists were followed in the 1970s by more alternative ones, hailing primarily from Germany and the Netherlands, who saw Tuscany as the perfect stage for their "back-to-the-land" fantasies. A faction of Germany's post-1968 Left is still known as the Toskana Fraktion, for they all own property there. These newer tourists saw their decision to move to rural Tuscany as a way of expressing their disdain toward the crass materialism of urban capitalism, which in some cases they had opposed in their political activism. Like elsewhere in those years, theirs was above all a retreat from the disappointments and demands of a political season that had coincided with their fading youth. For these tourists, Tuscany's Leftist political culture was a further asset, although it is far from clear what they actually knew about it.[11] In sum, for all their diversity, these residential tourists blissfully missed the pervasive signs of agricultural modernization, nor did they pay much attention to Tuscany's actual (as opposed to imagined) "peasant civilization," which was collapsing all around them. But they all noticed (and relished) the "landscape."

The Tuscan Landscape as Object of Preservation

Aristocratic aspirations and alternative passions coexisted with less pristine impulses. Swiss real estate agents, for example, began to buy land in the Chianti with the intention of building rural tourist villages. Land speculation became an increasing threat, although the prospect of making a killing in the real estate market was what had (at least in part) motivated the influx of residential tourists in the first place. In the largest town of the Florentine Chianti (Greve), within a few years in the late 1970s, 800 hectares of former agricultural land were parceled out into 600 lots, some of which as small as 100 square meters (Fiorentini and Massa 1979: 151). And all of this was happening as the rural exodus continued, albeit at a slower pace. It was at this crucial juncture that the Tuscan political Left began to discover the beauty of the Tuscan countryside and see it as a "resource" and set out to stem these speculative tendencies. The landscape came to stand for a rapidly disappearing rural society worthy of gratitude, nostalgia, and protection. Thus, Tuscany's leftist leaders also converted, albeit for their own reasons, to a civilizational understanding of landscape as a coherent system of signs.

To their credit, Tuscany's political leaders understood that every viable landscape, even a mythical one, must be populated. The first object and subject of conservation had to be whatever people were left on the land, even though these people were now so hard to characterize: They no longer belonged to tradition and peasant civilization, and yet they could be imagined as the new stewards of the land, standing guard against the destructive powers of unbridled market capitalism. But what kinds of people were left in rural Tuscany? And what kind of rural dwellers should be preserved? By and large, the burgeoning politics of social preservation relied on the construction of a fictional rural dweller, who embodied the progressive, postmaterialistic qualities imagined to have been shared by the traditional sharecroppers for centuries, through their struggles of the 1940s and 1950s. This postmaterialistic peasant farmer, simultaneously traditional and novel, would also happen to share some of the values embraced by the northern European residential tourists, not to speak of the European Community, soon to be moving (however ambiguously) from the vulgar instrumentality of the Common Agricultural Policy to the enlightened mandates of the European Model of Agriculture, with its promise to acknowledge the multifunctional character of European rural spaces beyond their mere productivity (Cardwell 2004). Now Tuscan

Communists left their cattle-raising projects behind and set out to conserve and valorize the "landscape," as was. In this pursuit, paradoxically, they were soon joined by many landowners, large and small, who owned thousands of decaying buildings discovered to be beautiful and in urgent need of renovation and valorization. Instrumental and emotional value were inextricably linked all the way through.

The problem was that postmaterialistic peasant farmers had to be created. Rural Tuscans had to be convinced that tourist villages and land speculation were threats, despite their short-term promises. The late 1970s and early 1980s saw the emergence of a series of regional laws with radically restrictive (and pedagogical) goals. One of the earliest, and arguably the most important, was Regional Law 10, issued in 1979, which regulated construction activities in rural areas. This law, at least on paper, all but froze the housing stock in rural Tuscany by forbidding the construction of new buildings, providing incentives (again thanks to the funds of the European Community) for housing restoration and strictly limiting the possibility of selling the buildings without the adjacent acreage. Despite its many limitations, this measure (and many others like it) radically restricted the supply of housing, thereby preparing the ground for its increase in value. The logic of manufactured scarcity that had been deployed for the protection of wine quality was now applied to the housing stock as well and by extension to the landscape as a system of signs. These kinds of legislative norms, coupled with more subtle and informal expectations, created the conditions of possibility for the production of symbolic value. They simultaneously created the object of valorization and the rules by which value was to accrue.

After vowing to protect the landscape from "speculation," a diverse coalition of actors set out to find new uses for the empty but potentially valuable rural houses. The most important of these novel uses was agrotourism, a practice imported from northern Europe and the Alps (Miele and Murdoch 2002; Sonnino 2004). The idea was for tourists to be hosted (and sometimes fed) on actually operating farms (although not necessarily in the same buildings as the farmers), thereby responding to urban people's need for contact with nature and tradition and to the farmers' need for extra revenue. In Tuscany this activity developed at first off the books and spontaneously, until the regional government agreed, after a long debate, to regulate it with a comprehensive measure, law 36, issued in 1987. On paper, this law was indeed a monument to a postmaterialistic conception of the countryside. Its stated goals were, among others, the preservation of the "patrimony" constituted by the rural houses and the diverse customs and products of rural Tuscany; the conservation of the natural environment and requalification of agricultural production away from a purely quantitative logic; and the equalization of the relationships between town and country (Angiolini 1989). Because an agrotourism establishment would pay half the taxes of a regular hotel or bed and breakfast (B&B), a whole series of rules was meant to discourage "fake" farmers from taking advantage of the tax credits attached to the law. The maximum number of bedrooms was set at fifteen, with no more than thirty beds; only farms with at least two hectares of arable land could open an agrotouristic activity; no new buildings could be raised for agrotouristic purposes; and so on. Above all, at least half of the revenue had to keep coming from agricultural activities, and each agrotouristic farm had to present yearly plans and reports demonstrating that that was the case. It goes without saying that this measure, meant to make sure that agrotouristic hosts would be authentic farmers, forced many operators in increasingly renowned areas to cook the books and hide part of their touristic business.

There is little doubt that agrotourism has been a huge success. There were 500 agrotouristic establishments in Tuscany in 1988; in 2004 there were 3,200. In the Orcia valley the spread of this activity has been even more spectacular: Over an area with a population of approximately 13,000 people, agrotouristic companies increased from fewer than fifty in 1992 to 352 in 2006, with a number of visitors approaching 100,000 and a number of presences exceeding 350,000.[12] This form of rural tourism represents the main source of revenue for a large portion of Tuscany's hill country. In some areas of Tuscany, this process of valorization has made real estate prices escalate. A ruined rural house in the Orcia valley with some acreage can sell for more than half a million Euros, partly because it can be turned into a lucrative agrotouristic establishment. This surge of tourist activity was followed (rather than preceded, as one might expect) by a barrage of international recognition. When, in 2004, UNESCO officially acknowledged the Orcia valley as a World Heritage Site, the game of mirrors on which landscape construction is based lay at the very center of the decision's justification:

> The landscape of the Val d'Orcia was celebrated by painters from the Siennese School, which flourished during the Renaissance. Images of the Val d'Orcia, and particularly depictions of landscapes where people are depicted as living

Figure 4.2 This cypress-lined road in the Orcia valley, now iconic, was built in the 1930s as part of a major state-funded reclamation project.   Dario Gaggio.

in harmony with nature, have come to be seen as icons of the Renaissance and have profoundly influenced the development of landscape thinking.[13]

In other words, the landscape of the Orcia valley had to be recognized as an icon because it had been recognized and depicted as an icon since time immemorial. If that were not the case, what would all those tourists be looking at (Figure 4.2)?

The self-fulfilling logic of these arguments, however, relies on (and masks) a massive amount of socially situated symbolic and political labor. Over the last two decades a complex hierarchy of socionatural entities has emerged in Tuscany, organized according to the stringency of the regulations they must adhere to and the scale of the regulatory bodies by which they are monitored—from National Parks to Protected Natural Zones of Local Interest (ANPILs) (Pagni 2005). For the Orcia valley to win the UNESCO designation, for example, the five communes of the area began coordinating their activities almost ten years before, by establishing a limited liability company called Valdorcia, Inc. (Valdorcia, s.r.l.), devoted to the marketing and branding of local sites and products.[14] Indeed, the company logo, which juxtaposes a cypress tree and a medieval tower against a stylized hilly background, is now widely used to advertise events and as a form of guarantee on the packaging of local products, such as wines and cheeses. This initiative then spawned a series of other coordinated efforts, including a common zoning and building plan, which culminated in the creation of an "artistic, natural, and cultural park," formally recognized by the regional government as an ANPIL.

To convey the gist of these kinds of initiatives, let us ask: What could be more incongruous than a swimming pool adjacent to a supposedly operating farm in a territory supposedly unchanged since the time of the Sienese primitives? As a matter of fact, however, almost all the agrotouristic establishments in the Orcia valley have swimming pools. But the zoning and building plan of the park's five communes demands that pools be lined with special nonrefracting tiles, deemed less offensive than regular ones, and surrounded by indigenous plants. No palmettos are allowed. There is no irony conveyed by these official documents, although the locals more than make up for such seeming lack of reflexivity by combining wry humor with a hint of resentment. And indeed this is serious business. It is by the symbolic labor of these norms, which are the product of often painful discussions, that iconic brands are created and reproduced, and it is on the reproduction of these brands' power that hinges the prosperity and viability of vulnerable communities.

Conclusion

This chapter has tried to examine the historical process by which rural Tuscany has assumed the status of an iconic brand by doing justice to its complexity and heterogeneity. To begin with, I hope to have demonstrated that there was nothing inevitable about the construction of rural Tuscany as an icon. This was a historical process full of contingency and negotiations. The cultural and symbolic value of Tuscany's rural landscape did not simply accrue from an uncontroversial and static reservoir of meanings. Instead, a variety of actors negotiated and contested these meanings for decades, constructing a dynamic compromise they could believe in. The narratives of authenticity on which the iconicity of the Tuscan landscape relies became hegemonic rather late, in the 1970s, emerging from the physical and metaphorical emptiness that followed the demise of the sharecropping economy and the peasants' exodus. Some of the valorization strategies implemented in the wake of the peasants' flight had very little to do with the creation of an iconic landscape.

Some of these strategies, such as extensive irrigation and cattle raising, were retrospectively regarded as incompatible with landscape "preservation," even though they failed for different reasons. Other valorization strategies, such as the implementation of vine and olive monocropping, were instead co-opted into a narrative of authenticity, even though they could easily have betrayed their modern and utilitarian origins.

In sum, the construction of authenticity, crucial to Tuscany's iconicity, was a thoroughly political process in which local leaders, as well as national and international stakeholders, produced a legible landscape, declared it the product of a coherent and unique civilization, and proceeded to preserve it, reproducing its value. The role of the local Communists was especially pivotal in this regard: They participated at least as much as the foreign tourists in the construction of a credible narrative of authenticity, and they did so out of genuine concerns for a society and territory saturated with historical myths and nostalgia. Their historical myths celebrated the dying world of the radical sharecroppers of the pre- and post-Fascist era, rather than the rituals of the medieval landlords or the gaze of the Renaissance artists, as was the case with many of the tourists. But these different narratives could coexist and, to a degree, even merge around the celebration of the region's "landscape."

The contingent and negotiated character of this process suggests that successful icons cannot be planned or promoted out of thin air; they need to be lived and imagined "from below" as well. In other words, narratives of authenticity, however constructed, must be believed in for nonutilitarian reasons as well, for an icon to acquire its power. Ordinary Tuscans came to aestheticize their territory in the wake of rapid change and trauma, coming to appreciate the landscape as a coherent system of signs. This process of aestheticization took place in dialogue with what John Urry (1990) and others have called the "tourist gaze," but this was never a simple process of the foreign tourists imposing a particular vision or sensibility. Rather, rural Tuscans have chosen to bear testimony to a disappearing civilization, imagining themselves as its heirs and stewards, but they have not done so merely to please the tourists. In a sense, the peasant civilization imagined (or believed to be true) by contemporary Tuscans is no more historically "accurate" than that imagined (or believed to be true) by tourists, and the same holds for the landscape that the former have built and the latter come to visit.

This finding dovetails with the conclusions of several studies in the sociology and anthropology of tourism. As the Maltese festivals, discussed in Jeremy Boissevain's influential ethnography, led to the reinvention of a credible identity for the locals as they interacted with an increasing influx of tourists (Boissevain 1979), the reinvention and "preservation" of the landscape has delineated the features of what authentic Tuscany should look and feel like to locals and tourists alike, in the face of massive change and disruption. If we understand the construction of authenticity as a heterogeneous process embedded in dynamic (or emergent) social relations (Cohen 1988), the product of such relations (the landscape) will appear as a crucial component of flexible local identities, negotiated in interaction with the tourists' diverse gazes.

This emphasis on negotiation does not mean that Tuscans do not participate in the commodification of their landscape, or that the authenticity they perform is not in some sense "staged," to use Goffman's expression. Viewing the Tuscan landscape as an iconic brand, however, directs our attention to the remarkable amount of socially situated labor that is meant to reproduce an extremely delicate, even implausible, balance between emotional and instrumental value. Much of this labor aims at erecting and reproducing symbolic frames, buttressed by legal measures, discursive devices, and material practices involving plants, animals, and even rocks. Tuscans tell themselves that this is sustainable tourism, often ignoring the conflicts and tensions that "preservation" engenders. These practices (sustainability, conservation, preservation, and so on) mask the vast amount of rapid, even traumatic, change experienced by these local societies in the last half-century. When branded, an iconic landscape becomes a fetish in a Marxian sense, a symbolic formation that disguises and erases the conditions of its own production, replacing them with legible, and therefore marketable, narratives. But if the beauty of a landscape relies on the legibility of its features, as some experts argue (Toesca 2004, Turri 2003), the task of social and historical analysis is to uncover legibility's conditions of possibility.

5 Impression Management of Stigmatized Nations

The Case of Croatia

Lauren A. Rivera

TOURISM IS ONE OF THE MOST POWERFUL SOURCES of international perceptions of a country's cultural, social, and political environment. As the world's most prevalent export and primary source of contact with foreign peoples and places (Baranowski and Furlough 2001), tourism exerts a powerful force on how countries are imagined globally. Tourism organizations, brochures, and professionals perform what is most important about a country's history and culture for visitors (Dann 1996). Essentially, these organizations and brochures make known the country's cultural wealth portfolio. Tourism industries are charged with communicating the symbolic value of a country and convincing travelers that a particular destination is worthy of economic and temporal investment.

In the case of the world's most established and well-regarded tourist destinations, successfully converting the symbolic value of a nation into economic capital in the form of tourism revenues may be a relatively less contentious process because such destinations are widely understood by international audiences to be legitimate, attractive, and desirable places to visit and invest. But how do countries with tarnished international reputations mobilize their cultural wealth for economic and political ends? In this chapter, I address this question by drawing from a case study of postwar tourism in Croatia. I analyze how the Croatian government has reconstructed the way it portrays Croatia's symbolic value to international audiences in the wake of the violent and highly publicized wars of Yugoslav secession in order to enhance the country's economic and political standing. I find that, in the postwar period, the state has represented Croatia's primary selling point as its similarity to its Western European neighbors. That is, it has presented Croatia's cultural wealth as being the wealth of others, in a sense free riding on some components of other countries' cultural wealth portfolios. I use the Croatian case alongside Goffman's work on stigma to understand this seemingly counterintuitive strategy and to develop a broader theoretical framework for understanding the conditions under which stigmatized countries are likely to pursue similar means of cultural representation. The chapter demonstrates the importance of impression management for the successful conversion of national cultural wealth into economic capital and informs debates about cultural isomorphism in an international context.

International Impression Management

In an international climate where global impressions have important economic and political consequences for countries, how do states with tarnished international reputations represent their history and culture on a global stage? I argue that Goffman's work on stigma is useful for illuminating this dilemma. In *Stigma* (1963), Goffman describes the representational strategies available to actors who possess characteristics considered shameful or embarrassing by mainstream society. Although the majority of empirical research examines stigma as an *individual* phenomenon, commonly a mental or physical handicap (Link and Phelan 2001), stigmatization is a broader social and cultural process that is applicable to the plight of collectivities. Goffman argues that stigma is a *label* applied by outsiders rather than an internal attribute; he notes that entire groups, such as nationalities and professions, can be perceived as "spoiled" (for a discussion of how a state may become stigmatized, see Rivera 2008). The concept of stigma can also be used to understand the impression management dilemmas faced by states with "spoiled identities." According to Goffman, stigmatized actors generally select among three strategies for interacting with the outside world, with the goal of acquiring legitimacy and avoiding embarrassment: (1) Actors can sever contact with nonstigmatized actors; (2) they can openly disclose the stigma; or (3) they can attempt to "cover" the stigma and, if successful, "pass" as unstigmatized. In the case of states, these responses translate into: (1) *isolation* from international circuits; (2) *public acknowledgment* of the reputation-damaging event, through practices such as commemoration, apology, or "dark tourism"; and (3) *strategic self-presentation* to cover the problematic associations. Four factors influence the likelihood that particular paths of representation will be pursued: whether a country is viewed as discredited or discreditable, the timing of stigma, the rewards associated with covering, and the role of competing narratives.

Goffman draws a central distinction between the strategies available to "discredited" versus "discreditable" actors. The former have stigmas that are certain (for example, visible, readily perceptible, obtrusive in social interaction, or definitively known to all interaction partners). Although discredited groups may try to minimize the attention paid to the stigma, believably "passing" is unlikely, and thus isolation or acknowledgment is the typical course of action. Conversely, "discreditable" actors have stigmas that are ambiguous or not readily apparent. Because awareness of the stigma may be manipulated through information control, discreditable actors are more likely to pass or "cover."

The *timing* of a stigma also plays a key role in the strategy selected. When a stigma develops early, actors are often socialized into the role of being outside the norms of society; they may accept this difference and pursue acknowledgment or isolation. Conversely, when actors develop a stigma after forming a self-concept as "normal," they are more likely to cover. After long periods of time, though, actors may switch from covering to disclosure because the stigma is sufficiently in the past and no longer poses a threat.

Despite actors' differential abilities to conceal their flaws, Goffman argues that, when possible, passing and covering are preferred courses of action due to "the great rewards of being considered normal" (Goffman 1963: 74). The likelihood of covering increases substantially when an actor perceives the stigma to be an obstacle to achieving desired material or symbolic goals, and it rises with the perceived importance of those goals. Exceptions occur when outsiders reward acknowledgment more highly than they do concealment.

Successful passing or covering requires skillful information control; there must be no discrediting "slips" in performance or "tells" picked up by knowledgeable audience members. Although all groups that cover face the possibility of exposure, the situation is more precarious for heterogeneous collectivities such as countries, where control over impression management is dispersed among numerous actors who may have conflicting ideas about what constitutes the group's identity and the appropriate strategy of representation. Thus, in discussing stigmatized countries, a modification to Goffman's model is necessary: Covering requires control of competing narratives. This can be achieved through *coercive control*, when a powerful organization, such as a state, suppresses alternatives or monopolizes opportunities for narrative performance (Merridale 1999) or through *indirect control*, when there are no strong competing alternative narratives (see Alexander 2004b). When analyzing the stigma response strategies of countries, it is thus essential to consider not only the dynamics between actors and audiences but also the control of scripts and stages.

Applying Goffman's insights to the level of states, we see that actively incorporating reputation-threatening elements of a country's history and culture into international representations is often *not* a preferred course of action due to the material and symbolic rewards associated with being perceived as being "normal." Yet, although often desirable, effective international impression management requires a complex interplay of structural, cultural, and contextual factors. In the remaining pages, I use an empirical case study of Croatia to examine under what conditions societies can successfully "cover" reputation-damaging events and exclude them from international representations of a country's cultural wealth.

Case Selection

Croatia represents an intriguing site for exploring how states with tarnished international reputations present their cultural wealth abroad. In the early 1990s, Croatia was one of three republics to undergo wars of secession from the former Yugoslavia. Although these conflicts began as wars for independence, the violence in Croatia and Bosnia soon transformed into attempts to create ethnically "pure" states and was waged primarily against civilians (see Rivera 2008 for details). The wars garnered extreme amounts of international attention, with news crews around the world reporting "ethnic cleansing" among Croats, Serbs, and Bosniaks (Judt 2005). Although local militias and police forces carried out much of the violence in Croatia, both the Croatian and Serbian governments have been directly implicated in the conflict, and government officials from Croatia and Serbia have been indicted for war crimes by the U.N. International Criminal Tribunal (Naimark 2001).

Croatia's war virtually wiped out its tourism, demolishing its image as a desirable travel destination and creating perceptions of the country as "war torn" and "savage." In the years immediately following the war, Croatia suffered from a reputation crisis and loss of status as governments around the globe issued travel advisories discouraging visits to the former Yugoslav states and international bodies imposed sanctions and curtailed diplomatic relations with them.

Recovering tourism, through reputation management, has been crucial for Croatia because tourism is the country's top industry. It is the country's primary export to and means of communication with the non-Balkan world (World Travel and Tourism Council [WTTC] 2002). Tourism is also a governmental activity managed by the Croatian National Tourist Board under the purview of the Ministry of the Sea, Tourism, Transport, and Development. Consequently, the tourism industry is extremely influential financially and politically within Croatia and constitutes a powerful "reputational entrepreneur" (Fine 1996). Despite the newness of Croatia's independence, the region has been a mass-market tourist destination since the late 1960s, so analysis of changes in presentation between the pre- and postwar periods is possible.

Methods

I analyzed international impression management in Croatia through tourism using a combination of content analysis of tourism brochures, interviews with tourism professionals, and ethnographic observation of tourist sites. To examine changes in official international representations of Croatia over time, I conducted textual analysis of all publicly available brochures published by the Yugoslavia National Tourist Organization (*Turistički savez Jugoslavije*) and the Croatian National Tourism Board (CNTB) from 1970, the first year that the Yugoslav government widely distributed tourism brochures featuring Croatia, to 2005, the first year when Croatian tourism had officially recovered. I coded descriptions of Croatian history, culture, attractions, and geography within brochures for what they presented as Croatia's primary attractions and distinctive characteristics. Following the analytic strategy of grounded theory (Charmaz 2001), I developed coding categories inductively and refined them in tandem with data analysis. I quantified frequencies of themes by category using the data analysis software package ATLAS-ti and compared them between time periods.

To gain insight into the "backstage" (Goffman 1959) of tourism promotion—the events and common understandings that have shaped the development of Croatia's tourism strategies—I conducted in-depth interviews with individuals integral in crafting and executing tourism policy, including government officials, consultants, policy analysts, hoteliers, and directors of national cultural institutions. I conducted thirty-four interviews with tourism professionals in three of Croatia's largest administrative centers: Zagreb, Split, and Dubrovnik. To complement these local perspectives with an understanding of Croatia's promotional activities abroad, I interviewed two CNTB representatives in Germany and the United Kingdom—two of the largest European markets for Croatian tourism. I recruited participants through a combination of random sampling from government directories and referral chains. Each semistructured interview lasted between sixty and ninety minutes. Interviewees discussed their experiences with tourism promotion in Croatia and their own conceptions of Croatian heritage.

As texts are never separate from social practices (Irwin-Zarecka 1994), I conducted observation in thirty Croatian towns over a three-month period during the peak tourist season. This supplements textual and interview analysis with deep contextual understanding of on-the-ground tourism activity in Croatia. During this time, I visited all major tourist attractions in each locale, observed how tourism professionals presented the country to visitors, and spoke informally with tourists. I kept a journal of field notes and used these data to supplement official narratives with firsthand observations of local attractions and tourism practices.

From War Zone to "The Mediterranean as It Once Was"

Before the recent war, Croatia was primarily a mass-market tourist destination, popular with Yugoslav and European tourists seeking an inexpensive beach holiday (Čavlek 2002). As noted in Figure 5.1, during the 1990s conflict, tourism in Croatia approached a standstill, but it completely recovered by 2005.

Such a quick rebound is exceptional within the tourism industry. It often takes decades for tourists to return to a country following war, and some countries never fully recover from perceptions of violence or instability (Pizam and Mansfeld 1996). Moreover, Croatia has received substantial international praise; the country has been featured in nearly every major travel publication and was even named "Destination of the Year" by *Lonely Planet* (2005) and *National Geographic* (2006).

In interviews, tourism professionals cited the country's aggressive postwar marketing campaign as the strongest factor contributing to tourism's speedy recovery. With the help of international consultancies, the CNTB undertook an intensive rebranding effort to "rebuild confidence in the destination" and create positive perceptions of Croatia abroad. This campaign consisted of

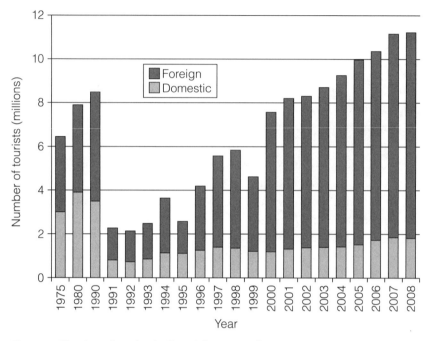

Figure 5.1 Number of tourists in Croatia by year and origin.
SOURCE: Central Bureau of Statistics, Republic of Croatia (2005, 2009).

tourism brochures, advertisements in international media sources, participation in international tourism fairs, expense-paid visits for foreign journalists, and training for domestic tourism representatives. Communications were produced centrally by the CNTB and were unified in design and content.

What War?

Notably, in its postwar tourism promotion campaign, the Croatian government omitted a crucial part of Croatian history—the war that initiated its independence. In its marketing materials, the state has chosen not to acknowledge the war to foreign audiences. Ironically, according to the "history" section of most CNTB brochures, the "official" history of Croatia ended precisely when the country was founded in 1991. In all postwar brochures under analysis, there was only one mention of the recent violence, and it is framed within a larger history of territorial struggles:

> The historical destiny of all beautiful countries has always been a destiny of repeated wars. . . . Despite many a war fought against Tatars, Franconians,

Venetians, Turks and Serbs, the Croats have succeeded in retaining their homeland whose abundant beauty reflects the richness of their tradition and culture. (CNTB 2003a)

The CNTB's decision not to recognize the war is linked to a relative absence of state-sponsored commemoration throughout the country. Although there is a national holiday marking the end of the war, until tourism fully recovered in 2005 there were no *national* monuments or *state-sponsored* museums dedicated to the war or private commemorative spaces mentioned in tourist publications or websites.[1] As of 2008, the Croatian History Museum had not expanded its collection to include exhibits pertaining to Croatia's postindependence history.

This absence is theoretically surprising, given that countries' founding moments tend to be important bases of identity, even when beginnings are less than glorious (Spillman 2003). Moreover, the state's choice not to publicly commemorate the war is unique in the context of tourism practices. Although tourism marketing seeks to foster an attractive and appealing image of host countries (Dann 1996), many states that have undergone reputation-damaging events in the twentieth century have not only incorporated such episodes into their tourist offerings but have actively marketed them. For example, concentration camps and war museums have become key tourist attractions promoted by national tourism boards in Germany and Poland; apartheid museums and "township tours" of racially segregated shantytown districts are heavily marketed by the South African Tourist Board; and genocide museums and memorials are integral to tourism in Cambodia and Rwanda. In addition to providing venues for citizens to mourn, such "dark tourism" (Lennon and Foley 2002) is often an economically appealing strategy for states because it can generate both revenue and employment. Moreover, these sites can provide positive public relations for a country, demonstrating that a state recognizes difficult moments in its past (Olick 2007). Croatia's choice not to recognize the war is thus surprising both theoretically and practically.

Exclusively European

Prior to the war, the Yugoslavia National Tourist Organization marketed Croatia's local distinctiveness as its primary attraction. When describing Croatia's primary attractions, brochures touted the region's unparalleled cultural diversity (61 percent), variety of landscapes (27 percent), and unique local culture (12 percent) as its defining features.[2] A mix of peoples and influences over the ages, Croatia was presented as a mosaic of Croat, European, Slavic, and Ottoman elements. Physically, Croatia was described as the Yugoslav republic with the most abundant natural resources and striking contrasts in scenery; it was not only a "land of a thousand islands" with crystal-clear waters but a region rich with alpine mountains, dense forests, emerald lakes, vineyards, and hot springs.

After the war, tourism materials shifted to portray the country's similarity to Western Europe as its most distinctive feature. Specifically, brochures tout Croatia's European heritage and history (55 percent), physical resemblance to Europe (26 percent), and topographic diversity (19 percent) as its main attractions. Similarly, descriptions of Croatian culture switched from strong local traditions (72 percent), complemented by Western and Eastern influences (23 percent), to customs identical to those in Europe (53 percent) or common internationally (21 percent). Particularly strong emphasis is now placed on stressing Croatia's ties to Western religions. Mentions of churches as tourist attractions have increased by nearly four times since the war, and depictions of Croatia as a country with a deep Catholic heritage have also increased substantially. In contrast, mentions of Islamic or Orthodox religious influences are absent in postwar marketing materials.[3] Similarly, after 1995, the country's past was rewritten in brochures—mentions of Slavic and Islamic historical figures and events have been virtually erased, and mentions of local history not tied to major European powers have decreased by half.

Although strong in all postwar tourism documents, the emphasis on Europe is most extreme in Croatia's newest promotional series. Implemented in 2002 with the tagline "The Mediterranean as It Once Was," the promotion stresses the country's "unspoiled Europeanness" and ties to Western culture, heritage, tradition, and topography. For example, its *Croatian Cultural Heritage* brochure (CNTB 2004b), which seeks to capture the essence of local life and traditions, asserts that "Croatian culture forms an integral part of West European culture." A CNTB press brochure (2003b) distributed to foreign journalists says, "The Republic of Croatia is a young, parliamentary state with a European culture and history. Although a young state, down the centuries its people have played a part in almost every noteworthy event of the Old Continent." Similarly, its capital Zagreb is described as "a distinctly central European city. Situated in the middle of the triangle of Vienna, Budapest, and Venice, it always has been and remains a part of the cultural circle of Europe."

Promotional materials make great efforts to draw parallels between Croatia and known European destinations. This process is most evident in presentations of Croatia's location and geographical features. References to Western Europe are used to describe Croatia's physical scale. A CNTB guide (2004a) notes, "By size, it is classified among the middle-sized European countries, such as Denmark." The brochures present Croatia as topographically similar to Western countries:

> Croatia is a country that is essentially both *Mediterranean and Central European in character* . . . preserved old Mediterranean towns with narrow streets and stone houses *reminiscent of those found in parts of Italy*, as well as spacious, green coastal meadows with dry stone walls which give the appearance of having been *transposed from the Irish countryside*. The mountainous regions of Croatia are characterised by extensive preserved forests, *similar to those found in Scandinavia*, by their romantic lakes, fast-flowing rivers and strikingly pleasing mountain villages *comparable to those in the Alps*, as well as by rugged, rocky and barren country with deep passes, crevasses and canyons in *the style of America's Wild West* . . . while the neighbouring hillsides are a sea of vineyards and enhanced by medieval forts and castles, *like those seen in Germany and Austria*. (CNTB 2003c; author's emphasis)

Given Croatia's former rule by powers such as the Roman, Venetian, and Austro-Hungarian empires, the inclusion of Croatia's historic ties to Europe in its promotional materials is not particularly surprising on its own. Presentations of national heritage often focus on glorifications of a country's past because the past is a symbolic resource that both unites individuals through a shared sense of descent and destiny and can provide a sense of legitimacy or status (Calhoun 1997). Emphasizing heritage in national ideology is especially common in newly established states, such as Croatia, that are striving to acquire legitimacy (Mitchell 2001). Highlighting a destination's historic roots is also common practice in tourism marketing because heritage and "cultural tourism" offerings are thought to attract affluent tourists who tend to want educational experiences on holiday (Dahles 1998). Furthermore, Croatia's geographic location may contribute to a heightened emphasis on Europeanness, given that states on the periphery of Europe tend to highlight their ties to the center to enhance their international standing (Herzfeld 2002).

It is surprising, though, that the Croatian government presents the country as being *exclusively* European. According to the country's official tourism communications, Croatia is unique because it is nearly *identical* to its Western neighbors. The CNTB general brochure (2003a) features a section titled "The Singularities of Croatia," which details the most unique aspects of the country. Yet according to the publication, "what distinguishes us from the others" is a litany of historical, cultural, and physical features that are *the same* as those found in other Western European countries (for example, a Roman amphitheatre nearly identical to the Colosseum in Rome). Like the majority of the CNTB's new marketing materials, the brochure presents the unique features of Croatia as those characteristics that connect the country with Europe and the world, with scant attention to local customs, traditions, heroes, or monuments not associated with major European powers. In fact, according to CNTB brochures, the major differences between Croatia and Italy are the former's lower prices and the better clarity of its sea.

Not Yugoslavia

In addition to portraying Croatia as "truly European," tourism professionals and materials draw strong *symbolic boundaries* (Lamont and Molnar 2002) between Croatia and its eastern neighbors, who are described as "Balkan" and "primitive." Marketing materials carefully point out that Croatian culture differs significantly from Yugoslav culture—the former being European and legitimate, the latter Slavic and less valuable. One CNTB brochure reports:

> Croatia is disproportionately and extremely rich in countless examples of works of art and architecture that rank among *the highest levels of European artistic achievement.* The problem of the wider recognition of Croatian cultural heritage and its rightful place in the annals of European art history has been exacerbated by the fact that *formerly this valuable heritage was erroneously presented as "Yugoslav" culture.* (2004b; author's emphasis)

Such efforts to dissociate Croatia from the East and from former Yugoslav states are also reflected in descriptions of the country's geographic position. Before the war, tourism brochures situated Croatia in Western Europe (35 percent), Eastern Europe (24 percent), the Balkans (17 percent), or on the border between Eastern and Western Europe (14 percent). After the war, ties to the East disappear. Post-1995 brochures situate Croatia squarely within Europe, particularly within Western Europe (78 percent) and the Mediterranean (19 percent).

The drawing of symbolic and geographic boundaries between Croatia, Eastern Europe, and other former Yugoslav republics is consistent with nationalist sentiment that has existed within the region since the late 1800s and surged before the recent conflict. Although the CNTB campaign certainly draws from such imagery, its content represents a rupture from purely nationalist claims because it: (1) omits the founding moment of the "Croat" state, which figures prominently in nationalist discourses, and (2) privileges the international and the similar over the national and the distinctive. Historically, nationalists used local (that is, Croat) heroes, events, and cultural practices *in addition* to Western influences to extol Croatian uniqueness and justify national sovereignty (Naimark 2001). These discourses were often framed against occupying powers (Tanner 2001) and did not claim that Croatians were identical to Italians or Austrians.

A Case of "Covering"

To summarize, the Croatian government has responded to the recent war through reframing Croatian history and culture in a way that excludes the war and describes Croatia in terms of its similarity to other countries. In essence, it has presented the country's cultural wealth as being the wealth of others. Why has Croatia adopted such a seemingly counterintuitive approach?

I argue that the "new image of Croatia" is largely an impression management strategy, similar to Goffmanian "covering," undertaken to regain a positive international reputation following the war and reestablish Croatia as culturally legitimate. According to the proposed framework of stigma management, Croatia is in a prime position to engage in concealment or covering. First, in most tourist areas, there are no longer visible imprints of war or instability. During the conflict, the majority of fighting and physical destruction were concentrated in the interior of the country, particularly in Slavonija, the Dalmatian hinterlands, and the areas surrounding Knin, away from Croatia's most popular coastal tourist destinations. With the exception of Dubrovnik, in many coastal resorts damage was confined primarily to hotels, which were used to house refugees displaced by the conflict (see Rivera 2008 for further discussion). Moreover, the CNTB has directed tourists away from former attractions such as spas and skiing in interior areas that still display significant damage. Consequently, according to conversations with foreign visitors, unless one knows about the history of Croatia, the casual tourist could not tell there was ever a war in the region, let alone recently. This is in contrast to neighboring Bosnia, which suffered extensive and highly visible physical damage and where "war tourism" has emerged in the form of memorials, museums, and guided tours in cities such as Sarajevo and Mostar.

Second, while evidence of war is no longer visible in the areas of Croatia most frequented by foreigners, the region's European heritage is. Centuries of rule under various European powers have had genuine influences on Croatian culture, particularly its architecture. In many places, the country looks like its Western European neighbors—Venetian-style structures dominate the coastline, and Austro-Hungarian facades line the historical quarters of Zagreb and other northern cities. The country's cuisine also possesses strong European influences. According to casual conversations with tourists and the reports of international journalists, visiting Croatia "feels" similar to visiting parts of Italy or Austria. Representing Croatia as the same as these countries is thus somewhat "believable" to most foreign tourists because this image is *available* and *resonates* (Schudson 1989) with how they experience the country.

Third, media representations of Croatia during the war have contributed to a "discreditable" rather than "discredited" reputation. Although the violence in the former Yugoslavia received tremendous media attention, and both the Croatian and Serbian governments have been directly implicated in the Croatian war (Naimark 2001), journalistic reports often framed Croatia as defending its territory from Serbian expansion. Moreover, many journalists and politicians assigned primary responsibility for the conflict to Serbia (Ramet 2005), particularly given Serbia's later involvement in Bosnia and Kosovo. Consequently, informal conversations with tourists reveal there is much confusion about "what exactly happened in Yugoslavia" and what Croatia's precise role was. As the assignment of guilt is essential for producing perceptions of national shame (Giesen 2004), such uncertainty gives Croatia more latitude to believably engage in impression management techniques, such as covering, than can states that have been labeled guilty on the basis of extensive documentation of atrocities (for example, Nazi Germany) or through more consensual media reports (for example, Serbia).

Fourth, Croatia had a substantial history of tourism completely apart from the war. Unlike countries such as Cambodia, where "dark tourism" industries evolved after political instability and rely on war sites to generate revenue (Lennon and Foley 2002), Croatia's tourism infrastructure is built primarily around the sun and the sea. The country enjoyed a positive reputation among

European travelers for decades before the war. According to Goffman, such a history of "normalcy" before the onset of stigma encourages the pursuit of "covering."

Fifth, because the concept of "spoiled" national identity is by definition a collective predicament and a multiplicity of social actors participate in processes of cultural representation, the distribution of cultural power within Croatia also affected the path of stigma management pursued. In the wake of the war, the Croatian government could essentially rewrite Croatian heritage for foreigners because the state controlled the means of image production. Few other powerful agents of memory emerged to resist the strategy or promote alternative narratives.

Conditions Influencing the Adoption of Strategy

Economic Conditions

Tourism professionals reported strong economic incentives for privileging European characteristics. After the collapse of the Yugoslav socialist economy and the subsequent war for independence, tourism emerged as Croatia's only viable means of generating revenue. During the war, Croatia suffered nearly $20 billion in damages, and two of its top industries, shipbuilding and manufacturing, were virtually wiped out (Landry 1998). Given Croatia's existing tourism infrastructure on the coast and history as a travel destination, tourism emerged as a viable moneymaker. Since the war, the Croatian economy has become dependent on tourism, which accounts for nearly 30 percent of formal employment in the country (WTTC 2002). Profitable tourism, though, now relies on *foreign tourism* (Institute for Tourism 2000), which in 2007 accounted for 18 percent of Croatia's total GDP, 36.7 percent of all exports, and 73.4 percent of total exported services (Chamber of Economy 2009). Annual foreign tourism revenues have increased by over seven times since the end of the war, from approximately $1.3 billion in 1995 to nearly $9.7 billion in 2007 (Croatian Chamber of Economy 2006, 2009). Due to high unemployment and lower salaries following the conflict, Croatians, who made up a significant percentage of tourists before the war, could no longer afford to travel as they used to. Some former Yugoslav travelers (primarily Serbs, Bosnians, and Macedonians) also curtailed travel due to economic constraints, border restrictions, and perceived discrimination in the immediate postwar period. A hotel manager explained: "Before we had about 70 percent Croatian and Yugoslav and 30 percent foreign guests in our hotel. Now that has reversed. . . .

Foreigners have more money to travel and to stay here." Moreover, due to significantly decreased hotel capacity resulting from the postwar refugee crisis, the tourism industry needed to generate more money from fewer travelers to remain profitable (Institute for Tourism 2000). Interviewees report that this predicament has resulted in a "rebranding" of the country from an inexpensive, mass-market destination to an upscale one, further increasing dependence on affluent foreign travelers.

To attract foreign revenue, the government had to demonstrate that Croatia is a safe place to visit and invest. As described by an international CNTB representative, "After the war, safety has become our biggest marketing tool." According to individuals integral in drafting the country's tourism strategy, the underlying logic behind presenting Croatia as a wholly European nation-state without significant Slavic roots is to dissociate it from negative images of war and instability in the minds of foreign travelers and investors. According to respondents, being associated with the war or Yugoslavia entails being perceived as a "backward" and "uncivilized" nation. A tourism policy analyst described the problem:

> All the press we were getting [during the war] ... sure we were finally a recognized name. Everyone had heard of Croatia, but they knew of Croatia for the wrong reasons. It was a war-torn nation. A Balkan nation. And that has all the wrong connotations. Savage ... they're all out there to slaughter themselves—to slaughter each other, actually.

There is a sense among locals that negative images of the country persist. A manager from a premier Dubrovnik hotel said, "The general opinion is we are all mad. That we are all fighting and killing each other. Still, even though the war has ended years ago." The devastating economic consequences of being associated with "the Balkans" were most evident in the aftermath of the 1999 NATO bombing of Serbia. Even though the war in Croatia had ended four years prior and the country was, in the words of tourism professionals, "completely safe," international tourism arrivals dropped 15 percent from 1998, due to misperceptions that the entire Balkan Peninsula was unstable (Čavlek 2002). Tourism officials thus believe that being perceived as Slavic or a part of the former Yugoslavia is detrimental to tourism revenues. A CNTB official explained, "It is important to make ourselves different from Yugoslavia in the minds of tourists.... If people know you are different from the troubles that were going on, you can convince people that it is it safe to come." Furthermore, as noted earlier, there currently are no state-sponsored memorials, museums, or sites dedicated to the war. This silence on the part of the tourism industry and cultural institutions stems largely from a perception among policy makers and professionals that drawing attention to the war will keep travelers from visiting Croatia. As summarized by an economic specialist, "The tourist board does not want people to think there ever was a war in Croatia. Because if they think of war when they think of Croatia, they will not come."

The CNTB attempts to create images of stability not only through distancing Croatia from "the Balkans" but by associating the country with the safe, familiar, and highly esteemed frame of Europe. A tourism policy analyst said, "Just by the fact that they're positioning themselves as 'Mediterranean,' they're trying to play to a known term, an understood term . . . a positively connoted term." Just as ties to reputable, high-status actors enhance an individual's prestige (Podolny 2005), linking Croatia with established and upscale destinations such as Italy and Austria is intended to signal to foreigners that Croatia is a stable, desirable, and legitimate travel and investment location.

Political Conditions

Political conditions, especially the desire for European Union (EU) membership, also contribute to the CNTB's focus on European qualities. Given Croatia's tenuous postwar economic situation, government officials see the availability of aid for EU candidate countries as a key source of revenue that can be used to repair infrastructure and stimulate the national economy. Interviewees reported that EU candidacy will provide Croatia with "access to funds, resources, and know-how that can make our development less painful and faster" (tourism policy analyst, Zagreb). In addition, interviewees saw membership as a means of attracting foreign investment, particularly in commercial real estate, and expanding employment opportunities. International consultants, who have played a strong role in shaping Croatia's economic development plans, have echoed such sentiments (for example, Landry 1998) In addition, all thirty-six respondents felt that EU membership will grow the country's primary industry: tourism. European integration is seen as a means of improving Croatia's image abroad by "proving" it is a safe, civilized nation. A Zagreb travel agent explained: "Being a part of the EU will have a great impact because we will finally be recognized as a part of Europe. . . . It will allow tourists to place Croatia—to put it in perspective." Such validation of the country's new image is hoped to increase foreign tourism. A Dubrovnik hotel manager concurred, "When we become members, I think tourists will then say, 'Now it's a good time to go. Now when it's EU, it's safe, it has to be good.'" EU membership should also increase the number of tourists by easing entry requirements.

Accompanying this strong desire to receive the economic and political advantages afforded by EU membership is a keen awareness that Croatia currently has few alternatives. Interviewees reported that the country currently lacks the ability to compete with others because of the economic stagnation it experienced during nearly fifty years of socialism and eighteen subsequent years of war and recovery. Consequently, the general opinion among tourism professionals is that Croatia needs the EU to survive. The tourism board has thus adopted a marketing strategy that emphasizes the country's European roots to demonstrate to outsiders "that we are similar to them and it is appropriate for us to be part of them" (CNTB marketing specialist, Zagreb). The pressure to "be like" Europe, however, is not entirely self-imposed. The EU has used the possibility of membership as a "carrot" to pressure Croatia into making desired political reforms. For example, accession talks were postponed until Croatia achieved satisfactory compliance with the International Criminal Tribunal for the Former Yugoslavia in 2005 (Commission of the European Communities 2006). To become a full member, Croatia must demonstrate to the EU that it has adopted "European" political institutions, such as a free press, minority rights, and democratic elections (NATO 1998). Such pressures highlight how the selection of impression management techniques is influenced not only by properties of the actor and the stigma but also by the expectations (Wherry 2007) and relative power (Link and Phelan 2001) of audiences.

Narrative Control

Although depictions of Croatia as exclusively European dominate the country's tourism discourse, this image is not necessarily an accurate portrayal of how Croatians perceive their own culture and national identity. National culture is not a unified construct. Even so, over half of interviewees *actively rejected* the cultural model promoted by the CNTB, expressing frustration that it is not representative of Croatian culture and history. Not surprisingly, nongovernmental participants voiced the most frequent objections. A travel agent in Split, Croatia's second-largest city, said, "Yes, we have a European history, and we have adopted many things from the people who have occupied us over the centuries. But we are not Italy. Or Austria. We have our own culture and our own way of life that is unique." Croatian culture is particularly complex. Various powers have ruled over different areas of present-day Croatia, but the resulting foreign influences vary sharply by region. Croatia's physical landscape, particularly its numerous islands and steep mountain ranges, helped preserve rich local traditions and customs (Tanner 2001). As a tour guide in Zagreb said, "What it means to be Croatian varies depending on where you are. If you were to ask a person from Dalmatia, you would get a very different answer from a person here in Zagreb or a person from the interior." Such sentiments are consistent with nationally representative survey data indicating that Croatians tend to identify significantly stronger with region of birth and region of ancestry than with "being European" (Cifrić 2004).

Given that the war had wide-reaching impacts in Croatia (see Kunovich and Hodson 1999), and the image of the country promoted by the CNTB is not congruent with that held by many of its citizens, why have there been few grassroots attempts to promote alternative narratives of history or culture? Groups of organized citizens often play a crucial role in memorializing contentious historical moments (Prost 1999). In Croatia, however, there are strong incentives for veterans groups and their families, who are often the strongest advocates of commemoration, not to lobby for recognition. The tactics used during the conflict routinely targeted civilians and violated Geneva Convention protocol (Naimark 2001). Despite backing the conflict, the Croatian government has now pledged "full cooperation" with the ICTY in locating and handing over wanted war criminals (Commission of the European Communities 2006). Consequently, although many Croats supported what they saw as the defense of their territory during the war and, in some communities, those who fought in the war are still seen as "heroes" (see Simons 2005), public acknowledgment of participation in the war now carries the threat (whether real or imagined) of national and international sanctions. In addition to legal concerns, it is possible that participants or their families may choose to remain silent out of fears of retribution or feelings of personal conflict.

According to interviewees and informal conversations with tourism workers, civilians also face incentives not to mobilize to promote alternative versions of the past. Although they may not agree with the image of Croatia promoted by the CNTB and may want to commemorate friends or family affected by the war, many are afraid of jeopardizing their economic livelihoods, which have become intertwined with successful foreign tourism. Many are "grateful for anything that brings more people" and, although inaccurate, the CNTB strategy seems to "work" (private accommodation owner, Dubrovnik). Many respondents contrasted the current tourism boom to the dearth of economic activity in Croatia immediately following the war and credit the CNTB's strategy for "bringing the people back." Under such conditions, few alternative public narratives have emerged, and the CNTB has implemented its version of history and culture with little opposition.

More than Marketing

Tourism is routinely criticized as presenting oversimplified versions of peoples and cultures for purposes of consumption (Urry 1995). In the Croatian case, however, the images produced by the CNTB are not only a matter of marketing communications. Regardless of its accuracy, the "new image" of Croatia is being institutionalized through new zoning laws, incentive programs, and cultural policies aimed at creating visible evidence of Croatia's European heritage (WTTC 2002). For example, the "Incentives for Success" program provides financial rewards for creating architecture and cultural programs in line with the image of Croatia as European (CNTB 2003b). Such cultural policies are important both for their symbolic value as indicators of "how the country's leaders perceive the culture and the value they place on different aspects of it" (Crane 2002: 13) and because they are transforming Croatia's physical and cultural landscape to realize this image. Moreover, the CNTB's promotional efforts also seem to be influencing how the country is imagined abroad. Since the launch of the "rebranding" campaign, major travel publications have shifted from depicting Croatia as a Slavic, socialist country, situated on the crossroads between the West and East, to portraying it as nearly identical to Italy (see Rivera 2008 for discussion).

Normal, but at What Cost?

In addition to being an incomplete portrayal of Croatian culture, some interviewees expressed concern that promoting Europeanness to the exclusion of locally distinctive characteristics (similar to a strategy of free riding) will harm Croatia in the long term. To remain profitable in a rapidly expanding, global tourism market, scholars have suggested that countries need to take on niche roles (Urry 1995). Without perceptions of uniqueness, Croatia may lose its ability to exact "monopoly rents" from travelers (Harvey 2001), and its tourism revenues may suffer. In addition, the country's economic dependence on international tourism may backfire as tourists have curtailed travel due to the global financial crisis.

This strategy's effects may also transcend the tourism industry and could affect the country's domestic political climate. Just as ethnic cleansing physically removed "nonnational" groups from the country, the CNTB campaign and concurrent cultural policies essentially purge non-European and non-Catholic cultural elements from presentations of national culture. Such exclusion may constitute a form of *symbolic violence* (Bourdieu 1977) against minority groups. As public narratives orient domestic policy (Somers and Block 2005), exclusion from official representations of national identity could exacerbate the already precarious position of Croatia's minority groups. Over time, such exclusion could fuel additional domestic conflicts or, given that greater incorporation of minority groups is a precondition for Croatia's European accession (NATO 1998), threaten Croatia's political position internationally. Although the CNTB's current image of Croatia is likely to yield significant economic, political, and social advantages in the short term, its long-term effects remain to be seen.

Alternative Explanations

One alternative explanation to address is whether the CNTB's extreme emphasis on European characteristics is an artifact of European expansion and/ or postsocialist recovery rather than a response to international stigmatization. Although Croatia's European Union aspirations as well as the transition from a socialist economy certainly influence the deployment of European imagery to acquire legitimacy, if this solely were the case, one would expect to see similar cultural campaigns deployed by other EU candidates, recent member states, and postsocialist states that have not undergone such profoundly stigmatizing events. However, recent studies of national discourses in two new members, Latvia (also a formerly socialist "borderland" state) and former Italian principality Malta suggest that this is not the case. Although these countries emphasize European elements in various presentations of national culture, they do not make claims of *equivalence* and also emphasize local distinctiveness (Cini 2001; Eglitis 2002). Such multifaceted strategies also occur in their tourism marketing.[4] Such findings suggest that although the EU and the transition from socialism may encourage a strategy that promotes Europeanness as a means of acquiring legitimacy (see Young and Kaczmarek

2008), it is not a sufficient explanation for Croatia's exclusive focus on Europeanness and specifically Italian identity.

As past management is an ongoing process (Olick 2007), it is also possible that Croatia's strategy of "covering" may be time sensitive. There is typically a period of *latency* before societies commemorate events which can vary from one week (Vinitzky-Seroussi 2002) to decades (Giesen 2004). International representations of Croatia may change as the country establishes itself more powerfully as a safe and trusted destination in Europe. As Croatia's economic situation becomes more stable and the war becomes more distant, civilian groups also may be more willing to mobilize for commemoration. There is anecdotal evidence to support this. Since the recovery of tourism in 2005, there have been small-scale attempts by locals in Dubrovnik to counter state silence. A gift shop in the Old Town now sells amateur video footage of the Dubrovnik shellings; a small memorial dedicated to residents who lost their lives during the attack was erected by local families in 2005; a private war museum was opened in Karlovac in 2009; and a memorial to fallen soldiers was erected in Karlovac in 2010. Similarly, the CNTB has begun to market select destinations in the country's interior through its website. Consequently, changes in representation should be monitored over time to see if the CNTB and other branches of the state present a more complex vision of Croatia as the country becomes more fully accepted by and integrated into the international community.

Conclusion

In the wake of war, to revive its tourism and enhance the country's economic and political status globally, the Croatian government adopted an international representational strategy similar to Goffmanian "covering." Through its tourism activities and cultural policies, the state has portrayed Croatia as having a cultural portfolio identical to its Western European neighbors. According to those responsible for the country's tourism promotion, this strategy of covering (or cultural free riding), was undertaken to convince foreigners that Croatia is a safe and highly desirable travel and investment location. Interviewees reported that, without such efforts, Croatia's remaining industry—foreign tourism—would falter, threatening the country's economic and political viability.

The CNTB can successfully conceal the war and present its cultural wealth as being the cultural wealth of other nations because doing so is *believable* to international audiences due to a combination of physical, historical, and cultural factors. Moreover, in the absence of other powerful agents of memory, the CNTB can present a cultural portfolio that serves its own economic and political interests, even when that image diverges from popular sentiment. Yet, more than just promotional tools, concurrent cultural policies promoting European rather than local culture seem to be structuring marketing communications of a singular culture into reality. If this exclusive focus on Europeanness continues, however, it may harm Croatia in the long run by providing it with little to differentiate it from nearby destinations and may exacerbate political tensions at home.

From the Croatian case, we see that a country's economic capital, its cultural capital, and its impression management activities are *mutually embedded*. Perceptions of a country's symbolic capital shape foreigners' investment decisions (Bandelj 2002) and the country's ability to attract economic capital. As such, concerns regarding the accumulation of economic and political capital also influence which "scripts" of national culture national governments choose to perform (Wherry 2007) on national or international stages and which events, objects, and characteristics are ultimately incorporated into or excluded from official representations of a country' cultural wealth.

In addition to demonstrating the importance of international impression management for the successful conversion, or *transubstantiation* (Bourdieu 1986), of a country's cultural capital into economic and political capital, particularly for stigmatized states, the Croatian case informs debates about cultural isomorphism in an international context. World polity theory posits that states are becoming increasingly similar due to the diffusion of a global "world culture" that emphasizes progressive Western values, such as democracy, respect for human rights, and world citizenship (for example, Meyer et al. 1997). According to this scholarship, states adopt structures and policies consistent with global norms because conforming yields enhanced legitimacy while violations result in costly penalties. The Croatian case suggests that isomorphism may also occur in the cultural domain but not necessarily in the straightforward manner predicted by world polity theory. It appears that states may not embrace all elements of "world culture" uniformly. In the Croatian case, the government draws from the world cultural notion of global citizenship, portraying the country as inextricably linked to Europe and the West, but it fails to incorporate another global norm—public contrition for violations of human rights (Olick 2007). World culture may thus be better conceptualized as part of a broader cultural *tool kit* (Swidler 1986) from which states and organizations draw to solve various material and symbolic dilemmas, rather than a "top-down" global monoculture diffused from the core to the periphery. Conceptualizing world culture in this manner may help scholars account for demonstrated variations (see Guillen 2001) in structure, policy, and culture between states and organizations in a globalizing world.

III

Converting Cultural Wealth into Economic Wealth

6 The Culture Bank

Symbolic Capital and Local Economic Development

Frederick F. Wherry

Todd V. Crosby

THIS CHAPTER DESCRIBES THE CULTURE BANK OF MALI in order to examine how the cultural wealth of a nation is utilized for local economic development. The Culture Bank represents a new model of microcredit because it uses local cultural objects as collateral for loans. Compare this with the Grameen Bank model, where people form groups for rotating loans and where the default of one individual becomes the responsibility of everyone in the loan group. In the Grameen model, social capital—the capacity to mobilize resources by virtue of social ties (Portes and Sensenbrenner 1993)—reduces the likelihood of a loan default. In the Culture Bank model, symbolic capital—the capacity to inspire deference in others by virtue of the meaningful icons and collective narratives one wields (Bourdieu 1984)—increases the likelihood that local cultural heritage is maintained, social relationships strengthened, and small-business loans collateralized. The Culture Bank unleashes the capital stored in the stories that people tell about handcrafted objects. These stories depend on the cultural wealth of a locale rather than on properties of the objects themselves.

This chapter opens by describing the origins and the development of the Culture Bank. This description emphasizes the similarities between the Culture and the Grameen Banks' lending models. The opening case study also provides the basis for discussing the difference between using social and symbolic capital as the basis for microlending and local economic development. The chapter concludes by explaining why symbolic capital is not merely a resource that can be used as a standard input that produces a predictable output; individuals are engaged in rituals that make these inputs real and that restrict how these inputs may be used for economic or other goals.

Origins and Operations

The Culture Bank began in 1995 in the village of Fombori in the Dogon region of Mali. Since 1995, three other Culture Banks have been built in different regions of Mali. The Culture Banks represent a new model of microlending that provides loans in return for local cultural objects as collateral. Similar to the Grameen Bank model, where clients form "solidarity" groups to gain access to credit and reduce lending risk (Woolcock 1998), the Culture Bank relies on social solidarity not only to enforce repayment but to further its goals of conservation and management of local cultural heritage. Using a unique loan system, the Culture Bank transforms local symbolic capital, namely the stories embodied in cultural objects, into a variety of forms of capital that provide tangible benefits to local people, creating an incentive for communities to manage their heritage resources sustainably.

The case study of the Culture Bank does not rely solely on a successful instance in which the bank was established and utilized symbolic capital successfully to promote economic development (sampling on the dependent variable). It may be plausible to think that symbolic capital leads to local economic development, but there may be cases in which there was plentiful symbolic capital but no economic development. Do these other cases mean that symbolic capital has a spurious effect on local economic development, or does this situation mean that a more interactive model is required to capture the dynamics of interaction and meaning making in various circuits of commerce? The second author worked as a Peace Corps volunteer in 1995 and was one of the founders of a failed experiment that depended on an input-output model of development (which will be explained momentarily). The same author worked with the community to found the now successful Culture Bank. His experiences with the unsuccessful and the successful Culture Bank models help us better understand how the cultural wealth of a nation may be placed in the service of local economic development (or not):

> When I arrived in Fombori in 1995, I was introduced to an enterprising group of local women who had acquired funding from the U.S. Embassy to create a local museum. The funding was intended to serve a number of functions:

(1) to protect their cultural objects; (2) to protect their archeological sites; (3) to manage and encourage tourism; and (4) to promote the sales of locally produced handicrafts. I worked with these women's groups to build the "Museum of Fombori" over the course of the first year of my service.

The way that the villagers came together to help build the museum depended on their categorical identities: The men built a modest adobe structure with three small galleries and a boutique and office space; the women gathered an array of objects stored under beds and in granaries to install in the museum. Typical ritual objects include masks and statuary, weapons, tools, cookware, jewelry, wedding blankets, archeological objects, and art objects. The objects in the museum were appointed in a way that tourists would appreciate and understand.

The local people of Dogon country may deposit a cultural object in the Culture Bank. The bank displays the object in its museum, where tourists pay an entrance fee to see the collection. The Culture Bank's system for assessing the value of the handcrafted object encourages cultural preservation, but it does not, at the same time, exacerbate the illicit traffic of cultural artifacts. The loan value depends on the amount of verifiable historical data that the client can provide about her object rather than on the amount of money the object could garner in the commercial marketplace. The verification process depends on indigenous understandings of the object's use value and of its symbolic power. These local standards for evaluating the cultural objects highlight the social and symbolic nature of economic value. The object is valuable because there is a community of evaluators who agree to the standards of evaluation; moreover, external audiences holding and wishing to obtain the objects assessed recognize these evaluations as valid.

What follows is an excerpt from a catalogue document at the Culture Bank. The wooden fetish described here has first been named and classified. The catalogue then offers a detailed description of the object, its place of origin, and the ethnic group insisting on its rightful cultural linkage to the object. The object may be pledged to the museum in exchange for a loan, purchased for the museum's permanent collection, or loaned to the museum (for the purposes of a community event or a religious ritual) without any expectation that the lender will secure a loan.

Museum Catalogue Document

Object Name: Wooden Fetish named "Nassourou"

Classification [circle one]: **Religious Object,** Tool, Furniture, Art Object, Jewelry, Musical Instrument, Weapon, Game, Clothing, Archeological Object

Detailed Description: This wooden statuette represents a woman sitting on a stool held up by pairs of twins. The statuette features three pairs of twins, which represent fecundity in Dogon culture, plus a single baby on the woman's back. Nassourou wears a headress and necklace of brightly colored beads made from plastic beads. She also wears a necklace of red glass beads. The statuette shows scarification on its cheeks. Around its waist the object is wearing a blue, indigo loincloth and waist beads of blue plastic. The ankles are also decorated with beaded anklets. The woman is reposed on a round stool.

Place of origin: Mori (Kono) NINGARI

Ethnic Group: Dogon (tòmò)

Materials: Wood, plastic and glass beads

Property of: Women's Group from the 1st quarter (Hawa Ongoiba, President)

Artiste: Amesa GUINDO

State of conservation: Very good

Restoration Measures Taken: Grapeseed oil has been applied to the wood to keep it from drying out

Date of collection: May 27, 1997

Date of Loan: May 27, 1997

Method of Collection [circle one]: Purchased, **Pledged,** Loaned (no loan secured)

Drawing or Photo of Object:

> Signature of Manager: <u>Amadou Dadié ONGOIBA</u>
> Signature of Owner: <u>Hawa ONGOIBA</u>

For the Pledge Value Assessment document, the bank's personnel ask the borrower the following questions: What is the object? How is it used? Who made it? Where did it come from? What do the symbols on the object mean? Can you describe the rituals the object is used in and how? The more questions the borrower answers, the more valuable her object is. Each class of object has a loan ceiling established by the bank's board, and the questions that the borrower answers are weighted on a 100-point scale. Answer all of the questions, receive 100 percent of the loan amount for that class of object; answer 70 percent, receive 70 percent. Loans usually start small, at around fifty or 100 dollars, and they are used to support or expand small businesses. All loans must be for the purpose of generating revenue (not for disposable consumption).

Pledge Value Assessment Document

I. Qualifying Question: (48% of Loan Limit value per the relevant class of object)

What is this object? This is a wooden fetish named Nassourou which belongs to a local women's group. It is used to help women get pregnant. It represents fertility.

II. Background Information Questions: (4% additional value for each correct question)

Who created this object? Amesa GUINDO, a blacksmith in Mori

When is it used? It is used during special women's ceremonies

What is the purpose of the object? To render sterile women fertile

Who owned it before? Amesa GUINDO

Who owns it now? The women's group of the first quarter

When (what year) was it made? Unknown

When did you get it? 1994

Where was it created (fabricated)? Village of Mori (Arrondissement de Ningari)

Where was it used? Village of <u>Fombori</u>

Where did you get it? We bought it in Mori (Kono)

Why did it interest you? It was beautiful and powerful

How did you acquire it? We bought it

How is it used? The fetish is kept in the women's « guinna » house. Sterile women make sacrifices to it in order to become fertile . . . Nassourou acts as an intermediary between the woman and God.

III. Supplemental Questions (Bonus): (500 FCFA chacune)

Are there any family stories or legends about this object or this type of object? Do not know.

What do the various elements and decorations on the object symbolize? The various sets of twins on the statuette symbolize fertility. . . . a woman who is very fertile.

How is the object made/fabricated? Do not know

Total % 100% × 20 000 FCFA **(Limite du prêt)** + 500 **Bonus** = 20 500 FCFA

Montant proposé par la Banque Culturelle : 20 500 FCFA

Village :Fombori

Numéro de prêt :01

The bank's board differentiates between classes of objects that belong to individuals versus those that belong to groups, establishing different loan ceilings for each. The board also has a special category of objects "of great value" that are widely recognized for their cultural importance to the Dogon people, and this category of objects has the highest loan ceiling. A council of elders intervenes when there is suspect loan information, and the council uses the lived experiences of its elders to adjudicate conflicting, ambiguous, or suspect claims.

Bank staff document, photograph, and catalogue the cultural objects before organizing them into a public exhibit. The borrowers retain ownership and access to the objects throughout the duration of the loans and are permitted to remove their objects temporarily for use in rituals or for other family occasions. After the borrower has repaid the loan, she may reclaim the cultural object or she may resubmit her object to the bank for a loan of greater value, increasing the incentive to maintain the object at the bank (cultural preservation).

While the system for establishing the size of loans would seem to be sufficient for the bank to succeed, it requires attention to the meaningful circuits of exchange happening in the community and to the political environment in which tourism is being promoted. The second author recalls how initial efforts at establishing the Culture Bank failed:

The museum opened its doors in 1996, but it was not met with throngs of tourists. The Tuareg rebellion had begun in 1990 and had only just ended, dampening tourism. The Tuareg ethnic group wanted autonomy and had been engaged in battles with the Malian government in 1990 after Tuareg separatists assaulted government buildings in the Gao area. The civil war these attacks sparked re-routed tourist traffic to southern Dogon country, away from Fombori. And it was only in 1995 when moderates from both sides negotiated an end to the conflict. In 1996 the separatists burned their weapons ceremoniously in Timbuktu to mark a new period of peace.

Because the museum depended on tourism for revenue, it could not survive the inconsistent flows of tourists who came to visit and who were willing to pay the museum's entrance fee. On days when there were no tourists, the building remained shuttered. The circuit of tourists animated the museum and delinked the power of the museum's symbols from the population and the rituals that made that power real. Only a few months after the museum opened, termites swarmed through it, damaging its interior and threatening the integrity of the cultural objects it housed. The objects had to be removed to a safer place. The museum temporarily closed.

A Relational Model

This failed effort to develop a cultural bank-museum reminds us that the stocks of symbolic capital at a community's disposal do not pay dividends in any way that one might expect because symbolic capital is not a fungible resource. This sense that symbolic capital would be fungible and straight-forwardly convertible into economic capital comes from the undertheorized concepts of capital. The metaphor of "capital" as developed by Pierre Bourdieu (1986) and popularized by James Coleman (1993) and Robert Putnam (1993) emphasized the direct conversion of one capital into another; however, in their conversations with local people, the founders of the Culture Bank would come to recognize that symbolic capital operates within a basket of various types of capitals, and, unlike a financial portfolio, a diversified basket does not spread risk. Instead, the meanings of the symbols, the understandings about how objects should be used, and the rituals that create the emotional energy that sustains enthusiasm and that bolsters the sense of the sacred interact in unpredictable ways. Symbolic capital constitutes earmarked resources, matched to appropriate purposes. As such, it is contested and relational. The second author captures the relational work involved in establishing the bank by noting what other activities had to accompany it to make it make sense:

> Trying to understand the waning enthusiasm in the project, the project leaders and I met with the women's groups and the village leaders and conducted interviews to assess the situation; we quickly understood that the local people simply had more urgent priorities: namely, tending their millet fields and

raising and trading goats, sheep, and cattle to generate money for food and medicine. The harsh environment of the Dogon country allowed for little leisure activity; in the absence of tourism, the museum was considered to be an unprofitable (and therefore unfeasible) enterprise.

In our conversations with people we explored with the community how we could revitalize the museum to make it more beneficial and engaging for the local people. First, it was decided to take the focus off tourism, an undependable source of income at that point, and rather focus on meeting the various needs of the local population. The people wanted literacy programs to help them with their businesses, so we transformed the museum's office into a classroom space and outfitted it with desks and chalkboards. Local teachers taught language literacy and numeracy classes so that adults and children could learn how to read and write in Dogon. Some people did not like the way the objects in the building were being displayed; we reworked the exhibition and redecorated the museum according to local tastes and because most local people could not read we recorded tours in local languages. Collectively, we identified a host of events that would engage the community including cultural festivals, educational seminars, and conservation workshops. In subsequent years, the Culture Bank became a central social space in the community, hosting craft workshops, business skills seminars, local language courses, local festivals, conservation workshops, health seminars, and a youth theater program. One annual harvest festival, which features dancing, drumming, and wrestling, attracts thousands of participants from Dogon villages miles away.

Within the bounded circuit of intercourse among the participants in the Culture Bank, there were shared understandings about how objects ought to be displayed and about what other development concerns ought to be integrated in the new bank. A number of different transactions intermingle in the bank with their own media for exchange—local festivals require the use of some ritual objects held by the Culture Bank, the preparation of particular types of food, the donning of ritual dress, along with periods of call-and-response; youth theater involves tickets along with the donations of various props and costumes; handicraft workshops involve the exchange of tools, equipment, supplies, patterns, and labor. These various circuits are dynamic, and their dynamism provides the energy needed for subsequent transactions, including the impetus for enforcing the collective expectations governing the transactions at the bank (see Collins 2004 on emotional energy in interaction ritual chains).

Converting One Form of Capital into Another

The Culture Bank model demonstrates how the symbolic capital of hand-crafted objects can be converted into social and economic capital as well as re-invested into the community's stock of symbolic capital, but these conversions are not straightforward. On the one hand, repayment rates for the small business loans were high with defaults reported as rare (Crosby and Ebbe 1998: 22). In 2000 the total amount of loans disbursed was $14,279. Ninety-four percent of borrowers repaid their loans, and the bank's museum collection stood at 440 objects in three galleries. Borrowers reported that their household incomes grew 51 percent for women and 70 percent for men borrowers between 1995 and 2000 (Deubel 2006; Gueye 2002). On the other hand, the sustainability of the bank and the loan schemes require that policy makers and development practitioners pay attention to the multiple functions of the bank and the various nonfinancial activities that happen at the bank, enabling these conversions of symbolic wealth into economic capital.

In addition to serving as a tool for local economic development, the Culture Bank also functions to promote cultural preservation and to generate emotional energy that can be utilized in bolstering or amplifying existing efforts. The importance of cultural preservation and the function that the bank can play in it are exemplified in the story of the Tabi stone. In the early 1990s the second author was a Peace Corps volunteer, living at the far northern end of Dogon country in the town of Douentza, where he witnessed Dogon cultural artifacts being trafficked by people trying to sustain themselves financially. He tells the story this way:

> One Sunday, a small man in a tattered robe, a ragged turban unwinding off the top of his head, came to visit to speak about a private matter of importance. The man spoke of a magical stone that he had unearthed near his camp, in the hamlet of Tabi, in the open desert about 100 miles northwest of Douentza. He and his older brother had reportedly gone out to chop wood for their fire. As he whetted his axe, some water fell on a large flat stone beneath him. As the water struck the stone, images began to appear: The first image was of a horse and rider; the second, of a snake; then a mysterious script. He believed that this stone was a magical talisman because it was found next to

an ancient archeological site that had once been inhabited by a powerful tribe of sorcerers. He had heard about our "museum project" from some friends and thought that the stone could be beneficial for his village. The little man had come to ask me to return to Tabi to examine the stone and to see if it could be used as the centerpiece for a village museum for their community. He also wanted an expert to read the script on the stone and to decipher the stone's meaning.

The day after the encounter, I left with friends for Tabi in a borrowed Toyota 4×4. We drove two hours through the desert to a lonely hovel on a windswept plain. The man disappeared into the hut to retrieve the stone only to return minutes later dismayed and empty handed. He called to a young boy seated nearby, asking about the stone. The boy said that the man's elder brother had taken the stone to the nearby market town of Boni to sell it. Distraught, the man led us to the family compound where we discovered that his older brother had just sold the stone several hours ago to a local merchant. I accompanied the man and his brother to the merchant's house, but we found only a smoldering fire and a woman pounding millet. She said that her husband had left for Douentza to take something to the market to sell.

We then headed back to Douentza where we found both the merchant and his buyer next to the marketplace in the town square. When I inquired about the stone, the buyer said that it was very powerful and very secret and had been in his family for many years. He could only allow the stone to be looked at for a "viewing fee" of US$ 20,000. After I offered to decipher the script and to assess the object's market value, the merchant paused, considered the request, and told me to return tomorrow. The planned transaction the next day never happened. The merchant had sold the stone to a local antiquities dealer in Mopti who, in turn, had sold it to someone in Bamako. By now, it was likely that the stone had left the country and was on its way to a museum or a private collection in Europe or the United States.

The quest for the stone of Tabi is rendered here as a mythical journey, as a search for the sacred and a (failed for now) battle against the profane. The quest itself requires hardship (a long journey in a borrowed vehicle), initial uncertainty (not being sure if the stone is real, if its acquisition and protection are possible), isolation from the comforts and familiarity of home (on a lonely, windswept plain), and the encountering of profane obstacles to the quest's completion (viewing fees and mercenary merchants). The seekers' determination affirms the worth of the sacred object. Its loss evokes a sense of righteous indignation, anger, and emotional energy that can be mobilized to preserve other cultural objects and to do battle with the mercenary merchants sure to populate the perpetual path.

The Cultural Wealth of Mali

The stone of Tabi derives its value from its inherent characteristics, the stories told about those characteristics, and *the place* where the stone was found. We focus on place to understand how cultural heritage sites seem to be imbued with magical powers and how these powers seep into objects found at or near these sites. This means that the symbolic capital of an object depends on its attachment to meaningful geographies, and these spatial meanings are officially recognized as World Heritage sites.

According to UNESCO, Mali has three World Heritage sites, namely Timbuktu, Djenné, and Dogon country. Of these three, Timbuktu garners the most international recognition. Just north of the Niger River, Timbuktu is known for its mosques made of mud bricks and for the 100,000 manuscripts dating from the twelfth century and from pre-Islamic times. Henry Louis Gates's production of *The Wonders of the African World* on the Public Broadcasting Service (PBS) in 1999 brought it greater notoriety and alerted the world that many of these manuscripts were disappearing into private collections and museums. Bill Gates, the Andrew Mellon Foundation, and the government of South Africa have funded activities to conserve the area's manuscripts in secure, climate-controlled libraries within the city.

While Timbuktu is perhaps Mali's best-known destination, Djenné is the oldest surviving city in sub-Saharan Africa. Tourists flock to Djenné every Monday to see the Konboro mosque, the largest mud structure in the world and to haggle for souvenirs in the bustling market square. Yet cultural plundering also plagues Djenné. After Roderick and Susan McIntosh and Téréba Togola excavated the Djenné-Jeno site and *National Geographic* published an article detailing the archeological richness uncovered there, pillagers arrived in droves, digging for terracotta figurines. Many of these illicitly traded statutes have shown up in rather unexpected places, including at the presidential palace of Jacques Chirac (Huey 2009).

Unlike Mali's other World Heritage Sites, Dogon country derives additional value from the craftsmanship of its artisans and the scarcity of its original artworks. In the early 1900s the works of Picasso and Braque spurred interest in "primitive" African art from Mali among Western art collectors. In the 1950s with the publication of *Dieu d'eau*, which described the people and the arts of Dogon country, museum curators and art collectors began to buy the area's art works in large quantities. In 1957 in an art gallery in Los Angeles, Lester Wunderman encountered Dogon art and has since established a sizable collection at New York's Metropolitan Museum of Art (Imperato 1988). By the 1960s local traders had rummaged through many of the burial caves in the Bandiagara Escarpment for cultural artifacts (Leloup, Rubin, and Serra 1994). By the 1990s scholars and journalists again decried the ravages of the market on Mali's tangible cultural heritage, described as the "rape of Mali" (Brent 2006).

Malian cultural heritage had become embodied in musicians like Salif Keita, Ali Farka Toure, Amadou and Miriam, and Oumou Sangare. A cultural focal point for West Africa, Mali played host to the Festival in the Desert and the International Photography Festival. The Malian *bogolan* became an iconic representation of Africa, and Dogon statuettes became externally recognized indicators of African culture and civilization. These are the totems of the metaphorical tribe.

Totems and Symbolic Capital

Durkheim's work on totems serves as the basis for our understanding how symbolic capital works. In *The Elementary Forms of Religious Life*, Durkheim recognizes the totem as "the flag of the clan, the sign by which each clan is distinguished from the others, the visible mark of its distinctiveness, and a mark that is borne by everything that in any way belongs to the clan" (Durkheim [1912] 1995: 208). Some of the most effective totems are simple, enabling cognitive anchors to moor ideas in place. In other words, there is no ambiguity in what the totem means for its adherents. Durkheim uses the example of the color black as a symbol of mourning to impress on us how cognitive anchoring works. Because black is a symbol of mourning in Western society, it evokes feelings of loss and lamentation. The color sets off a chain of associations in the mind of its beholder, enabling "much more complete and more pronounced" emotional reactions to the situation than would have been manifest otherwise (Durkheim [1912] 1995: 221). The sacred character of the totem does not inhere in the animal, plant, or object itself. The totem reflects both the divinity and the social group. The divinity represented by the totem stands above and apart from the social group. The social group remains dependent on the divinity for protection and for nurturance. Similarly the social group requires the individuals comprising it to subsume individual interests for the sake of the collective.

These same dynamics can be found in modern-day totems that outsiders to a social group recognize as marking the distinctiveness of a group's traditions. For insiders, the totem represents an essential quality of the group's identity that transcends the qualities of the individuals making up the group. The belief that their group has essential characteristics depends on the social performance of that belief rather than on the inherent qualities of those characteristics; for example, the religious totems in Dogon country are deities who preside over the Dogon people, and the rituals in which these totems figure prominently demonstrate the connection between the totem and its clan. Part of this connection emerges in the fact that the totem and the ritual in which the individuals are interacting with the totem inspire an emotional response in its adherents. This emotional response enables the participants in the ritual to express righteous indignation at perceived violations of the sacred totem (Collins 2004).

In its surface manifestation, a totem seems to command respect, nearly irrespective of the material costs or benefits resulting from its respectful recognition. Not the totem but the sociability surrounding it explains its supernatural power. Durkheim writes: "Because social pressure makes itself felt through mental channels, it is bound to give man the idea that outside him there are one or several powers, moral yet mighty, to which he is subject" (Durkheim [1912] 1995: 211). Although the power of the totem seems to be external to him (god), Durkheim contends that these powerful entities come from society. As individuals come to believe that these powers exist, they subsume any of their own interests that might conflict with the supernatural, and they behave as if these supernatural powers will buttress their own pursuits:

> In the midst of an assembly that becomes worked up, we become capable of feelings and conduct of which we are incapable when left to our individual resources . . . we can . . . explain the curious posture that is so characteristic of a man who is speaking to a crowd—if he has achieved communion with it. His language becomes high-flown in a way that would be ridiculous in ordinary circumstances; his gestures take on an overbearing quality; his very thought becomes impatient of limits and slips easily into every kind of extreme. This is because he feels filled to overflowing. . . . This extraordinary surplus of forces

is quite real and comes to him from the very group he is addressing. . . . It is then no longer a mere individual who speaks but a group incarnated and personified. [Durkheim (1912) 1995: 211–212]

One can imagine rituals in which individuals feel the force of the leader as they recite a chant. Each ritual action, each chant echoed by the group becomes amplified for all present and is perceived to be an extraordinary surplus of forces.

Durkheim believed that this surplus of forces would compel people engaged in religious ritual to respect the sacred and to protect it from pollution by the profane; however, not every individual involved in a ritual feels the same sense of conviction about protecting the totem. While Durkheim reviewed the religious rituals of groups with high social closure—limited networks with outsiders that render the group's internal sanctioning mechanisms the primary source for reward and punishment (Coleman 1990; Portes and Sensenbrenner 1993)—many of the groups we study today have low social closure. Consequently, the group's professed solidarity may more easily be assured than its adherence to rules regarding how to treat the sacred and how the profane. As a result, one encounters reports of sacred objects being traded from one merchant to another, but these sales, as the story about the stone of Tabi suggests, do not happen without some recognition of what "ought" to happen. While one family member sought advice about how to preserve the stone of Tabi, another family member sought a commercial opportunity to supplement his income. Likewise, the newspapers have reported the pillaging of caves in the Bandiagara escarpment where tombs contained valuable, sacred objects.

The power of these totems lies not in whether all individuals adhere to the rules of the ritual but in whether members of the group and some members of outsider audiences readily acknowledge that some violations of the sacred are egregious and whether this recognition inspires action to right the wrong (Wherry 2008b). Because totems and the qualities they represent are a collective resource, a broad group of individuals can free ride, making claims to the resource and sometimes using that resource in ways that deplete it. If members of external audiences recognize the collective resource as universally valuable and worthy of protection, these violations of the sacred generate an emotional reaction and a sense of commitment for protecting a scarce and threatened resource. In other words, violations of the sacred enable the mobilization of material and political resources that might have remained dormant otherwise.

Portes and Sensenbrenner (1993) theorize the sense of belonging to a group sharing a common fate as bounded solidarity and describe it as a source of social capital—defined as the capacity to mobilize resources by dint of one's social ties. They predict that, if a class of people faces a common external adversary or a common threat, a feeling of "we-ness" will emerge among members of the group. In this way, bounded solidarity is a situational by-product, and once it is obtained it provides a basis for reciprocal exchanges and for altruism. Within some ethnic communities, bounded solidarity enables the establishment of scholarships for members of the group and for charitable donations when a member of the group finds herself in trouble (for example, legal defense funds, a destroyed home, injuries resulting from a hate crime). Bounded solidarity made possible by the symbolic power of a totem (or a set of totems) leads community members and those outsiders who respect the community's totems to offer aid in times of trouble, but this aid usually consists in protecting what symbolizes the community rather than in directly helping an individual member of the community.

Portes and Sensenbrenner (1993) offer a comprehensive scope of variables that promote bounded solidarity in their exploration of immigrant communities. These variables include the following: (1) distinct phenotypic or cultural characteristics and the existence of prejudice against these characteristics; (2) blockage of exit opportunities; and (3) situational confrontations. The authors offer a passage from *The Communist Manifesto* to illustrate how bounded solidarity emerges:

> With the development of industry the proletariat not only increases in number; it becomes concentrated in greater masses, its strength grows, and it feels that strength more. The various interests and conditions of life within the ranks of the proletariat are more and more equalized . . . The collisions between individual workmen and individual bourgeois take more and more the character of collisions between two classes. (Marx and Engels [1848] 1948, pp. 17–18, cited in Portes and Sensenbrenner 1993: 1324)

Marx and Engels's treatment of this we-ness suggests that it is structurally determined. The bounded group is exposed to conflict over a long period of time before solidarity emerges.

Those observing a particular totem see themselves as belonging to it or being nonmember observers of it. Their stance depends on their sense of sharing the same fate as those rallying around a particular totem. Durkheim ([1912] 1995: 238) writes: "What is fundamental to totemism is that the people of the clan, and the various beings whose form the totemic emblem represents, are held to be made of the same essence." In other words, what one worships is what one is. There are national totems around which people rally because these totems represent "the essence" of a nation and the best of its people. These indicators of membership in a national community act as a rallying point for ritual interactions and as a glue binding together the collective.

What makes the totem resonate as real is its placement in a circuit of commerce. Viviana Zelizer (2001, 2005a) coined the concept of circuits to indicate how meaningful and dynamic negotiations occur within various sites, including banks, and how the dynamic relations within those sites encompass different spheres of social life. Zelizer identifies four characteristics of a commercial circuit: (1) Its boundaries are well defined, and its actors exercise control over what types of transactions cross its boundaries. These transactions consist of (2) distinctive media (objects, legal tender, collateral bank notes, and the like) and (3) various categorical definitions of the types of transfers taking place within the circuit (donation, loan, compensation, gift). (4) The participants within the circuit have a shared understanding of what their relationships are with one another, and their actions within the circuit confirm, modify, or contest what those understandings are. These four interrelated characteristics suggest that it would be a mistake to treat symbolic capital as if it is an additive rather than an interactional resource.

Conclusion

This chapter has highlighted the potential of a nation's cultural wealth to be harnessed locally for economic development and the importance of highly particular, highly specific representations of national culture and local traditions for generating economic value at the community level. Development practitioners have been seeking new tools for ameliorating conditions of poverty, and tourism ministries, along with tour operators and producers of cultural commodities, have tried to harness all the attributes that might add value to their products and services. The Culture Bank offers an example of how these goals may be achieved by paying greater attention to the symbolic resources at a community's disposal by virtue of its country's international reputation and its local endowment of cultural riches. The case study also warns against facile approaches to development, with a set of standard inputs assumed to produce local economic development. To these promises and pitfalls of symbolic capital the conclusion turns.

The case of the Culture Bank reminds us that the strategic use of symbols does not replace material resources. Instead, the symbolic complements and interacts with the material conditions facing the villagers. The stone of Tabi leaves the village not because its symbolic power is not great but rather because the material conditions of the merchants are poor. The initial attempt to establish the Culture Bank fails not because symbolic capital cannot be converted into economic capital but rather because symbolic capital does not work like a financial instrument. One form of capital depends heavily on the other forms of capital in its orbit. When these orbits are considered holistically and when the broader material conditions of the community are addressed, symbolic capital becomes a powerful tool for local economic development.

The Culture Bank works well because it uses structures that may be appropriated for microlending and cultural preservation; however, these structures depend on existing circuits of commerce, restricting how those structures may be appropriated (Zelizer 2005b). This means that plopping down a culture bank wherever stocks of symbolic capital exist will not work. One has to build on existing circuits by incorporating activities that local people are already doing and that they consider important for the cultural and material life of the community. Attempts to pursue an input-out model rather than a relational model of development are likely to fail because culture does not work in any way that its appropriators wish it will. This is not to say that cultural wealth cannot be harnessed. Obviously, it has, and it will be again, but the ways that it becomes activated must be recognized.

7 Converting (or Not) Cultural Wealth into Tourism Profits

Case Studies of Reunion Island and Mayotte

Madina Regnault

"ALTHOUGH IT IS CLEARLY FAR FROM BEING A PANACEA, cultural tourism can often provide an attractive socio-economic development option for many societies" (Smith 2003: 56; see also Lanfant 1995). Focusing on Reunion Island and Mayotte, the two French territories located in the southwest Indian Ocean, the purpose of this chapter is to show to what extent cultural heritage can provide the basis for socioeconomic development through the blossoming of the tourism sector. The chapter also addresses how the process of generating income from cultural heritage calls into question whether the touted cultural heritage is rooted in local traditions or is staged solely for the purpose of income generation. These two questions should be considered concomitantly because they recognize the possibility that socioeconomic development based on cultural heritage has the potential to undermine the value of heritage. Cultural heritage tourism is becoming a profitable market that attracts, at the local level, numerous players trying to benefit from this growing tourism sector. At the macrolevel, public authorities create specific discourses to cater to tourists' expectations.

Both Reunion and Mayotte possess cultural wealth portfolios based on an important stock of cultural capital (Bourdieu 1986) that is mostly an "embodied cultural capital." According to the Bourdieusian definition, this cultural capital includes local beliefs, traditional practices, knowledge, know-how, and languages. What makes these various forms of cultural capital "authentic" and belonging to a single people in a particular place is both ambiguous, sometimes contested, and continually worked on (Cohen 1988; MacCannell 1973; Taylor 2001). Specifically, this chapter focuses on how several players involved in cultural tourism, including policy makers, craftspeople, and tourists, attempt to manage the impressions linked to the cultural wealth of these two islands. The Durkheimian approach is also useful for conceptualizing culture, especially in defining what commodified culture means in societies based on an intangible heritage. The construction of "capitalizing" culture has to be understood in a changing environment where the local cultural values and beliefs are always adapting, reinventing, re-creating, and rethinking themselves in reaction to both external and internal influences. The way people perceive themselves and their own collective identity (whether national or communal) is strongly related to the way this identity is represented and understood by tourists.

Methods and Data: Multisited Ethnography, Multiple Roles, Multiplication of Interlocutors

The study is based on semistructured interviews and participant and nonparticipant observation. I conducted interviews with different local policy makers directly involved in the cultural and/or the touristic field, including fourteen in Mayotte and nineteen in Reunion. The interviews covered questions about the image of the island, the main cultural resources, and the link between cultural and tourism policies. I also conducted more than 130 hours of participant observation (around forty hours in Mayotte and ninety-two hours in Reunion) by first involving myself in the "tourist role." Doing so, I took part in twenty-two excursions and organized trips and cultural animations designed for tourists; specifically, seven in Mayotte and fifteen in Reunion. Using this method helped me to witness the more spontaneous and genuine reactions of the tourists that could not have been revealed in an interview setting. Eleven months later, I returned to the islands for a more sustained period of observations. I observed local shows and sales of handicrafts. I complemented this by conversations with tourists (thirty-two in Mayotte and forty-five in Reunion) and asked them questions about how they perceived the local culture, heritage, and identity. These foreigners were interviewed when they were participating in excursions that emphasized local cultural heritage or in more intimate cultural demonstrations, such as traditional weddings, music shows, or spiritual events.

Drawing (or Not) from the Stock of Intangible Cultural Heritage

This chapter uses UNESCO's 2003 Convention for the Safeguarding of Intangible Cultural Heritage to identify the various components of cultural capital being used in the tourism sector. UNESCO's definition of cultural capital includes the "practices, representations, expressions, knowledge, skills—as well as the instruments, objects, artifacts and cultural spaces associated therewith—that communities, groups and, in some cases, individuals recognize as part of their cultural heritage." The five domains of "intangible" cultural heritage recognized by UNESCO are: (1) oral traditions; (2) performing arts; (3) social practices, rituals, and festivals; (4) knowledge about nature and the universe (cosmology); and (5) traditional craftsmanship.

Referring to the UNESCO definition, the first domain of intangible heritage is "oral expressions and traditions, including language as a vehicle of the intangible cultural heritage." In Reunion and Mayotte various oral expressions are important. Most common in Reunion are tales, which were traditionally transmitted in the creole language but are nowadays translated, written, and published (Honoré 2003). Also in Mayotte, local tales used to be transmitted only in the local languages (*shimaoré* and *shibushi*), but now they are translated into French for the sake of foreigners (Soilihi and Blanchy 2002). As conduits of traditional roots of these oral societies, these published tales are extremely appreciated by foreigners. But, more than the tales themselves, it is often the whole context of tale telling and oral traditions that attracts the tourists. For example, in Mayotte, the tales used to be told by an elder in a village or under a huge baobab on the beach. However, a tourist would rarely come by such an "authentic" experience because these were not usually shared with outsiders (in addition to becoming increasingly rare among the locals as well due to the country's rapid modernization). How oral traditions are maintained, transmitted, and performed affects how well they may be transformed into economic wealth. One could imagine that tourist organizations might try to stage an authentic experience of tale telling, but such a staging might garner only marginal economic rewards. At the same time, a village elder telling tales may generate symbolic value that others may capture to generate economic capital. It is because the villager is not trying to garner economic rewards from the tale telling that his or her tale telling is so profitable (for example, Wherry 2008a).

The second domain of intangible heritage encompasses "performing arts." Reunion is home to famous dances and music like *Maloya* and *Séga*. In Reunion, because music is everywhere in everyday life, the tourist automatically becomes a part of this specific atmosphere. Furthermore, the natives easily share their musical heritage and experience of performance with foreigners. But, contrary to the local people who know and have never forgotten the painful intangible heritage of this music that comes from the slave times (see Sudel Fuma 2004 and Benjamin Lagarde 2007 about *Maloya*), foreigners often simply perceive its apparently "joyful" aspect. This disconnect between what the songs mean and how different audiences experience them highlights why one cannot simply look at the cultural portfolio of a country's folk music and know how its different categories of music will be received. The meaning of the music depends on the interactions between the performers and the audience. In Mayotte, there are other specific performing arts such as *Mgodro* and *Mrengue* that are also easily accessible to foreigners because they are present both in the private and the public sphere.

The third domain of intangible cultural heritage, as defined by UNESCO, concerns "social practices, rituals and festive events." In Reunion, there are festive events of different cultural and religious roots. According to Nelson H. H. Graburn (1983: 28), in the anthropology of tourism, further research should analyze "the significance of the interaction between institutional development and tourist culture . . . , particularly those establishments which may not directly be part of the industry but which have great significance for tourism." In Graburn's framework the festival is one of the most important events because it provides a setting for the interaction between the local community and the tourists. In Reunion, tourists enjoy the spiritual diversity and like to participate in traditional celebrations, such as the *Dipavali*, that is a Tamil celebration. More and more foreigners go to see this religious and cultural event that translated as "the Festival of Lights" because of its "spectacular" aspect and the "beauty of the colors and the lights," as a French tourist I met there told me. Interestingly, the public and secular municipalities are involved in the promotion of this religious celebration, especially in the cities with a significant Tamil population, such as Saint André.

In Mayotte, Muslim and African-inherited traditions have left a deep mark on traditional practices and events. The most important event is the "*Haroussi*," which is the name of the comorosian wedding (see Figure 7.1). This huge, colorful, and spectacular event is extremely appreciated by foreigners, so much so that there is a growing presence of Western people during the traditional weddings in Mayotte. The intrusion of strangers into the private sphere can be explained by an increasing quest for new emotions in a world where people are "looking permanently for innovations in other cultures and are interested in 'exotic' and 'authentic' cultures" (Schuerkens 2003: 219).

Figure 7.1 A traditional wedding ceremony in M'tsapéré (Mayotte). Madina Regnault.

The fourth UNESCO domain of intangible cultural heritage is "knowl-edge and practices concerning nature and the universe." By creating in 2004 the honorary title of *Zarboutan nout kiltir*, the Regional Council of Reunion has decided to honor the guardians of local knowledge and practices, such as the *Granmoun* (meaning the elders). In Mayotte, every generation is pro-foundly respectful of the *Fundis* (a person who possesses a particular local knowledge or know-how). Many tourists today—especially "romantic tour-ists" as Urry (1990) dubbed them—engage in tourism to find their roots and answers to existential questions, so partaking in events that transmit "knowl-edge and practices concerning nature and the universe" is of substantial inter-est to them. However, local activities concerning "nature and the universe" are largely kept secret and closed to strangers in both societies. According to a *Fundi* I met in Mtsamboro (North of Mayotte), this is because this special knowledge has to be passed on from generation to generation, by and for peo-ple of the same village or the same area. To the extent that local knowledge, local cosmologies, and the practices they enable remain relatively inaccessible to outsiders, both sites continue to have a durable source of symbolic wealth (Wherry 2008a).

Finally, the fifth UNESCO domain of intangible heritage is traditional craftsmanship. Handicrafts are less important in Reunion and Mayotte's collective culture than the intangible elements. The foreigners surveyed in the two islands largely confirmed that fact, yet handicrafts are part and parcel of the international tourism experience. On the ground, this means that handicrafts are on offer in the marketplace, even where there is no strong local tradition of craftsmanship intended for the tourism commercial circuit. These expectations of international audiences enable the invention of a tradition. In other words, the symbolic resources expected of a particular place may lead to its creation, or this situation may lead to the use of substitutes from other locales to meet market demand. In the event that such market demands lead to the use of substitutes rather than to revivification of the old or the invention of a new authenticity, the capacity of traditional craftsmanship to generate economic capital may be weak (see, for example, Wherry 2008a).

In both Reunion and Mayotte, I asked tourists to tell me what they thought was the most important aspect of the country's cultural offerings. I found that only a minority of the tourists I interviewed identified "tangible cultural heritage" (such as types of housing, musical instruments, or handicrafts) as the country's most important cultural offering. Only one out of the thirty-two tourists I spoke with in Mayotte said that tangible cultural heritage was for her the main cultural wealth of the island. In Reunion, the trend was similar, as only two out of the forty-five tourists I encountered said that the intangible cultural heritage was the main cultural wealth that attracted them. Where tourists differed was in their perception of the "intangible" versus the "human" heritage of each place. By "human heritage," I mean not the expressions of the cultural specificities and expressions of these people, which I categorize as "intangible cultural wealth," but the local people *themselves*. Twenty-nine out of the forty-five foreigners interviewed in Reunion ranked human heritage as the most important cultural offering in Reunion, while twenty-one out of the thirty-two tourists I interviewed in Mayotte identified intangible cultural heritage as the most important cultural offering there.

In sum, the five different domains of the intangible cultural heritage of Reunion and Mayotte represent the basis for cultural tourism on these two islands. As Graburn (1983: 11) writes, "tourism is a 'modern ritual' in which the populace 'gets away from *it all*,' the '*it all*' being ordinary workaday, mundane life, particularly work, which includes the workplace, homework and housework." The fact that Reunion and Mayotte's cultural heritage is based on an oral culture and symbolic resources is of great appeal to Western tourists who try more and more to escape "it all" through a transient immersion in far-away lands. However, Reunion is able to convert cultural wealth into tourist arrivals much more successfully than Mayotte.[1] The following sections try to explore the reasons for this discrepancy. I argue that creating an image, based not on local realities but on political motivations, could be an obstacle to an effective promotion of tourism, resulting in lower tourist arrivals.

Reunion Island

Making Reunion's Cultural Wealth a Tourist Attraction

At the end of the 1980s the public authorities of Reunion Island began to pay more attention to tourism as a way of economic development. At that time, the image of Reunion portrayed to potential tourists was mainly based on Re-union's nature, and not on its culture, because it was promoted as the "Intense Island." At the end of the 1990s, the public authorities decided to reenvision the image of Reunion by highlighting the richness of its people with its mixed background, cultures, and traditions. Picard (2005: 46) demonstrates how, at that time, "economic wealth became less a product of cultivating the land for its agricultural surplus, than for gardening it for its aesthetic and symbolic 'fruits.'" Consistent with this, public officials in charge of Reunion tourism changed the official slogan to "Reunion Island, a World in the World." It has proved to be a particularly rewarding choice in terms of impression management (Goffman 1959), making an argument that costs nothing but brings a lot of appeal to the place. Based on the discourses of the vacationers who gave me information about the motivations behind their destination choice, it appears that tourists are particularly attracted to this island presented as a paradise where very different and mixed populations coexist peacefully.

Still, converting cultural wealth into tourist Euros and dollars is not a straightforward matter. First, when one deals with intangible cultural heri-tage, it is unclear what exactly one can sell to tourists and how to do it most effectively. Moreover, this process has been made difficult in Reunion by the fact that official cultural policies for the island are not linked to the tourism ones. The cultural policy of Reunion has been well developed since the end of the 1970s, emphasizing the history of Reunion people and especially the slavery past. It is clearly a policy "made in Reunion for Reunion people," as a tourism representative for ODIT France[2] told me. In such a context, it is thus difficult to develop coordination between the tourism and the cultural sectors. Added to that, there is certain distrust of such a potential coordination from the cultural policy makers. As the person in charge of the cultural infrastructures at the Conseil Général de La Réunion told me,

> When we work on the field of culture, we are having high expectations and we feel a little, hmm, dirty doing tourism. Culture is something noble. . . . It is true that tourism has this 'marketing' side, 'popularization,' whereas we have a quality approach. We agree to have a partnership, but we have to be sure of the quality. We refuse to produce a speech that was not confirmed at the scientific level and is a bad popularization.

However, despite such hesitations, it appears that, by comparing the evolution of the discourses of policy makers interviewed during the three periods of my fieldwork, Reunion's decision makers are more and more aware that the development of cooperation between the two public policies is a significant opportunity.

They have started to realize that supporting the development of interconnected policies of the cultural and touristic sectors is a good strategy for economic reasons. Tourism is clearly a lucrative sector on the island. According to the institution in charge of tourism in Reunion (the Comité Regional du Tourisme), the tourist monies spent in Reunion were estimated at 137.1 million Euros in 2008 and increased 6.1 percent from 2007 to 2008. In this context, elaborating an appropriate strategy of cultural tourism would certainly be a way to create economic capital and contribute to lowering unemployment in this island, where the unemployment rate is the highest of all the French *départements*.

Second, there are noneconomic considerations that have to be taken into account. States promoted cultural commodities also to promote the cultural image of their countries (Graburn 1976; Wherry 2005).[3] The promotion of particular cultural sectors of the economy is possible not only because they can be readily converted into economic wealth but also due to a public commitment to native culture promotion. Such actions are often motivated by an urge to take a stand in opposition, or at least in reaction, to a cultural model that was strongly imposed by the conquerors and the colonizers. As a duty of memory, and sometimes as a commitment, local policy makers reaffirm their cultural specificity and try to construct a specific image of the society they belong to. This thesis applies perfectly to Reunion because the past evolutions show a cultural reaffirmation built in opposition to the former French model of cultural assimilation. However, in Reunion, the authorities did not build an image by making a clean sweep of the past. As Wherry (2005) suggests, each country "work[s] its reputation for culture according to how the nation-state define[s] itself and in response to a set of historical contingencies." Reunion's public authorities appropriate their historical heritage by making "heritage tourism" a profitable sector with the promotion of *lieux*, places, that I refer to as *sur-lieux*. This concept has to be understood in reference to the famous concept of *non-lieux* created by Marc Augé (1992) to define specific spaces that exist in the contemporary "surmodernity" period. These spaces, principally associated with transit and communication, are characterized by the fact that an individual doesn't appropriate them because they don't have their own identity; they don't have a history; they are *non-lieux*. In his work, Augé implicitly positions these *non-lieux* in opposition to all the other *lieux*. In my view, the *non-lieux* are not the antithesis of the *lieux*, but, in fact, the *non-lieux* are an inversion to the *sur-lieux*. The *sur-lieux* could be defined as spatial matrix of immense symbolic capital and intangible heritage that, more than other *lieux*, are appropriated by the people of a specific community because they have a strong history, a strong past, and a strong identity. This is especially the case of what Pierre Nora (1984) called the *lieux de mémoire* (realms of memory).

I have observed the reactions of the tourists in these *sur-lieux*, that are, on Reunion Island, mainly linked to the slave trade's history. Many tourists I met in these places are deeply touched by these sites, and they try to appropriate them by comparing them to places that are familiar to them. But sometimes these appropriations are made in inappropriate ways, as was clear in a case of one American tourist visiting the Lazaret (see Figure 7.2)—a place where slaves were quarantined—when she said that she was overwhelmed to visit this "equivalent of Ellis Island."

Tourists' Perceptions of Reunion's Culture: The Rainbow Wealth

In my survey of tourists visiting Reunion, I was able to get at some of their perceptions of the island's cultural wealth. One of my questions aimed at comparing the impression the local leaders wished to make with the perceptions foreigners held about the local human and cultural capital. I asked the tourists to select from a provided list those things that they thought were characteristic of the island identity. In an overwhelming majority, the foreigners chose the word *mixed* to define the identity of Reunion's inhabitants as

Figure 7.2 A tour guide explaining Lazaret history. Elizabeth McCann.

the main and most important criterion. I argue that this complete accordance with the image highlighted by the local authorities could be explained both by the fact that is a cultural reality as well as because it is constructed as such. The official emphasis on diversity is so imbedded in the foreigners' perceptions that this is the criterion that immediately come to their minds.

Despite these general impressions, there were also some differences in tourists' views of the local identity. For instance, in the village of Hell-Bourg, I met a couple of retired French tourists (around sixty-five years old) and a couple of young Belgian tourists (the young lady was twenty-two, and her partner was twenty-five). Their views about the local identity were strikingly different. The older couple explained to me how wonderstruck they were by the cultural diversity and even showed me a picture they took of a Creole child with red hair, to support what they were saying. In contrast, Damien, the young Belgian tourist, said:

> When you arrive on the island, you are totally surprised by the mix of cultures, and you really think that all the different communities live together. If you think so, it is because this is what you see first and because the authorities have constructed this ideal image. . . . It is only when you go in isolated areas

and when you speak with the population, and you spend time with them, that you see "behind the postcard" and see that there are strong inequalities and impossible dialogues between some groups of populations. (Hell-Bourg, October 2009)

An Example of a Successful Cultural Tourism Project: The Label "Creoles Villages" in Reunion

"Creole Villages" is a network of fifteen villages that emphasizes the cultural wealth of Reunion through excursions offered to tourists. This label is characterized by the image of friendly, warm, welcoming places, where tourists are supposed to be "in direct contact with an authentic and traditional culture" (Villages Créoles 2010). When I personally traveled to these villages, the first thing that came to my mind was that there was nothing "authentic" about them. These places seemed to have become completely commodified and turned into a business where guides feed the tourists with the same and impersonal speech over and over again. It resonated very much with Greenwood's (1977: 179) report of "the culture brokers [that] have appropriated facets of a life-style into the tourism package to help sales in the competitive market."

Furthermore, during the high season, tourists are sometimes more numerous than the inhabitants of the small villages visited. This point can be linked to the issue emphasized by André Rauch (2002), who explains how, in a touristic region with a strong density of vacationers, natives feel transformed. Their own identity is threatened in two ways as they become *allochtons*:[4] On the one hand, they temporarily become a minority and lose their privileges, to the point that they may not feel at home anymore; on the other hand, they are forced or convinced to "act their difference" to attract the visitors' interest. However, it can also be the case, as others have argued that, for the natives, engaging in representations of their local culture is also a way to reconstruct and reappropriate their own identity. In her article published in the book *Inégalités et Spatialité dans l'océan Indien*, Marie-Gisèle Dalama (2005: 253), who studied the case of these "Creoles Villages," explained that the quest for authenticity is sought after not only by the tourists but also by the local populations. Outside of the *Hauts* (that is, the inside lands), tourism is seen as a conveyor of distribution of the Creole image. Inside the *Hauts*, tourism is seen as a tool for identity construction, a kind of retrospective psychology for the inhabitants of Reunion.

Mayotte

Exploiting Mayotte's Cultural Wealth by Cultural Tourism, a Contradictory Process

In contrast to Reunion, the strategic impression management of Mayotte for the purposes of tourism development has happened only recently. It is only since the creation of the *Club outre-mer* in 2003 within the Economic Interest Group (GIE) Maison de France—which specializes in the analysis of markets and the promotion of all the overseas destinations—that Mayotte has started to develop a local tourism policy. The main official body, the Comité Départemental du Tourisme de Mayotte (CDTM; the Mayotte Tourism Departmental Committee), which engages in public relations and tourism promotion, saw its budget rise 69 percent in 2006 (1.5 million Euros) compared to the 2005 figures. CDTM aims at implementing a country and town planning policy (reception and housing facilities, especially in rural areas), trainings, and communication tools and plans to be part of the committee ranking tourism structures, to promote quality seals for small, unrated structures; to establish partnerships with the Cultural Cooperation and the Craftsmen's Network; and to intensify regional partnership on common tourist products (Direction of Tourism of the French Ministry of Economy, Finance and Employment 2007).

On its website's homepage, the CDTM presents the island as such: "It is comforting to note that in the third millennium, when the whole world is listed and catalogued into innumerable possibilities for organized travel, there are still some destinations which have been able to preserve their independent rhythm of life and their centuries-old traditions." Even though the authorities have begun to define a strategy to promote Mayotte as a tourist destination, as concerns cultural tourism on this island, the process is still fragile, unfinished, and full of contradictions.

As in Reunion, the first obstacle for the conversion of cultural wealth into economic value is the intangible aspect of the local heritage in Mayotte. Another challenge is that the development of the cultural sector is *not* a priority for the local authorities in Mayotte, as it is for local authorities in Reunion. More specifically, the Schéma d'aménagement du tourisme (Tourism Development Plan) of the CDTM does not really attach importance to the cultural sector. But the most important obstacle is political. There is a strong opposition between the will to value a cultural heritage that can be a source of economic capital and the distrust toward this same heritage. It reflects the

challenges facing the policy makers. They are having difficulty in positioning themselves with regard to the strong Muslim and African specificities of
this really special French territory. On the one hand, these characteristics are
simply stated as facts, for example, on the website of Mayotte's Tourism Office, where Mayotte is presented as a land that "still maintains its living African roots" (p. 5 of the official guide) and where the Islamic "religion is today
omnipresent in daily life" (p. 6, ibid). On the other hand, these specificities
are not effectively emphasized through actions or activities of promotion. The
policy makers seem reluctant to adopt a clear strategy toward this local culture because this would fit poorly with the character of the island's official
French culture. Still, my interviews of the Mayotte locals revealed that they
used to be perceived as on the fringe of the French Republic and not an integral part of it. A young student from Mayotte living in Montpellier (France
mainland) told me, "Before coming here [to Montpellier] I considered myself
as both Mahorais and French, but since I am here, it is difficult to have the
sensation of belonging to France since the majority of French people don't
know that Mayotte is a French territory and where it is located."

Because of this common ignorance about Mayotte's Frenchness, local
authorities choose to stress Mayotte's belonging to France and evoke a comparison to Reunion, saying that Reunion is not the only French territory in
the area. This is made extremely clear with the slogan on the posters put up
in Mayotte airport, proclaiming: "Mayotte, the other France of the Indian
ocean." It is likely that highlighting symbolic resources that are not embedded
in local conditions, but on a political construction, and not internalized by
local populations, is an obstacle to effective touristic promotion. The situation
is complicated by the fact that even within the group of public officials, there
are differences in the logic of impression management employed. Administrators working in the Conseil Général de Mayotte (General Council) and the
municipalities emphasize local cultural elements such as languages, Muslim
religion, beliefs, music, and the like. On the other hand, administrators from
mainland France and those working at Mayotte Prefectures (which depend
on France) emphasize the French culture and the fact that Mayotte is tied to
France.

Why Support Cultural Tourism in Mayotte?

As in Reunion, at Mayotte there is a sense that there are economic reasons for
marketing cultural heritage via the development of tourism, which is also a

vehicle for certain native groups with a particular knowledge or know-how to be integrated into the market world. In a speech made in Mayotte on May 20, 2001, the former French president, Jacques Chirac, highlighted that the crafts are one of the privileged carriers of the social and professional integration of women. While reducing gender inequalities by increasingly including the women of Mayotte in market activities, cultural tourism development has considerable favorable economical effects as it is a source of employment.

Noneconomic reasons also have to be taken into account. Within less than one decade, many important cultural changes in Mayotte have turned this initially traditional society upside down, and the future changes will be even more brutal. On March 31, 2011, Mayotte officially became the 101st *département* of the French republic. As I have argued elsewhere, this institutional evolution will necessitate many cultural changes to fit in with the values of the French Republic (Regnault 2009). Because France is a secular (but traditionally Catholic) country, many religious (Muslim) elements would have to be outlawed. In this context, beyond being simply an economic issue, emphasizing and promoting symbolic capital through the tourism sector is also a cultural necessity. Tourism might be for Mayotte's inhabitants—as it was in Bali, as described by Picard (1992)—an opportunity to become aware of their cultural wealth, preserve it, and build pride out of it.

"Exotic" Mayotte: Tourists' Perceptions of the Island's Cultural Wealth

To compare the discourses created by the policy makers and the vision of foreigners, I met several tourists from different countries of origins and asked them what they thought was most characteristic of Mayotte's identity. The term first chosen was *Muslim* and, close after that, *African origins*. The term *French influence* was chosen most infrequently. Contrary to Reunion, where the impressions of the tourists are in accordance with the images created by tourism officials, in Mayotte, the official image created (emphasizing the fact that Mayotte is French and that it is the "other France of the Indian Ocean") is far from aligned with the audience's perceptions.

Political Issues and Difficulties with Cultural Tourism in Mayotte

The diverse interviews I had with tourists, public authorities, and private actors in Mayotte led me to the same observation: Cultural tourism, as a structured policy, does not exist in Mayotte. There are only a few and rare private initiatives that offer cultural performances. There have been several attempts, but they seem to have great difficulty getting off the ground for various reasons, which could be due to a certain disinterest for the development of this sector. For instance, in Boueni (South of Mayotte), a project called the "Village Tobé" has enabled the training of 130 persons in eleven professions involved in crafts and also the creation of several handicrafts retail outlets. Wherry has shown that because "impression management is a process in which local improvisations influence and are influenced by non-local expectation" (Wherry 2008a: 121) some local actors could contest or misunderstand the way they are asked to perform. This is exactly what happens with the Village Tobé project in Boueni. While the project's goal was to "protect a traditional heritage in the respect of the cultural values of Mayotte's society" (as stated in a working document about the project), some craftspeople had, at the beginning, refused to go along with this image. They thought that showing traditional objects was against integration into modernity, and they were afraid that outsiders would get an impression that these traditional objects were part of Mayotte's current society. Confronted with this unexpected situation, the person in charge of the project had to engage in several actions aimed not toward the tourists but toward the local actors to convince them of the legitimacy of the project. In the end, the local community did lend its support to the project, boding well for its success; the authorities decided to transform it into a larger-scale program, including several different types of economic activities. However, these could not materialize due to a lack of management and financial support, leading to the general failure of the Village Tobé project. This was not an isolated case. Another project, called the "Village Vacances," located in Kani-Kéli (south of the island) was also supposed to be an appealing place for the tourist. It would offer cultural services—such as handicrafts or culinary products—to both local populations and tourists in a unique natural environment (Mount "Choungi"). However, financial and managerial difficulties similar to those in Village Tobé constrain its development.

Currently, another project is gathering many hopes. This is the project of the Ecomusée de l'Habitat (Ecomuseum of Housing) supported by the Comité Départemental du Tourisme de Mayotte. The aim of this ecomuseum is to present the history and the characteristics of the diverse traditional housing of Mayotte and the way the inhabitants were used to living. While promoting this cultural wealth, the project would convert it into monetary resources by developing touristic activities in the region. While this project was presented by the CDTM as its "flagship project" for 2009, internal conflicts resulting from a lack of coordination during the process of nominating a new person in charge have delayed its development for many months. By the beginning of 2011, the project seemed to have been completely forgotten, marginalized, by the local authorities.

Importantly, as Raissa Feno, appointed in May 2009 by the municipality of Chiconi (on the West side of Mayotte) for the promotion of arts and crafts, pointed out, around fifty talented and inventive craftspeople exist in this small area of Chiconi and around, but their activities are not promoted or publicly supported. This is consistent with a general lack of sustained support for handicrafts in Mayotte.

As Colloredo-Mansfeld (2002) shows, the potential for some artisan economies to be integrated in the commercial marketplace is predicated not only on economic factors but also on expressiveness and communication, which seem to be lacking in Mayotte. While there may have been economic demands for handicrafts on this island, there hasn't been a strategy to develop and promote them. However, as Colloredo-Mansfeld argues, the value of the crafts relies on the social performance of the artisans and how well matched the audiences' expectations are with the underlying messages of the performance. A performance is believable in part because the audience wants it to be so, given what the audience thinks it knows about the performers and about the narrative those performers ought to proffer.

Souvenirs from Elsewhere

While the level of public support for cultural tourism is very different on Mayotte and on Reunion, it is interesting that to some extent the response by local actors is quite similar, especially as concerns handicrafts. Local handicrafts and artifacts made in Reunion and in Mayotte are rare. They are mostly specific objects made for many generations by the natives of those islands, including utilitarian objects made from the weaving of vegetable fibers in Reunion and wooden utilitarian objects that served in the house or in bush in Mayotte. Neither of these objects seems to be attractive as handicrafts to sell to tourists. Hence, in both Reunion and Mayotte, private players have adapted themselves to the tourist market, so to speak, and succeeded in getting around the problem of the lack of local specific handicrafts by answering tourists' expectations with regard to "authentic" cultural commodities that they can take

Figure 7.3 A retail outlet of handicrafts made in Madagascar, in Mamoudzou's Market (Mayotte). Madina Regnault.

with them back to their home countries. Tourists in Reunion and Mayotte can easily buy some "souvenirs," but these are handicrafts that are, in the overwhelming majority, imported from Madagascar (Figure 7.3).

It is thus surprising to find objects (like baskets made in raffia) with "Mayotte" written on them and then learn that they are not made in Mayotte but in Madagascar. A Malagasy saleswoman said to me, "I am not ashamed to say that this is their [Mayottes'] fault. They are idlers. There is a market, if they do not want to give the tourists what they are expecting, we will give the *vazahas* ["white outsiders" in Malagasy] what they want."

Graburn (1983) demonstrated how important souvenirs are for tourists, as they are the proof of their intimate contact with the "other." Graburn (2000) added that the more educated and status conscious the traveler, the more concerned that person will be that his or her souvenirs are authentic. In fact, it seems that sometimes the need for this proof of the encounter with the "other" is more important that the genuine authenticity of the proof itself. After all, the proof does not have *to be* authentic itself; more important is that it *looks* authentic to the uninitiated eye. I met a Frenchwoman from a small town near Toulouse in the market of Saint-Denis de La Reunion when she was buying some souvenirs, and she told me, "Of course I know that these handicrafts are not from here, but what can we do when we have nothing locally made to buy? We can't come home without anything for our friends or relatives. And you know what, for them, it is exactly the same whether it is made in Madagascar or here in Reunion!" Contrary to what I originally thought, this woman was totally aware of the inauthentic aspect of the handicrafts and was even ironic about it. This posttourist, who has "ironic detachment from experiences and situations" (Smith 2003: 35), has different personal experiences from those of the cultural tourists, who have "earnest interactions with destinations and inhabitants" (Ibid.).

Conclusion

The cases of Reunion and Mayotte show the extent to which it is possible for small territories to convert, or not, cultural wealth into tourism profits. Taking after Hobsbawm and Ranger's notion of the invention of tradition (1983), the process is that of the capitalization of tradition. In other words, tradition in Reunion and Mayotte is a very diverse and appealing symbolic resource that has been invented and reinvented and that is now trying to be transferred into economic capital.

As the comparison of the official promotion efforts and impressions of tourists on these two islands reveals, the outcomes are quite different because Reunion is much more successful in cultural tourism than Mayotte. I traced the reasons for this difference to the political nature of impression management at the state level. As Donald V. L. Macleod and James G. Carrier (2010) suggest, it is crucial to take into consideration the issues of power while analyzing the promotion of local culture in the touristic prospect. If diverse voices exist to push different portrayals of a tradition, as in Mayotte, there is little chance that consistent support for cultural heritage, including promotion and financing, will ensue. Moreover, it is likely that there will be a dissonance between tourist impressions and public intentions, yielding official promotions less effective than they could be. Even if the private actors were the first to understand it as such, Reunion's and Mayotte's public authorities are also well aware that cultural tourism can bring benefits. Projects based on cultural intangible heritage are multiplying, and there is also a wish to develop specific handicrafts that are locally made and not imported. However, such projects can be successful only when integrated into a system of coordinated public policies that build a consistent image of the island's cultural wealth aligned with local people's expectations.

Moreover, the notion of the capitalization of tradition makes visible the fact that, during the capitalization process, the local traditional values are staged for the tourists. This means that what the indigenous people live and embody is not the same as what the foreigners receive and choose to pay attention to. In a relational process, not only is the local tradition capitalized for tourism, but tourism also creates neotraditions that are what tourists anticipate to see, hear, and live.

Nevertheless, if the risks of mutations and misunderstanding exist when we look into the case of Western tourists' experience, future research would be well served to pay attention to a specific type of tourism that is proportionally extremely important[5] in these islands, namely *"tourism affinitaire,"*[6] consisting of people who are visiting friends or relatives (Musso 2005) to spend their holidays on their island of origin. As put forward by Appadurai (2001), notably through his concept of ethnoscape, in a world of increasing migratory flows, the deterritorialized groups are never totally deterritorialized; they remain strongly connected to their cultural roots.

IV

The Cultural Wealth in
Global Value Chains

8 Constructing Scarcity, Creating Value

Marketing the Mundo Maya

Jennifer Bair

IN OCTOBER 1989, *National Geographic* featured a cover story about a path called the *Ruta Maya*, or Mayan Route, which winds through a multicountry region of Mesoamerica rich in ecological and cultural diversity. Although it was said to have some relationship to ancient trade routes, the *Ruta Maya* was essentially a tourism product devised by several of the region's governments, in conjunction with the editor of *National Geographic*. This initiative, which later came to be known as the *Mundo Maya*, promotes the distinctive resources of the Mayan region, both natural and human, with the aim of attracting visitors and generating revenues. Like other ventures in heritage tourism, it is an effort to market what contributors to this volume are calling cultural wealth and to leverage that wealth into economic development.

In this chapter, I bring the analytical framework of global value chain (GVC) analysis to bear on the *Mundo Maya* to investigate how this conversion of cultural wealth into tourist dollars occurs. I explain that the *Mundo Maya* project represents a collaborative effort to upgrade the region's tourism offerings beyond the "sun, sea, and sand" model typical of Mexico and the Caribbean. For it to succeed, potential visitors must be convinced that, among the possible destinations from which they can choose, the Mayan world is unique and, therefore, valuable. This effort to market the *Mundo Maya* is fundamentally an exercise in promoting the region's cultural wealth, and I show that such an exercise not only necessitates a set of decisions about how the qualities and characteristics of a particular place and its people should be presented to the consumer but that it also involves contentious negotiations, and potentially even conflict, among various stakeholders about how and by whom the region's cultural wealth should be defined and valuated. While this case study of the *Mundo Maya* provides an opportunity to consider what is distinctive about attempting to leverage cultural wealth into development, I conclude that it ultimately points to the politically and socially constructed nature of value more generally and therefore has broad implications for understanding the developmental dynamics of global value chains.

The chapter proceeds as follows. The first section provides a brief overview of the sociology of development and discusses the emergence of global value chain analysis as a way to understand national development trajectories within the global economy. In the next section, I provide a brief tutorial to the GVC approach, focusing on the upgrading corollary at its core. The third section presents a case study of the *Mundo Maya* as a tendentious exercise in marketing cultural wealth as a scarce resource and therefore a valuable tourism product. The fourth section draws out the implications of this analysis, emphasizing that the contested nature of cultural wealth is at the center of an uneasy relationship between the *Mundo Maya*'s promoters, who act as if the cultural and ecological richness being offered to tourists are self-evident features of the Mayan world, and the inhabitants of this region, who do not necessarily or uniformly share the meanings that elites have attached to the natural and social landscapes in which they live.

Developing the Wealth of Nations in a Global Economy

From the days of Adam Smith, economic development has been equated with the production and trade of physical goods. In the twentieth century, this association between material production and the wealth of nations was reflected in the prioritization of industrialization as the sine qua non of successful development. While countries pursued industrialization via import-substituting strategies during and after the Second World War, by the century's end development strategies across the global South were reoriented toward production for export. As the objective of autonomous industrialization gave way to the pursuit of comparative advantage in international markets, many developing countries sought to leverage one of the primary resource endowments they enjoyed—namely, cheap labor (Frobel et al. 1978). With the shift to export-led strategies, countries across Latin America, Asia, and parts of Africa have become incorporated into cross-border and transnational production networks for the manufacture of products such as clothing, toys, footwear, and electronics.

For development scholars, the demise of import substitution presented serious challenges to dominant theories of development, from modernization to dependency theory, and left the field searching for a paradigm that would help shed light on the causes and consequences of the South's conversion to an export-oriented development model. Recently, various approaches have emerged to fill this gap. Over the past decade and a half, the literature on global value chains (Gereffi et al. 2005; Gibbon and Ponte 2005) and related constructs, including commodity chains (Bair 2005; Gereffi and Korzeniewicz 1994; Talbot 2004), global production networks (Henderson et al. 2002; Hess and Coe 2006), and the *filière* (Raikes, Jensen, and Ponte 2000) has grown rapidly. This composite global chains literature now engages a diverse set of conceptual frameworks for studying global commodity production and trade, including actor-network theory (Schurman and Munro 2009), convention theory (Ponte and Gibbon 2005), and transaction cost economics (Gereffi et al. 2005). Although these approaches differ in important ways (Bair 2009), they share an interest in the relationships that connect people, places, and processes across space to each other, and ultimately, to world markets.[1]

The fragmentation and spatial dispersion of production documented in the value chains literature indicates that a significant portion of manufacturing activity has shifted from the global North to the global South; accordingly, the industrialization gap between developed and developing worlds (with the exception of sub-Saharan Africa) has dramatically narrowed (Arrighi, Silver, and Brewer 2003). While there is a lively debate within social science about the relationship between globalization and poverty and about the inequality between and within nations (Firebaugh 2003; Lee, Nielsen, and Alderson 2007; Wade 2004), there is relative consensus that widespread industrialization, once regarded as the linchpin of development, has not altered the underlying structure of a stratified world-system, nor has industrial convergence between North and South resulted in a significant convergence of living standards between citizens of the global South and their counterparts in the North. To understand this outcome, it is necessary to understand where, how, and by whom value is created and captured within the global economy.

This is the primary objective of global value chains analysis, which also purports to provide insights into how firms (and, presumably, aggregations of firms in geographical and political units like regions and countries) can change their position within global production networks to secure better outcomes. Studies of global value chains have proliferated rapidly in recent years, with a relatively small number of manufacturing industries dominating the empirical literature. Chief among these are apparel (Bair and Gereffi 2001; Gereffi 1999), electronics (Borrus, Ernst, and Haggard 2000; Sturgeon 2002), and autos (Humphrey and Memdovic 2003; Sturgeon, Biesebroeck, and Gereffi 2008). There is also a growing body of empirical research on value chains for primary products, primarily agricultural commodities such as coffee and cocoa (Gibbon 2001; Ponte 2002; Talbot 2004).

Service industries have received far less attention, despite the contemporary importance of this sector. From a development perspective, the absence of GVC research on service value chains sector is particularly problematic when it comes to tourism, which has long been important for many developing countries, not just as a leading service industry but as a major contributor to overall GDP.[2] International institutions such as the World Bank and the United Nations noted tourism's potential as a mechanism of development decades ago. Because it drew on existing resources, such as natural scenery, tourism promotion was thought to be an ideal development strategy for countries that were unable to afford expensive infrastructure or other large capital investments (even if tourist projects are often, in practice, accompanied by these kinds of outlays). Some enthusiasts of tourism as a development strategy even saw it as an alternative to industrialization, arguing that it might allow developing countries to "advance from a primary sector-based situation to one based on an expanding service sector, omitting the normal industrial phase of economic growth" (Crick 1989: 315).

Eventually, this initial enthusiasm gave way to considerable debate and even controversy about the benefits and costs of tourism for developing nations. Much of this debate has centered on the economic implications of tourism, with some studies suggesting that the participation of multinational hotel chains and all-inclusive tour operators result in significant "leakage" of potential revenues from host countries. Other concerns focus on the social and cultural implications of international tourism, with critics charging that encounters between affluent visitors and impoverished locals are less likely to generate mutual understanding and appreciation than resentment of the former by the latter. The recognition that many tourists are motivated by a search for authentic difference, often represented by the beauty of exotic locations or the novelty of local peoples and traditional practices, has led to new reservations about the possible commodification of natural and cultural resources for foreign consumption (Greenwood 1977; MacCannell 1976).

Recent research on tourism has attempted to move beyond the polarities that structured earlier debates. These more measured assessments suggest that tourism can generate positive outcomes for local residents, particularly when it is small in scale and involves the consumption of locally produced goods and services (for example, when tourists eat locally grown instead of imported foods), but that the economic benefits of tourism are neither guaranteed to occur nor likely to be evenly distributed when they do (Cano and Mysyk 2004; Hernandez Cruz et al. 2005). Recent studies show that tourism frequently exacerbates existing inequalities within a host community but that locals are adept at negotiating the opportunities and costs that it provides and are frequently able to leverage interaction with tourists toward their own objectives (Little 2008; Rekom and Go 2006).

Despite the importance of tourism to many developing economies, and the claims and counterclaims that have been made about its role as a mechanism of (under)development, the tourist industry has received little attention within the global value chains literature.[3] This chapter does not attempt a conventional GVC analysis of tourism, which would involve identifying the different kinds of actors participating in the chain and then tracing the distribution of costs and benefits among them. While such empirically oriented and applied analyses are useful, my aim here is to use GVC theory and its corollary insights about upgrading to explore the relationship between cultural wealth and development within the tourism value chain.

Upgrading along the Tourism Value Chain

A global value chain is defined simply as the full range of activities involved in the conceptualization, creation, distribution, and consumption of a good or service. The GVC framework addresses questions of development by directing attention to the role that organizations occupy in international trade and production networks understood as global value chains. While not all value chains cross international borders, GVC analysts contend that geographically dispersed but organizationally complex and functionally integrated production networks are a defining feature of the contemporary world economy. What differentiates GVC analysis from alternative theories of development is the insistence on participation in these global circuits of commerce as a necessary, if not sufficient, condition for economic development. By focusing on interorganizational networks as an infrastructure of globalization and, at least potentially, a mechanism of development, GVC analysis departs both from neoclassical trade theory, which assumes that a country's participation in global markets reflects the comparative advantage of particular factor endowments, and from institutionalist theories that emphasize the competitive advantages resulting from different institutional configurations, including various aspects of state policy, and the particular business systems or varieties of capitalism they engender.

A key concept within the analytical vocabulary of the GVC paradigm is governance structure, which refers to the power dynamics that exist along a chain. Defining the governance structure of a chain involves identifying which actors are able to make decisions about how resources and responsibilities are allocated among the participants and what criteria shape these decisions. Governance is critical for understanding the possibilities that exist for actors to leverage their participation in a chain into desired outcomes, such as technological learning or increased profitability. Because not all positions in a global value chain are created equally, studies of particular chains aim to identify the various activities occurring at different links in a chain, as well as the specific returns that accrue to each of these activities relative to others.

Research on a wide variety of industries, including both manufactures and nonmanufactures (coffee, fresh fruits and vegetables, and the like) has shown that the highest value-added links in many GVCs tend to be those that deal with "intangibles"—that is, activities that have to do with the conception, design, and marketing of a product as opposed to its actual physical manipulation and transformation:

> As "intangible" aspects of production (i.e. marketing, brand development, design) become increasingly important for the profitability and power of lead firms, "tangibles" [production and manufacturing] have become increasingly commodified, leading to new divisions of labor and new hurdles for developing-country producers to overcome if they wish to enter these chains. It is almost certainly a pervasive trend . . . that the barriers to entry in intangibles are growing faster than those in tangible activities." (Gereffi et al. 2001)

Gereffi and his coauthors' formulation points to the relationship between upgrading, barriers to entry, and rent. Another way to explain their observation that intangible activities have "become increasingly important for the

power and profitability of lead firms" is to suggest that they are characterized by greater rents than tangible activities (Kaplinsky 2005). For this reason,
value chain participants trying to move beyond the tangible links that are
described by Gereffi and his coauthors as increasingly "commodified" might
set their sights on *upgrading* to these intangible activities.

Upgrading is the core of GVC analysis as a theory of development. From
the GVC perspective, development is an ongoing process whereby actors try
to upgrade their position in global value chains to secure the rents that are
guaranteed by scarce resources.[4] To be enduring, rents need to be protected by
barriers to entry because it is these barriers that maintain scarcity (Guthman
2009). And herein lays the paradox of upgrading as a development strategy:
At the level of the individual producer or firm, successful upgrading involves
overcoming the barriers to entry that insulate a particular link in the value
chain from excessive competition. However, as successful upgrading occurs
and those barriers to entry are eroded, the scarcity that assured higher returns is undermined by increasing competition. And so begins a new cycle, as
some of the now downgraded firms try to construct new barriers to entry to
insulate themselves from competition in the hopes of again securing higher
returns, at least for a time.[5]

The upgrading paradox helps explain another apparent paradox that was
noted earlier—namely, the fact that the gap between North and South has not
appreciably narrowed despite the widespread industrialization of the latter.
It is precisely this expansive process of industrialization that has generated
excessive competition at the "tangible" links of value chains. The conversion
among developing countries to export-led growth strategies over the past
three decades, and the resulting proliferation of suppliers vying for incorporation into value chains, has generated a fallacy of composition dynamic,
putting downward pressure on the returns to manufacturing and challeng-
ing the long-held belief in industrialization as the prescription for the developmental cure (Kaplinsky 1993; Mayer 2002). For this reason, much applied
GVC research of the sort sponsored or conducted by institutions such as the
U.N. Industrial Development Organization or the World Bank has focused on
identifying strategies for developing-country producers to upgrade beyond
basic manufacturing to links in the chain characterized by less competition
and therefore greater security and better returns.

Research and development activities figure prominently among the "intangible aspects of production" affording better returns, but so too do activities

such as design, branding, and marketing. As Gereffi and his colleagues emphasize (2001), intangible activities of this sort are important for the production of many tangible goods, and there is a small but growing corpus of empirical GVC research examining who does them within a particular chain, where they are located (that is, under what conditions are they colocated with the production of tangibles), and how they influence the organization of the chain's tangible activities. This literature tends to underscore the challenges that most value chain participants and especially developing-country firms confront when trying to upgrade to these intangible activities, which are characterized by higher returns but concomitantly also by the higher barriers to entry that secure those rents.

Less is known about the dynamics of value chains in which the end product is not tangible, including the services provided by the US$940 billion international tourism industry. The tourism value chain differs in a number of important ways from value chains for tangibles, such as manufactures or agricultural goods. While a typical global value chain may span several production sites, linking people and processes in developing countries to each other and ultimately to foreign consumers, the tourism value chain flows in the opposite direction, bringing the consumer to the product. Indeed, in this particular chain, the place itself is what is to be consumed.

As the market for international tourism grows, and cheaper travel brings more destinations within the reach of the tourist, competition among sites intensifies, and the average rate of return to tourism declines. As GVC theory would predict, this fuels a variety of upgrading efforts, as government agencies promoting tourism, often in conjunction with private sector actors, try to reposition their product within the tourism market. Upgrading in this industry typically involves moving from inexpensive package vacations, which generate minimal spillovers beyond the "all-inclusive" resort enclave, to various, higher-end niche markets, such as ecotourism, culinary tourism, and cultural heritage (or, simply, heritage) tourism. The rents associated with niche tourism are higher because the supply of specialty tourism destinations is smaller and more differentiated than, say, the large number of warm weather locales offering tourists a relatively standardized sun, sea, and sand product.

For purposes of this chapter, I am particularly interested in heritage tourism because what is being marketed in this strand of the tourism value chain is the cultural wealth of a region.[6] Drawing on GVC theory and its upgrading corollary, there are several reasons to expect that heritage tourism may be particularly auspicious for development. First, as with other kinds of tourism, consumption of a destination's cultural heritage has to occur in situ. Consequently, this value chain is less spatially fragmented and thus creates greater opportunities for the local appropriation of value, as compared with value chains that connect exporters (often in the global South) of tangible products such as clothing, computers, and coffee to consumers (often in the global North). More importantly, if the cultural wealth on offer in a particular destination is sufficiently differentiated from what can be found elsewhere, and if it cannot be easily or readily replicated, this scarcity should provide protection from excessive competition and thus afford higher returns.

In the remainder of the chapter, I explore these hypotheses through an analysis of one such effort to leverage cultural wealth into heritage tourism and thus development. Marketing the *Mundo Maya* as a heritage tourist destination requires constructing the region's cultural wealth as a scarce, and therefore valuable, product. This involves a problematic conflation of the two types of cultural wealth that Bandelj and Wherry indentify in their introduction to this volume: (1) "cultural goods," such as UNESCO World Heritage sites; and (2) "intangible attributes," such as reputational assets or symbolic capital. The *Mundo Maya* is abundant in cultural goods, boasting no fewer than twelve UNESCO World Heritage sites. Among these are the archaeological sites of Copán in Honduras and Chichén Itzá in Mexico. Indeed, *Mundo Maya*'s promoters strive to forge a connection between these physical vestiges of pre-Hispanic civilizations and the contemporary Mayan societies that tourists are encouraged to visit. In other words, while Bandelj and Wherry's typology differentiates between material and symbolic assets as analytically distinct dimensions of cultural wealth, in the case of the *Mundo Maya* such distinctions are difficult to sustain in practice, precisely because the former is used to define the latter. Achieving this synthesis of the region's "cultural goods" and its "intangible attributes" is the central challenge of marketing the *Mundo Maya*, and it is a process rife with potential complications.

Marketing the *Mundo Maya*'s Cultural Wealth

Mundo Maya is a collaborative project among the governments of Mexico, Guatemala, Belize, Honduras, and El Salvador. Though the origins of this initiative are hazy, they appear to stem from conversations among government officials of Central American countries in the second half of the 1980s. These discussions centered on the possibility of reviving old plans for regional cooperation that had been abandoned in the wake of the political violence and social upheaval that had gripped the region for most of the preceding decade. In 1987, representatives from the Central American countries plus Mexico formally endorsed the concept of a multinational tourism project in Mesoamerica that was given the name *Ruta Maya*, or Mayan Route.

Considerable impetus for the project was provided by a cover story published around the same time in *National Geographic* magazine. Written by one of the magazine's editors, Wilbur Garrett, the article contained a brief reference to the as-yet-undeveloped tourism initiative that had been approved by the region's governments. Most of the article, however, was written as a travel narrative, inviting the reader to accompany the author on his journey along a Mayan Route that was described in text and presented visually in a set of lavish photos accompanying the article. This trip takes Garrett and the reader through a region of stunning natural beauty and ecological diversity that is also dotted with significant archaeological sites attesting to the former presence of a sophisticated, pre-Conquest civilization (Garrett 1989).

Garrett described the *Ruta Maya* as an entirely novel approach to international tourism, based on a "bold concept" requiring five different countries to "put aside their differences . . . and collaborate in . . . an ambitious regional project designed to showcase and preserve their shared cultural, historical and environmental heritage" (1989: 424). While he noted that this heritage was at risk, especially from increased population pressure, the *Ruta Maya* initiative was presented as a possible solution because it "would increase environmentally-oriented tourism and sustainable, nondestructive development to provide jobs and money to help pay for preservation" (ibid: 436). Similar language was used by government officials, who described their objective as developing "an integrated tourism program compatible with environmental conservation and sensitive to the protection of the cultural and historical legacy of the region" (cited in Burtner 2004: 455).

The appearance of the *National Geographic* article galvanized the project's supporters, who were excited by the scenario that Garrett's article described and concerned that potential tourist dollars "were slipping away due to disjointed information about the Maya and non-coordinated infrastructure throughout the indigenous zones" (Brown 1999: 295). This initial enthusiasm notwithstanding, the project moved forward in a halting fashion. First, a name change was proposed from *Ruta Maya* to *Mundo Maya*; the latter was thought to be more inclusive of the diverse tourist attractions that the region offered. In 1992, four years after the initial agreement by regional governments to pursue the project, and three years after the publication of Garrett's cover story, the Organización Mundo Maya (Mundo Maya Organization) was formed, and a constitution for the organization was ratified by the governments of the five member countries (Burtner 2004). Eventually the Mundo Maya Organization incorporated private sector representatives from each of these countries, as well as a representative from the European Economic Commission, which provided financial support for the initiative.

Suggestive of the project's rather inauspicious beginning is the fact that plans to launch it have been announced numerous times. The Inter-American Development Bank first pledged support to this "landmark" program in 2000, when it made a US$1.3 million grant to "finance an investment plan for the 500,000-square-kilometer area" (IADB 2000). In 2003, the IADB announced a strategic alliance among the Mundo Maya Organization and three international institutions to inaugurate the Mundo Maya Sustainable Tourism Development Project. These institutions included the National Geographic Society, Conservation International, and Counterpart International. The Bank also reported that negotiations were underway with potential donors to support a US$150 million investment plan including "projects in the areas of planning and regional integration, archaeological restoration, development of local parks and protected areas, tourism and social infrastructure, tourist microenterprises, training and streamlining border crossings" (IADB 2003). In August 2007, another announcement of the *Mundo Maya*'s official launch was made, this time by Mexico's secretary of tourism, who reported that the *Mundo Maya* initiative "would be presented for the first time as an integrated tourist project at the International Tourism Trade Fair" in London (Secretaría de Turismo 2007; author's translation).

Initial assessments of the project suggest that, despite the abundance of cultural wealth in the region, the *Mundo Maya* has thus far proven rather disappointing, at least in comparison to initial expectations (Adelson 2001; Torres and Momsen 2005). Particularly controversial have been proposed infrastructure projects that critics claim are barely disguised efforts to implement the disputed Plan Puebla Panama, a US$50 billion package of infrastructure investments, mostly dedicated to transportation, energy, and telecommunications and intended to facilitate the economic integration of the region

(Grandia 2007; Vigna 2006). In other words, existing criticisms of the project focus on the disjuncture between the ostensible objectives of the *Mundo Maya* initiative and the way in which the project is being implemented. Specifically, concerns center on the extent to which the discourse of sustainable development that is being used to describe the project is a form of "greenwashing" that aims to make the initiative sound more appealing to stakeholders without implying any specific commitments to the local communities affected by the anticipated influx of foreign tourists.

While these criticisms are important, I want to draw attention to the specific challenges that the *Mundo Maya* project poses for those seeking to market the region's cultural wealth. The ostensible goal of the *Mundo Maya* project is to promote a form of tourism that is sensitive to the ecological and cultural richness of the region and to the needs of local communities, which are supposed to be its primary participants and beneficiaries. In this sense, *Mundo Maya* is not dissimilar from many similar efforts in Latin America and elsewhere, in which countries are trying to move up the tourism value chain by developing specialty tourism products (Greathouse Amador 1997). What is innovative about this project is its scope: The Mayan heritage that is being promoted as the centerpiece of this initiative refers to a pre-Conquest civilization encompassing a region that today straddles five different countries. While these countries share a Mayan past, they also share a tendentious history, replete with conflicts over the very borders that are supposed to be rendered invisible for foreign tourists on their travels along this Mayan route. A particularly interesting element of the *Mundo Maya* project, then, is the collective action problem created by its international character. The participating governments essentially need to downplay the distinctiveness of their own claims to Mayan history and heritage to construct a singular, scarce, and therefore valuable Mayan world. Thus, to market the *Mundo Maya*, promoters have to *differentiate* the cultural wealth of the region from the many ventures in heritage tourism *outside* of Mesoamerica with which it is competing. This, in turn, necessitates a *standardization* of the Mayan world's cultural heritage *within* the region.

Achieving this degree of standardization and uniformity within the region is complicated by the fact that the physical assets representing the Mayan world's cultural wealth are not evenly distributed across it: Of the twelve UNESCO World Heritage sites located throughout the five-country region, fully half are located in the five Mexican states that comprise its northern frontier: Chiapas, Tabasco, Yucatán, Campeche, and Quintana Roo.

Fundamentally, *Mundo Maya* is a heritage tourism project based on marketing the Mayan past, particularly those tangible cultural goods, such as pyramids and other ruins, that attest to the achievements of this civilization. Creating demand for the Mayan past is, however, complicated by the Mayan present—that is, the large number of real, existing Mayans who inhabit the region and who have a very different relationship to the landscapes in which they live than either the tourists in search of an authentic Mayan experience, or those actors, chief among them government officials, tour operators, and representatives to the Mundo Maya Organization, who are promoting the *Mundo Maya* as a window into a glorious but long-receded past. Thus, the *Mundo Maya* project inevitably involves the negotiation and management of the region's current inhabitants, whose ambivalence about the marketing of the region's archeological and cultural landscape threatens to disrupt the carefully constructed congruence between the *Mundo Maya*'s "cultural goods" and its "intangible assets."

Marketing the *Mundo Maya* as a site of heritage tourism, and cultivating demand for its cultural wealth, involves the construction of two kinds of continuity. The first kind of continuity is continuity across time—specifically, the fashioning of a direct and unbroken connection between the ancient and modern Maya. Take, for example, one of the pictures accompanying the *National Geographic* "*Ruta Maya*" piece, which features a shirtless young male of Mayan descent (Figure 8.1). The caption appearing below this photo strains to establish the youth's place in a transhistorical Mayan universe: "Stepping out of time, a young Maya bears the classic features of his forefathers. Though decimated by war and disease, Maya still outnumber European descendants in much of their homeland" (Garrett 1989: 425). Thus, the discursive construction of the *Mundo Maya* as a marketable product relies on narratives of cultural homogeneity and ethnic continuity: The people living along the Mayan route today are understood to be the direct descendants of the ancient Mayans who constructed the cultural artifacts that are still in evidence. It is this ancient civilization that is the raison d'etre of the *Mundo Maya* project, and it is the abundant archaeological evidence of that civilization that makes this such a compelling region for heritage tourism (Arden 2002).

Figure 8.1 A young man of Mayan descent pictured in
National Geographic's "Ruta Maya" story. David Alan Harvey/
National Geographic Stock.

The second kind of continuity that is being asserted by the *Mundo Maya*
project is continuity across space, in the sense of claiming as a single Mayan
people citizens of five countries with different colonial pasts, different political and economic presents, and different experiences of incorporating indigenous populations into their state-building projects (Castañeda 2004).[7] Even
within one of these countries, Mexico, Mayan self-identification is a more
complicated and relational process than a straightforward genealogical understanding of ethnic identity would suggest. The ambivalence that some Yucatec Mayans feel about identifying *as Mayan* is shaped by the way in which

what it means to *be Mayan* has been politicized by the Zapatista movement in Chiapas and the pan-Mayan movement in Guatemala—areas, again, with regional histories and political trajectories that differ from those found in the Yucatán. A group of American archaeologists who have been working in the region for several years describe the identity work done by tour promoters, guides, and others, who lead tourists to

> . . . assume that the Maya were and are an ancient culture that developed over a vast area, who, despite the arrivals of the Spaniards and the dramatic consequences of European colonization, had and maintained a homogenous indigenous Maya identity. But in fact, not all people referred to as Maya think of themselves or call themselves Maya, indigenous, or Indian. (Magnoni, Arden, and Hutson 2007: 355; also Medina 2003; Castañeda 2004)

Thus, the lukewarm reception that the *Mundo Maya* project has reportedly received among some citizens of this supposed Mayan world may reflect ambivalence about the type of heritage tourism it presents—namely one that markets a standardized Mayan product and a collective pan-Mayan identity that does not necessarily reflect the way that local residents understand themselves and their communities (Evans 2005; Magnoni et al. 2007).

Throughout the *Mundo Maya*, identification as Mayan or indigenous is an interpellatory process; it is connected to the ways in which citizens are recognized by and make claims vis-à-vis the state. In the case of Mexico, where state formation has been intimately tied to the agrarian question, it is a process interwoven with struggles around land and property rights. More often than not, these historical struggles have contemporary resonance in the context of ongoing processes of political economic reform. For much of the twentieth century, land in Mexico was organized and held under a particular system of tenure called the *ejido*. Historically, the residents of these communities, *ejiditarios*, had usufruct rights to lands that were heritable but not alienable. The ejidal system, established in Article 27 of the Mexican constitution, was the centerpiece of the country's postrevolutionary agrarian reform and the concrete realization of Zapata's call for land and liberty. The juridical status of this system was changed in 1992, when President Salinas oversaw the passage of a sweeping new agrarian law designed to enable the emergence of a market in land. After these reforms, it became possible for *ejiditarios* to petition the government for title to the land, thus granting them formal ownership rights and the ability to sell or rent it legally. Despite these changes to the constitutional status of the ejidal system, *ejidos* continue to organize much of rural and semirural life in contemporary Mexico.

This is the case in Yucatán, where ejidal communities can be found throughout those northern and western portions of the state that were once home to large plantations growing henequen, a natural fiber that was used to make rope before the development of synthetics. Beginning in the nineteenth century, the henequen economy dominated the social organization of Yucatán for well over a hundred years (Wells 1985). The fiber was grown and harvested primarily by immigrants and Mayans who labored under a system of debt-peonage that extended beyond the Mexican Revolution and well into the twentieth century. In the 1930s, during an intense period of land reform, Mexican President Lázaro Cárdenas expropriated some of the property belonging to the henequen plantation owners and redistributed it to formerly landless workers, creating many of the Yucatán's *ejidos* (Brannon and Baklanoff 1984; Joseph 1988).

Some of these ejidos are scattered among the cultural goods of the *Mundo Maya*. Consider, for example, the archaeological site of Chunchucmil, a community located in the northwestern part of Yucatán, near the border with Campeche. Chunchucmil is the site of Mayan ruins that are currently being excavated by a group of American archaeologists. This team of archaeologists has established a field site in the area and has prioritized the involvement of local communities in its work. The scholars involved in the Chunchucmil excavations are motivated less by the desire to produce academic archaeological knowledge than by the goal of using "academic archaeological inquiry as a foundation from which to generate tourism within the local communities" (Arden 2002: 380). In articulating this objective, they have been at pains to differentiate their vision of locally developed and administered heritage tourism from what they regard as the more commercial and less beneficial *Mundo Maya* project. Yet their efforts to develop the archaeological site at Chunchucmil and create a "living museum" that would feature local residents educating tourists about ancient Mayan civilization have encountered some resistance from the population living among the ruins on land that encompasses five different ejidal communities.

The ambivalence of local residents about the living museum at Chunchucmil can be read, at least in part, as a contestation over the meaning of cultural wealth and its relationship to development (Breglia 2006). From the vantage point of the archaeologists working at the site, the development of tourism would allow the local residents to benefit economically from a cultural heritage that these scholars regard as the rightful patrimony of Chunchucmil's residents. But at least some of the intended beneficiaries are concerned that an influx of tourists and the development of a living museum might threaten their access to the land, which they also regard as their rightful patrimony, as well as both source and manifestation of their cultural wealth. These anxieties are not unwarranted because lands deemed to be of historic or scientific value can "be taken away at any time when the nation-state determines they are of archaeological importance to the national patrimony" (Arden 2002: 393). Thus, the Mexican state can make claims to archaeological sites and ruins like the ones at Chunchucmil, arguing that they represent the *patrimonio cultural* (cultural patrimony) of the nation (and in the case of those cultural goods that have been designated as World Heritage sites, of all humanity). Yet some residents of Chunchucmil, in explaining their relationship to the land and to their communities, refer to a *patrimonio ejidal* (Breglia 2006).

The invocation of different patrimonies can be read as a struggle over the control of the region's cultural wealth and the appropriation of the value that it generates. This interpretation would suggest that what is stake in the conflict between the *Mundo Maya*'s promoters and the inhabitants of the region is the extent to which local communities are stakeholders in the project, having input into the way in which their cultural heritage is being marketed and sharing in the material wealth and other benefits that increased tourism is expected to generate. And, indeed, it is precisely the exclusion of Mayan communities from meaningful participation in the *Mundo Maya* initiative that has been emphasized by some of its critics. For example, Evans observes that "questions of ownership, access, and management of heritage sites and collections, although increasingly raised by indigenous groups and their vocal leaders, seldom feature in tourism promotion and planning or in strategies for community and local economic development" (Evans 2005: 43-44).

These concerns, which highlight the degree to which a project like the *Mundo Maya* exploits or benefits the local communities whose heritage is being put on offer, are clearly important in evaluating heritage tourism as a strategy for sustainable regional development. But they do not fully capture the tension that is articulated when the state's claims to the Mayan world as cultural patrimony of the nation confront the claims of Chunchucmil residents to their land and livelihood as the ejidal patrimony of the community.

Rather, what is being expressed by these claims and counterclaims is the lack of congruence between these actors' understandings of what constitutes cultural wealth. Thus the conflict underlying these distinct visions of Chunchucmil's patrimony is not exclusively distributive in nature—or rather, the distributive struggle that it expresses is interwoven with struggles over meaning that cannot be separated from questions of value.

What is the significance of this foray into Mexican history? What is its relevance to the specific project of heritage tourism discussed in this chapter and to the analysis of upgrading via the marketing of cultural wealth more generally? My point is that projects such as the *Mundo Maya*, which attempt to market a region's cultural and historical experience, are ripe for contestations over the very meaning of that culture and history. This occurs when stakeholders in such initiatives make different and possibly competing claims about what cultural wealth is, who should get to define it, and how or even if it should be converted into material wealth and economic development.

Although the controversy over the proposed living museum at Chunchucmil suggests that not all inhabitants of the *Mundo Maya* are enthusiastic about this venture in heritage tourism, a similar project may be well be embraced by locals elsewhere, precisely because the multinational *Mundo Maya* is a socially and politically variegated landscape, despite the best efforts of promoters to present it as a single, scarce, and therefore valuable, entity. Even within Mexico, there may be important differences in the way that the *Mundo Maya* project is playing out. For example, van den Berghe (1995) reports that the growth of heritage tourism in Chiapas has elevated the status of indigenous Mexicans in the eyes of the local mestizo elite because the latter, who are the principal economic beneficiaries of increased tourism, eventually realized that tourists come to Chiapas because of its profile as an indigenous area. Thus, the commercialization of Mayan culture inherent in marketing it to foreign tourists may have the unanticipated consequence of valorizing this culture at home.

What Is Value?

The *Mundo Maya* project is just one among many initiatives being developed by countries trying to upgrade along the tourism value chain to forms of specialty tourism that are believed to be more economically, socially, and environmentally beneficial. Further research is needed to assess the extent to which heritage tourism does indeed generate a premium (what GVC analysts would describe as its "value-added" relative to the commodity tourism that sun, sea, and sand vacations represent) and to determine how that value is distributed among various stakeholders. My somewhat different goal in this chapter has been to inquire into the potential challenges that arise from a development strategy based on the marketing of a region's cultural wealth and to suggest that these challenges might be relevant for thinking more broadly about the value being created in global value chains.

Admittedly, the strand of the tourism value chain that I have discussed here is unique; because heritage tourism ultimately rests on exploiting the "cultural exoticism of the touree" (van de Berghe 1995: 581) it is particularly ripe for the kinds of competing claims about the definition and valuation of cultural wealth that I have outlined here. However, I believe that the issues raised are relevant for global value chain analysis more generally because they diagnose larger questions about how the pursuit of upgrading and development can recognize and accommodate multiple definitions of value, especially as value comes increasingly to be associated with what GVC analysts call "intangible" aspects of the production process, which often involves the construction of meanings and narratives around goods and services.

For example, in their contribution to this volume in Chapter 9, Ponte and Daviron note the importance of "symbolic value" for actors looking to upgrade within global value chains. Consistent with Gereffi and colleagues' finding that tangible aspects of the production process are increasingly commodified relative to intangible ones, Ponte and Daviron conclude that developing country producers have to control the symbolic as well as the material value of their exports to avoid "a race to the bottom." Their study of the South African wine industry analyzes the challenges and potential pitfalls implied in converting cultural wealth into a characteristic or attribute of a good or service that gives value to the consumer and which he or she is willing to pay for. As I noted in the preceding pages, many such efforts center on defining the intangible qualities of one's product in such a way as to differentiate it from those being offered by competitors. This process of differentiation, which is, in turn, critical for constructing the product's scarcity and thus generating its value, is one that Ponte and Daviron recognize as essential for the efforts of South African producers to upgrade along the wine value chain.

While, from a GVC perspective, Ponte and Daviron are right to emphasize the control of symbolic value as a means to the end of upgrading, my discussion of the *Mundo Maya* suggests the value of inquiring more fundamentally into the meaning of value itself. Most research on upgrading within global value chains focuses on how actors within the chain can capture more value, but work in this tradition too rarely interrogates how that value is defined, by whom, and toward what end, leaving the narrowly economistic concept of "value-added" as the default definition. Ironically, then, for a framework that is ostensibly focused on the creation and capture of value, value has been something of a black box within this approach. While value chain researchers may, like Pandora, have good reason to keep this box closed, it is by looking inside that we can begin to produce a better sociology of development.

9 Creating and Controlling Symbolic Value

The Case of South African Wine

Stefano Ponte
Benoit Daviron

IN THE INTERNATIONAL DEVELOPMENT LITERATURE, upgrading is seen as one of the main ways through which farms, firms, or industries in the global South can respond to the challenges of globalization and increased competition. The concept is often used in analyses of global value chains (GVCs)[1] to entail a combination of making better products, improving processes to make these products, and/or taking over new functions. GVC work has been especially concerned with documenting the eschewed distribution of value added along chains to the detriment of actors based in the South. The existing work on upgrading has mostly dealt with issues related to the material attributes of products, to skills and knowledge that are applied to the production and circulation of products, and to organizational and institutional forms (including standards) that are at the core of upgrading efforts in the South (see, among many others, Bair and Gereffi 2003; Gereffi 1999; Gibbon 2001; Giuliani, Pietrobelli, and Rabellotti. 2005; Neilson and Pritchard 2009; Schmitz 2006). In only a few instances has the GVC literature dealt explicitly with the symbolic attributes of products. These attributes are built on reputation and cannot be measured by human senses or technological devices. They are part of what Gereffi (2001) and Bair (Chapter 8 in this volume) call "intangibles" (as opposed to tangible production and transformation processes). Yet symbolic attributes are different from other intangibles in the sense that they are transmitted to consumers through "signs," such as slogans, nomenclatures, indications of geographic origin, labels, and brands.

Bair (Chapter 8 in this volume) differentiates between two ways in which "cultural wealth" comes into play in GVCs. One is where culture (in her case study, heritage tourism) is the product generated and consumed in the value chain. A second is where the cultural component of material goods becomes an important site of value creation and struggle over its control. This chapter complements Bair's contribution by focusing on the symbolic resources that are incorporated in the design, production, processing, and marketing of South African wine.[2]

Creating and controlling the value arising from symbolic attributes is particularly important in the global South because the terms of trade for agricultural commodities and even for labor-intensive manufacturing, which are mainly valued for their material quality attributes, have been historically decreasing (Kaplinsky 2005). As consumption in the global North is increasingly about signs and identity than the material components of products, access to lucrative markets for Southern producers depends on the mobilization of symbolic resources such as place, fairness, rurality, authenticity, or sustainability. As Slater argues (1997), contemporary consumer culture is a site of contestation over social and cultural resources and arrangements (what this book calls the "cultural wealth of nations") that underpin the mobilization of material resources (see also Richey and Ponte 2011). "As consumption has become an ever more central means of enacting our citizenship of the social world, struggles over the power to dispose of material, financial and symbolic . . . resources have become central to the cultural reproduction of the everyday world" (Slater 1997: 4-5). The flip side of such consumer culture is that production moves beyond materiality and toward identifying and (re) valorizing symbolic resources that are part of the cultural and/or natural wealth of developing nations—one way of getting out of the spiral of doing more for less.

In our earlier work (Daviron and Ponte 2005), we showed how the global value chain for coffee was characterized by a paradox in the late 1990s and early 2000s: a "coffee crisis" in producing countries, with international prices at the lowest levels in decades, and a "coffee renaissance" in consuming countries, with the growth of specialty and "sustainable" coffee consumption and the fast expansion of coffee bar chains.[3] We demonstrated that the coffee paradox could exist because farmers and other producing country operators sell the material attributes of coffee. Consuming country operators create and appropriate value by selling the symbolic attributes of coffee.[4] Therefore, we argued that one of the main challenges for producers in the South is to find ways to create and control the symbolic attributes of products.

In this chapter, we further develop this line of argument through an understanding of upgrading as the ability or inability of producers in the South to create and control the value accruing from the symbolic attributes of products. Symbolic value can be generated through a variety of processes, such as the creation of trademarks, geographic indications, and sustainability labels. This requires specific institutional setups, investments (in marketing, certification, promotion), and collective action from producers. It often involves struggles over what kinds of symbolic resources are brought into play. In wine, for example, symbolic value can be extracted from the geographic features of a location, from the specific or unique cultivation and winemaking practices, from branding or label design, or from the collective quality reputation of an area, region, or country. Symbolic value can also be generated by the "fairness" of trading practices, by environmentally friendly cultivation methods, or from the fact that the wine was made or sold by socially disadvantaged groups (as is the case in South Africa).

Investing in one of these symbolic resources, or a specific combination, rather than another, entails different distributions of rewards for different groups. Struggles also emerge on the interpretation of these symbolic resources—such as the operational definition of what is "fair," what is "good quality," or what "sustainability" is. Such interpretations have direct consequences on production practices and costs and benefits. Finally, the social groups or actors who create, harvest, or mobilize symbolic value may not be the same as those who reap the rewards. For example, a coffee sold under the brand "Kilimanjaro" in Japan capitalizes on the symbolic value of the east African mountain and its easily recognizable shape. While the owner of the brand captures such symbolic value, coffee producers do not necessarily do so, unless a system of protection of the geographic indication "Kilimanjaro" is put into place.

In the next section, we briefly highlight the limitations of focusing on the material attributes of products to improve producer welfare in the South. We also highlight the analytical value that the concept of GVC upgrading can provide. We distinguish two elements of value creation: one based on material quality and one based on symbolic quality. This framework is then applied to explaining successes, struggles, and pitfalls of upgrading through symbolic value creation in the South African wine industry. In light of the South African experience, we conclude by reflecting back on the issue of upgrading from the perspective of symbolic value creation and control.

Commodities, Value Chains, and Upgrading

Commodity Management

Until fairly recently, the main instruments used to improve returns to agro-food producers in the South had to do with tinkering with the relative *material* scarcity of a product in an international market. Products were not seen as an agglomeration of different kinds of qualities but as commodities defined by grades and standards based on material quality attributes. The issue of management of commodities actually dates back to the nineteenth century, before the advent of the "development project" of the post-World War II era. From the end of the nineteenth century until 1920, the management of international commodities was considered a "private problem." Associations of farmers or estate owners tried to influence price formation by organizing collective infrastructure to store commodities. Collective action of this kind was attempted in cocoa, rubber, tea, and coffee. After World War I and the Great Depression, the management of commodity markets became increasingly an affair of the state. The "commodity problem" moved from being a farmers' problem to being an issue of national wealth and growth (McMichael 2000). With the adoption of import substitution strategies and a central focus on industrialization in the 1960s and 1970s, the "national issue" dominated policy making to the detriment of farmers' interests.

The counterrevolution in development economics of the 1980s and increasing concern for poverty introduced a new shift, with a focus on deregulation, market liberalization, and export-oriented growth. In this framework, commodities did not have a special place in trade and development policy. Countries were advised to export whatever product generated comparative advantage for them—whether primary commodities, labor-intensive manufactures, high technologies, or services (but not labor, due to increasing political concerns over immigration in the global North). In the 1990s, new preoccupations started to be raised in relation to "unfair" trade practices in commodity trade, especially in terms of agricultural subsidies in developed countries and the skewed distribution of value along chains. New attention has been placed on commodities, from the cotton and commodity initiatives presented during the WTO Doha Round negotiations, to fair trade and related certifications and codes of conduct guaranteeing the "sustainability" of production and trade. It is only in this more recent period that "symbolic" attributes of a product (its "fairness" or "sustainability") have started to make inroads in the debates on how to improve welfare of producers in the South.

A related discussion on commodities has dealt with whether markets for labor-intensive manufactures work in substantially different ways than for agrofood commodities. Developing countries (except for sub-Saharan Africa) are increasingly exporting manufactured goods instead of primary commodities. One interpretation of this tendency is that the setting up of global value chains and production networks organized by transnational corporations involves actors in a large number of localities in the production/transformation process. As a result, an increasing proportion of international trade is characterized by exchange of components and intermediary products rather than exchange of final consumer products (see, among others, Feenstra 1998).

Yet various studies carried out in the 1990s and 2000s have also shown that increased exports of labor-intensive manufactures by developing countries have been accompanied by deteriorating terms of trade—due to the use of unskilled labor and the adoption of the same export strategy by several countries (the fallacy of composition) (Kaplinsky 1993, 2005; Kaplinsky, Morris, and Readman 2002; U.N. Conference on Trade and Development [UNCTAD] 2002). Kaplinsky in particular argues that the commoditization of export-oriented manufacturing produces "immiserizing employment growth"—a kind of growth that is based on falling wages.

But is this the whole story? Are developing countries and their labor forces and farmers doomed to increased competition with each other that drives down prices and wages? In this chapter, we argue that quality is not just a matter of "material goodness" and that there are other paths of upgrading in agrofood production via symbolic value creation and control. At the same time, we show that these paths are fraught with difficulties and require appropriate collective action, institutional setups and well-designed regulation.

Global Value Chains and Upgrading

Global value chain analysis has addressed some of the questions posed in the preceding paragraphs but is still mostly focused on issues of *distribution* of value, rather than value *creation* and subsequent *control*. GVC analysis examines how and under what conditions developing countries participate in international trade and seeks to identify the opportunities they offer. In GVC analysis, the international structure of production, trade, and consumption of commodities is disaggregated into stages that are embedded in a network of activities controlled by firms. This approach allows the identification of the "place" (both in the value chain and in broader geographical terms) where specific "quality attributes" are produced and the examination of how value is distributed between different actors. GVC analysis also discusses the dynamics of upgrading into "higher" (technology, value-added, scale) positions in global markets—which involves acceptance of terms, rules, and measuring devices defined by key agents or institutions.

A large part of the development implications of the GVC framework is related to the notion of *upgrading*. Based on the historical evolution of the global chain for apparel and electronics, Gereffi argues that the continuous process of externalization driven by large marketers and/or retailers provides opportunities for developing countries (see Gereffi 1999, among others). These opportunities are linked to a progressive control in developing countries of an increasing number of transformation stages. For developing countries' subcontractors, participation in GVCs brings benefits in terms of organizational and technological learning, technology transfer, and positive backward linkages with local supply industries.

In the GVC literature, the upgrading process is examined through the lenses of how knowledge and information flow within value chains from "lead firms" to their suppliers (or buyers) (Gereffi 1999). Upgrading is seen as the process of acquiring capabilities, integrating new activities, and gaining access to new market segments through participating in particular chains. The argument is that upgrading in various forms can be stimulated through learning from lead firms rather than through interactions between firms in the same functional position (horizontal transfer in clusters) or within the frameworks of common business systems or national systems of innovation (Gereffi 1999; Gibbon and Ponte 2005). The reach and limitations of upgrading have been shown to also depend on the kind of governance structure of the value chain (Humphrey and Schmitz 2002).

Although much of the early GVC literature privileged one kind of upgrading (functional), other categories of upgrading have been subsequently highlighted. Humphrey and Schmitz (2002), for example, use four categories of upgrading: (1) process upgrading (achieving a more efficient transformation of inputs into outputs through the reorganization of productive activities); (2) product upgrading (moving into more sophisticated products with increased unit value); (3) functional upgrading (acquiring new functions, or abandoning old ones, that increase the skill content of activities); and (4) intersectoral upgrading (applying competences acquired in one function of a chain and using them in a different sector/chain). Other analyses (Gibbon and Ponte 2005) also give recognition to the importance of achieving greater economies of scale as a means of securing a stable and profitable supplier position in value chains dominated by global buyers or retailers.

As mentioned earlier, little discussion has taken place in the GVC literature of the potential and pitfalls of upgrading trajectories focused on symbolic value creation and control. But before we apply such an approach to the case study of South African wine, we first need to draw analytical distinctions between material and symbolic quality attributes of products.

Material and Symbolic Quality

Most economic analyses of quality assume that agents have an "objective" idea of quality, which entails predetermined preferences that do not change in relation to the behavior of others. In these formulations, quality attributes are often classified depending on the ease with which they can be measured. *Search* attributes are those that can be verified at the time of the transaction (the color of a wine, for example). *Experience* attributes can be assessed only after the transaction has taken place (the taste of wine). *Credence* attributes cannot be objectively verified (or it is very expensive to verify them) and are based on trust (for example, whether wine is organic).

Attributes are also linked to the *product* itself (such as wine appearance, taste, absence of taints) or to *production and process methods*. These methods may include aspects related to authenticity of origin (geographical indication), safety (pesticide residues, levels of toxins), and environmental and socioeconomic conditions (organic, fair trade).

These classifications assume that the "evaluators" of attributes have identical capacity to assess them. In reality, these capacities vary dramatically between individuals and across time, countries, and cultures. Economic agents (especially consumers) make quality decisions also on the basis of imitation and/or the achievement of "distinction" (Bourdieu 1984). Finally, the way attributes are "measured" varies depending on what convention is used to set accepted reference values and measurement methods (Ponte 2009; Ponte and Gibbon 2005).

Material Attributes, Physical Transformations, and Measurement

In much of the economic literature on quality (among the "classics," see Akerlof 1970; Darby and Karni 1973; Nelson 1970; Shapiro 1982) material attributes of a product are seen as embedded "within" the product. These qualities are referred to as "intrinsic" and/or "objective" and are conceived as independent from the identity of sellers and buyers. They result from previous physical, chemical, or biochemical processes that create and/or select some specific physical parameters. Yet, in a transaction, the value of material quality attributes relates first and foremost to the existence of measurement operations and devices and to the accuracy of these measurements. On the one hand, qualities are attributed to products based on measurement that itself creates objectivity. On the other hand, acceptance of what kind of operations and devices of measurement should be used to measure what aspect of quality depends on a set of understandings that are shared or accepted by those involved in transactions. In other words, what is acceptable under a quality convention at a particular point of a value chain, in a particular location, enmeshed in specific collective identities, organizational setups, and local "cultures" is not necessarily accepted in other sites. As we have argued elsewhere, governing a GVC is thus also about spreading common quality conventions along a chain or being able to operate translations and accommodations along it (Ponte 2009; Ponte and Gibbon 2005).

Material attributes can be measured by using human senses (vision, taste, sense of smell, hearing, sense of touch) or by mobilizing sophisticated technological devices (for example, spectrographers). The measurement of attributes can be direct or indirect. Often, an attribute cannot be measured directly or only in a costly manner. Sometimes, another attribute can be used as a proxy for the one to be measured (for example, the color of a piece of fruit to measure taste). The use of proxies supposes a previous building of equivalencies and common understandings between the different measured values of the proxy and the values of the "real" attribute. In other cases, attributes that were originally measured with different metrics are compared (and "translated") through a common metrics, a process that Espeland and her colleagues call "commensuration" (Espeland and Sauder 2007; Espeland and Stevens 1998).

The ability to measure an attribute or to commensurate two different attributes will depend on the resources (equipment and skills) owned by the transactors at the time and place(s) of transaction. It will also depend on the possibility to deliver measurement fitting a legitimate or dominant metrics or to commensurate it into such metrics. Asymmetric resource endowment between actors is a first and basic source of specific distributions of value along a chain. As a buyer, a potential source of profit is being able to identify the exis-tence of a specific attribute that the seller cannot evaluate. As a seller, masking a quality defect that the buyer cannot discover at the time of transaction can also be a source of profit. However, it is likely that the buyer eventually will discover the problem. If this happens, he or she will not buy from the same seller next time or will apply a quality risk discount. But asymmetry of infor-mation is not the only source of capturing value—the fewer and the larger the buyers are, the more difficult it becomes for sellers to capture value from the material attributes of products on sale. Thus, measuring a valuating material quality is not simply a technical process but is shaped by the selection of mea-surement indicators and devices, by their possible commensurability, and by the political economy defining the conditions of exchange.

For a given commodity, the supply and demand of material attributes are determined by the technologies used in the production and in the transfor-mation of this commodity. But technologies are neither unique nor fixed. Then, for a seller or buyer, the ability to impose his or her own technological constraints clearly depends on the power relations with the other side of the transaction. The history of material quality for natural rubber is a good illus-tration of the relation between material quality attributes and power relations. Until the 1950s, U.S. tire manufacturers defined quality for rubber. Rubber was exchanged in sheet form, and quality control was based on visual inspec-tion. However, after 1960, Malaysia radically changed both the physical pre-sentation of rubber traded on international market (from sheet to block) and material attributes used to define quality (from visible defaults to chemical composition). Malaysia was able to do so because, at that time, it was harvest-ing more than 60 percent of world production but also because a government entity was strictly monitoring the national value chain and controlling ex-ports. At the same time, this change allowed Malaysia to increase the value of the rubber produced by smallholders, a "low-quality" rubber compared to the one produced by large plantations (Daviron 2002).

Creating and Controlling Symbolic Value

Symbolic quality attributes cannot be measured by human senses or complex technological devices. They are based on reputation. In the agrofood sector, they are often embedded in trademarks, geographical indications (for wine, but also other agrofood products), and "sustainability" labels. Trademarks enable what we would call the symbolic "consumption of an enterprise." Geographical indications facilitate the symbolic "consumption of place." Sustainability labels make it possible to "consume ethics."

According to economic theory, the quality of a product that bears a trademark is not measured directly but is identified with the "name" of a firm or a brand. Trademarks are distinctive signs. Consumers use them to identify products with specific attributes. Trademarks are socially useful because they reduce information asymmetries between producer and consumer when the valued attributes cannot be measured easily. Reputation is the key determinant of value creation (or destruction) in this case. Reputation is acquired through repeated consumption experiences and advertising. According to Chamberlin (1933) and the industrial organization school, price formation for brand-name goods can be analyzed in relation to monopolistic competition. From this perspective, the promotion of a brand name is part of the differentiation strategies enterprises adopt. The objective is to decrease price elasticity of demand in order to control selling prices.

In everyday life, trademarks, brands, and firm names, and the related reputations that build consumer confidence, acquire value to some extent independently from the material attributes of a product. They are not just proxies for difficult-to-measure material attributes. Consuming specific branded goods distinguishes the consumer from some people and identifies him or her with others. The value given to trademarks exemplifies the increasing role of ideas, culture, and symbols in consumption and the importance of consumption in the definition of identities.

But trademarks can acquire value only when there is a legal framework protecting their use: intellectual property rights. Without legal protection, other firms would use the reputation associated with the brand name of a specific firm. According to Rangnekar (2004), the legal protection of brand names has two objectives—to enable the appropriation of investment made in developing a brand name and to maintain the information role of the brand name as indicator of source. A third objective is to guarantee the capture of rents (see Kaplinsky 2005). This takes place when an enterprise buys a good, or inputs, with quality defined by easily measurable attributes and sells, after some transformation, another good qualified by a brand name.

An indication of geographical origin (IGO) is, in some way, similar to a brand name. It creates differences in the opinion of consumers and makes it possible to organize some differentiation strategy in term of price and quality.

Its existence and value also depend on the creation of a protective legal framework limiting the use of the quality sign. The rationale for the legal framework is the same as that which applies to brand names: protection against misleading use and against the dilution of meaning. The main difference between brands and IGOs lies in the collective nature of property of IGOs. This entails that all the enterprises present in the area protected by an IGO can use the indication as long as they meet the required technical specifications.

In France, a first law enabling the organization of appellation for top-quality wines was passed in 1935. This law gave birth to the Institut National des Appellations d'Origine (INAO). Within this legal framework, any *appellation d'origine contrôlée* (AOC) is confirmed by a ministerial decree defining the geographical area for production, the technical specifications, and the assent conditions. Every AOC has an association representing and safeguarding the producers of the area. This association is in charge of elaborating, jointly with the INAO, the text that serves as a basis for the ministerial decree. The association is also in a position to control the maximum quantity produced—through the use of planting rights and by setting a maximum yield per hectare. This initial legal framework was complemented in 1955 by a law enlarging the appellation system to cheese and in 1990 by a law that allows appellations to be developed for any agrofood product (Lagrange, Briand, and Trogon 2000).

The main instrument protecting geographical "origin" in Europe is the EU legislation 2081/92, which was fiercely discussed prior to its enactment. The French system was seen as incompatible with the creation of a unified market in Europe. Many European actors (public and private) wanted to limit any regulation about quality sign to food safety and fraud issues. For these actors, regulation protecting geographical appellation would be disguised protectionism limiting competition and innovation. On the contrary, France, Italy, and Spain argued that it was necessary to create a European regulation to limit the use of geographical names that qualify specific products (Valceschini and Mazé 2000).

EU legislation protects agrofood products that have either quality characteristics "essentially due to" a particular production, processing, and preparation environment linked to a geographical area (protected designation of origin, or PDO) or quality that is "attributable" to a particular area and to production, processing, and/or preparation that take place in that area (protected geographical indication, or PGI) (Ilbery and Kneafsey 1999). In this system, no reference is made to the material quality of the product itself. The (unwarranted) assumption is that quality is guaranteed by the geography of production. In terms of territoriality, PDOs are clearly stronger than PGIs. With a PDO, the whole value chain, from the production of the raw material to packaging must be done in the region of origin. Moreover, the product characteristics must be linked not only to the natural attributes of the region (climate, soil, and so on) but also to some cultural attributes. In a PGI, just one part of the value chain must be located in the region giving its name to the product, and no cultural attribute of the region is considered.

The so-called TRIPS (Trade-Related Intellectual Property Rights) agreement of the WTO deals with indications of geographical origin. Agricultural quality signs are just one of the components of the TRIPS agreement, which covers a broad range of topics (patents, trademarks, rights of authors, and the like). In ways similar to what happened in the European debate, the TRIPS negotiations mobilized strong opposition against any international legal acknowledgment of geographical appellations. For the opponents, among them the United States, geographical appellations are an example of nontariff barriers to trade. Another key issue at stake is whether the system of trademarks can be used to protect "locality" (as the United States argues) or whether these labels belong to a collectivity—thus individual companies or persons cannot own the intellectual property right attached to the name of the territory (as argued by the EU) (Barham 2003: 129). Under the latter system, no individual entity is allowed to move its production outside the region and retain the label of origin.

Article 22 of TRIPS is dedicated to the protection of geographical indications. It states that "geographical indications are, for the purposes of this Agreement, indications which identify a good as originating in the territory of a Member, or a region or locality in that territory, where a given quality, reputation or other characteristic of the good is essentially attributable to its geographical origin." According to Boy (2002), the TRIPS agreement institutes a weaker version of geographical indication, the one illustrated in European legislation by the PGI, not the PDO. This version protects the consumer more than the product or the producer. Under the PGI system, a firm not located in the concerned area can be interdicted from using the geographical indication only if it can be demonstrated that it creates confusion among consumers.

Because of the collective nature of the property rights defining the use of IGOs, small farmers and small manufacturers located in areas covered by geographic indications may be able to generate and control extra value for "symbolic production." However, the existence and utility of IGOs as means for farmers to capture value is related to two conditions: an existing legal framework supporting and protecting them and the ability to build vertical alliances with other actors in the value chain (see Barjolle and Sylvander 2000; 2002). At present, the legal framework being elaborated within WTO is less protective of farmers' interest than is the historical framework created in France around AOC wines. Moreover, the ability to build vertical alliances is clearly weakened or contested by the current process of spatial disintegration of value chains. Both tendencies are limiting the possibility of using IGOs to increase farmers' incomes and to provide a stimulus for building stronger producer organizations.

In addition to trademarks and IGOs, a third kind of "sign" can provide information on products to consumers: "sustainability" labels. These labels are awarded to products provided by enterprises or organizations that meet specific criteria. These criteria concern the technical and/or management processes. They can define the characteristics of inputs (for example, organic), the characteristics of labor (for example, "child labor free"), and/or the characteristics of machinery and equipment used in transformation processes (for example, food safety). They can also define rules regarding the way decisions are taken or profits are distributed (such as fair trade) and the procedures for segregating certified products from "noncertified" products (traceability). In other words, labels are based on "process-oriented" standards, a kind of standard previously used to coordinate production *within* firms. These process-oriented standards can be elaborated by a large number of entities: a group of enterprises (for example, Global-GAP), associations and NGOs (such as Fairtrade Labelling Organizations International), and a combination of public entities and private associations (organics in the United States and European Union). Most of them include a sustainability dimension; that is, they are conceived in relation to current definitions of "sustainable development."

To be able to use a label, enterprises or organizations are usually inspected by a third party—the certifier. The certifier guarantees that the enterprise respects a set of predetermined criteria. Any label supposes inspection of the technical process and/or the management methods. For agricultural producers, the implementation of labels is introducing a radical change in the relations with the enterprises buying their products, where product control is replaced by control of production and process methods, including labor monitoring. Labels ensure control of the production process without having to vertically integrate. Like historical agricultural standards before them, the new standards and certification processes supporting these sustainability labels allow the existence of market transactions. They facilitate a much more extended governance of the value chain without the use of formal hierarchical relations.

A distinction should be made at this point between process standards and labels dedicated to: (1) organizing relations within a value chain; and (2) providing distinctive signs for consumers. Retailers and/or the food industry can use the latter for differentiation strategies and to charge higher prices—as long as the use of these standards is not generalized. With the diffusion of common codes and standards, the social, environmental, or sanitary practices cease to be a differentiation variable. As this happens, retailers cannot use them to set higher prices at the consumption level.

Labels are distinctive signs, but, unlike trademarks and IGOs, access to them is much less restrictive—as long as standards are met. Thus, at least in theory, any enterprise or farm can apply to use a label, irrespectively of its location and identity. Nevertheless, the contents of the standard (the list of criteria and their value) are defined by a specific enterprise, organization, institution, industry association, or regulation. The actors in position to define the standard place themselves in a key governing position in the value chain (see also Ponte and Gibbon 2005). Once more, the ability to mobilize collective action is decisive. Cooperatives, industry associations, standards organizations, regulatory agencies, and large firms cooperate and/or compete in defining standards that describe symbolic attributes and in selecting what standard management systems should be adopted. Such decisions have important repercussions on the distribution of economic returns along a value chain (see Ponte 2008). Deciding, for example, that only smallholder cooperatives can qualify for fair trade status in coffee entails strengthening collective action in the South. At the same time, it does nothing to safeguard working conditions in commercial farms. Selecting which symbolic resources to extract from the cultural wealth of nations, how such resources are to be defined and marketed, and who qualifies for their benefits are key decisions that shape not only value distribution along a chain but also the relative distribution among different groups of actors that operate in the same position in a chain. In the next section, we show how these decisions guided symbolic value creation and struggles over its control in South African wine.[5]

South African Wine: Symbolic Value Addition and Struggles over Its Control

South African Wine: A Brief Overview

In international wine circles, South Africa is classified as a "New World" producer, along with Australia, New Zealand, Chile, Argentina, and the United States. It is also considered a relatively new player due to the recent (re)opening of its export market with the end of sanctions and the transition to the postapartheid regime of the early 1990s. This is somewhat misleading, as the first vineyards were planted in the Cape peninsula by Dutch settlers as early as 1655. Constantia wine was very popular in Europe at a time and apparently was a favorite of Napoleon. At the beginning of the nineteenth century, wine represented almost 90 percent of exports from the Colony (Vink, Williams, and Kirsten 2004). But by the end of the century exports had almost collapsed. In 1861, the United Kingdom—the main importer of South African wine at that time and again today—and France signed a trade agreement that made French wines cheaper to import. The spread of phylloxera in the late nineteenth century destroyed most of the vineyards in the Cape (Ewert et al. 2002).

In the early twentieth century, the new giant cooperative, the Koöperatieve Wijnbouwers Vereniging van Zuid-Afrika (KWV) was granted the statutory powers to regulate the industry. KWV controlled sales and stabilized prices and later managed a quota system regulating new plantings, varietal choices, and vine material imports. This period was characterized by a focus on high yields and volume over quality and an overall preference for the production of brandy and fortified wine. Throughout the twentieth century production (and presumably consumption) increased right until the advent of the new "quality era" in the early 1990s (Williams 2005). Exports, on the other hand, fell to an all-time low in the late 1980s (Vink et al. 2004). However, they had never been more than a minor part of total wine production. In 1988, they represented only 0.8 percent of total output, compared to 5.1 percent in 1964, for instance. Table wines, in turn, formed only a small proportion of total exports. Whatever was exported in the form of table wine was done by the KWV, in accordance with its export monopoly. As a result, very few South African growers or cellars had any experience in foreign markets when the

KWV's regulatory powers came to an end and sanctions were lifted in the early 1990s.

It was only in the 1990s that a veritable renaissance of the South African wine industry took place—following the opening of international markets, the (relative) novelty of South African table wine, and a weak rand. The material quality of wine has increased dramatically in the last fifteen years through product and process upgrading. Furthermore, wine has been exported increasingly in bottle rather than in bulk (at least up to the mid-2000s), the proportion of production of "noble varieties" has grown, and a larger number of top-quality wines have become available. In other words, the South African industry is now providing its main export markets with wines of higher average quality and the preferred wine styles, alcohol content, and grape varieties. This success story has been built on improvements in organizational setups in viticulture and winemaking operations, on improved economies of scale, and on supplying reliable quantities of basic wine, but also on building a set of institutions, infrastructure, and regulation aimed at improving the creation of symbolic value.

The Wine of Origin Scheme

The first element of the symbolic quality infrastructure in South Africa is the wine of origin (WO) scheme, which is a set of regulations, first introduced in 1973, that guarantees the origin, grape varietal, and vintage of wines. Currently, all wines for export need to be certified under the WO scheme, while wines for domestic consumption are subject to these regulations only if the producer wants to specify origin, cultivar, and/or vintage on the label. The WO scheme is administered by the Wine and Spirits Board (WSB), a government agency that performs control functions and carries out sensory analysis of all batches of wine submitted for certification.

South Africa stands somewhere in the middle of the spectrum of management systems for geographic origin, perhaps closer to the New World systems than the Old World ones. France has the oldest and most sophisticated system in the world, with specific limitations on what cultivars can be planted within certain areas, which vineyard techniques can be used, when the harvest can take place and what can be the maximum yield, what the character of grapes needs to be for specific labels, and what winemaking techniques can be used. Grape varietal names are rarely specified on wine, and brand names tend to be not as important as in the New World (with the exception of Champagne).

The bottle will showcase the name of the individual producer and/or bottler.[6] Australia, on the other end of the spectrum, relies mostly on brands and varietal names for consumer recognition and has developed a basic wine of origin scheme delimiting areas mainly in response to EU requirements. In South Africa, there are several "layers" of geographical indications, from broad regions to individual vineyards, but no specific limitations on varietal, grape quality, viticulture, and winemaking techniques are imposed.

In South Africa, the broadest *geographical units*, below the generic "wine of South Africa" indication, are "Western Cape," "Northern Cape," and the new addition "Kwa-Zulu Natal." Most of the wine of high quality is produced in "Western Cape," while the drier "Northern Cape" produces bulk wines of basic quality and wine for distillation. "Kwa-Zulu Natal" produces a minuscule quantity. However, within "Western Cape" there is a large diversity of geography, climate and soils; thus, these indications are of only very general character. The next layer in the WO system is the *regions* (such as "Coastal Region"), which are a combination of several districts, portions of districts, and other smaller origins. They are usually built around a common broad geographic trait, such as a river or a plateau. *Districts* are also built around macrocharacteristics such as mountain ranges and rivers but with a more specific character than regions. They still encompass a variety of soil types. "Stellenbosch" is probably the most recognized district internationally.

Wards are where soil, climate, and ecological factors start to have a distinctive and more easily recognizable impact on the character of wine (or they should, anyway). Ward indications such as "Constantia" and "Franschhoek" enjoy a good reputation for high-quality wines, but so also do emerging areas such as "Elim" and "Elgin" for "cool climate" varieties such as sauvignon blanc. *Estate wine* is wine made of grapes grown within the borders of one or more bordering farms, as long as they are farmed as a unit and made into wine on a cellar placed within this unit. The regulations on estate wine have been changed several times and are subject to some debate. The most recent changes entail that "estates" are no longer recognized by the WO scheme— only "estate wines" and units registered for the production of estate wine. The smallest production unit that can be certified under the WO scheme is single vineyard wine, made with grapes coming from a single cultivar and a single vineyard not exceeding five hectares. This is a fairly new system (the first wines were certified in 2005), and it is still unclear whether it will have many takers among high-quality producers. It is specifically inspired from the French idea of the "clos" (a specific vineyard with unique characteristics that was enclosed by a wall). But in the South African system, differently from the French, there is no requirement that the soil characteristics and structure in the vineyard be uniform. WSB is also considering the development of a certification system for so-called terroir specific wines (TSW). These wines would have to show identifiable and homogeneous characteristics with respect to topographical, climatic, soil, and geological patterns (as in the French definition of *terroir*). This would be a further step in South Africa toward the demarcation of geographic origin according to the European model, but it is unlikely to be backed up by strict rules on quality, cultivar choice, and specific vineyard techniques.

The quantity and proportion of "certified wines" that are examined by WSB increased dramatically in the 2000s. However, of all certified wine, a large majority still specify only the broad geographical unit. Other, and more specific, origins under the wine of origin scheme applies to a minority of total certified wine, while estate wine accounts for a tiny proportion of total certifications (see Ponte and Ewert 2009 for details). In other words, the WO scheme has so far failed to promote wines of origin from smaller territorial domains in the export market, relying instead on larger denominations such as "Coastal" or the very broad "Western Cape." As influential wine critic Jancis Robinson recently argued, this reflects a failure to further develop symbolic value in the industry (*Financial Times*, November 7, 2009). This means that the benefits of symbolic value addition via origin promotion are smaller than they could be—a fact reflected by the lower average prices obtained by South African wines in comparison to Old World wines (Cusmano, Morrison, and Rabelotti 2010). At the same time, they are also spread more widely because the geographical demarcations are broad. Also, the absence of more specific regulation on vineyard practices and quality and a weaker institutional setup than in IGO systems in Europe provide more flexibility to producers to experiment and innovate in vineyard management and winemaking.

Brand South Africa and Private Brands

On the footsteps of the Australian wine industry model, South Africa has invested more in promoting its more generic "Brand South Africa" abroad than in wines of origin per se. In 1999, the industry association WOSA (Wines of South Africa) was set up to explicitly improve the symbolic value of "Brand South Africa." While, in the 1990s, the simple fact that postapartheid South

Africa had wines to offer in the international market was sufficient to attract attention and curiosity, the novelty factor had rubbed off by the end of the decade. WOSA is funded by a levy per liter on all bottled wines exported. It carries out generic promotion of South African wine and coordinates South African wine presence in international wine fairs, including hosting its own biennial Cape Wine trade exhibition. WOSA also brings wine and lifestyle journalists regularly to the Cape.

WOSA has since 2004 embarked on a collective marketing initiative called "Variety Is in Our Nature." The idea is that the enormously rich biodiversity of the western Cape can be translated into a great variety of wines and conversely that appropriate stewardship of the wine lands can preserve this biodiversity. The image symbolizing this initiative is an appropriate combination of a grape leaf and a *Protea repens* (also known as common sugarbush), a typical flower of area. What WOSA wants to portray is South Africa as a "dynamic country of enormous diversity . . . [with a winemaking tradition blending] the restrained elegance of the Old World with the accessible fruit-driven styles of the New World . . . [yielding] wines which eloquently express the unique *terroir*, extraordinary biodiversity and fascinating people of the Cape" (Wines of South Africa [WOSA] 2005: 5).

About 90 percent of wine production in South Africa is said to occur within the Cape Floral Kingdom. According to WWF and WOSA, the growth of the wine industry can endanger some areas of vulnerable natural habitat (like *renosterveld* and lowland *fynbos*). This commitment is showcased in the Biodiversity and Wine Initiative (BWI) and in the integration of biodiversity guidelines in the Integrated Production of Wine (IPW) scheme (see the following discussion). BWI is said to present "a great opportunity to both the wine and conservation sectors. The wine industry benefits from using the biodiversity of the CFK as a competitive marketing advantage, and from contributing to sustainable natural resource management . . . The conservation sector benefits from pioneering biodiversity best practices in the wine industry and conserving the CFK's most threatened habitats" (Ibid.). In practice, this means that, before planting new vineyards, producers need to carry out a botanical audit and draw up a plan to preserve endangered and significant species. Some producers have set aside natural areas that will remain undeveloped in perpetuity.

Unfortunately, WOSA's motto sits rather uncomfortably with two facts: first, that grape growing is a monocrop cultivation method that destroys rather than enhances biodiversity; and, second, that the industry is not diverse in its *human* nature, especially at the managerial and ownership levels. While there is disagreement within the industry on whether the diversity tack has created a unique positioning of South African wine abroad, what is clear is that this effort to create symbolic value is based on contested interpretations of the interaction between viticulture and biodiversity and that the failure to meaningfully integrate previously disadvantaged groups in the mainstream of a white-dominated industry (see a more detailed discussion in the following pages) does not sit well with a symbolic focus on diversity.

Efforts have also been made in the South African wine industry to improve symbolic value through private brands. Although there is still room for improvement in technical operations and in cost rationalization in the country, branding and marketing are seen as the main way forward by business analysts, both at the industry and individual company levels. In this realm, developing a "personality" for a wine, "lifestyle" messaging, and packaging are deemed to be especially important (see Loubser 2001; Rabobank 2004; Wood and Kaplan 2005).

South Africa is seen in the U.K. wine trade (its main export destination) as lacking in the number of big brands that are needed to drive significant growth. It is seen as too dependent on the flagship brand Kumala (owned by American drinks conglomerate Constellation). Other brands of South African wine, however, are also growing healthily, such as Namaqua (from giant ex-cooperative Westcorp, recently renamed Namaqua) and FirstCape (from a joint venture of several cooperatives and BrandPhoenix of the United Kingdom). A number of cooperatives and ex-cooperatives have become more engaged in direct marketing and branding through joint ventures (which may also involve co-ownership of a brand, rather than just marketing agreements), some with very successful results (Goudini/FirstCape, Swartland, Westcorp/Namaqua).

Yet the most successful brands of South African wine in the United Kingdom, its main export market, are now owned or co-owned by U.K. companies—while the market share of traditional South Africa-owned brands (with a few exceptions) has remained fairly stagnant (Ponte and Ewert 2009). The few South African producer-wholesalers and marketers who used to have their own agencies in the United Kingdom and Europe are either divesting from them or entering in joint ventures with Europe-based branders and marketers. This is a sign that even though symbolic value is being created via branding, it is largely captured by actors outside South Africa.

Certifications, Labels, and Wine Tourism

Another element in symbolic value addition in South African wine has been the introduction of a variety of certification and labeling schemes and codes of conduct. In 1998, the industry put in place the Integrated Production of Wine (IPW) code of conduct, a semiregulatory system that provides guidelines for "good agricultural practices" for farms and "good manufacturing practices" for cellars to produce wines that are "healthy, clean and environmentally friendly" (IPW 2004). Although compliance with IPW can be achieved with a relatively low score, it seems to have helped creating environmental awareness among South African growers.

A number of other voluntary certifications, covering a wide array of aspects—for example, labor conditions, production, processing, food safety, and quality management more generally—have also been put in place. Some of these are linked to assuring that the material attributes of a wine are "safe" and thus do not add symbolic value in any significant way. In this category we find the ISO 9000 and ISO 14000 series of standards on quality management and environmental management, respectively, or British Retailer Consortium (BRC) and ISO 22000 certifications for food safety and quality management.

Others, however, explicitly target symbolic value in trying to address issues related to the social and environmental conditions of wine production and trade. Among these, we find the Wine Industry Ethical Trade Association (WIETA) code of conduct, based on South African labor legislation (Bek, McEwan, and Bek 2007; du Toit 2002), organic and biodynamic certifications, and fair trade, which aims at guaranteeing fair conditions in production and trade (Kruger and du Toit 2007). While the WIETA initiative is faltering, having been embroiled in criticism (du Toit 2002), political wrangling and contestation over the meaning, interpretation, and application of "ethical trade," fair trade wine has been quite successful in terms of market expansion, especially in the United Kingdom through the Thandi brand. The interesting aspect here is that the South African fair trade movement managed to convince Fairtrade Labelling Organizations International (FLO) to include specifically South African requirements into the definition of fair trade certification for its wines. In other words, South Africa was able to adapt a global certification system aimed at enhancing symbolic value to its own needs.

In terms of symbolic value addition, it is also useful to briefly highlight the role that wine tourism plays. Wine tourism is a well-developed industry in the Cape, with a number of organized wine routes. Cape Town is part of the Great Capitals of Wine network. Many cellars are open to the public and have tasting facilities on site. Over forty properties also have restaurants. Scenic beauty and many flagship properties displaying Cape Dutch architecture (and some interesting contemporary architecture as well) add flavor to the "Cape wine experience." Additionally, some fair trade tourism initiatives in South Africa have explicit links to wine. For example, the Spier Hotel (located in the Spier wine estate) was the first luxury hotel in South Africa to be certified under the "Fair Trade in Tourism" initiative. While this is not the place to delve into details of wine tourism, we want to highlight one aspect: Wine-tasting rooms and related hospitality infrastructure are the main places where most tourists come into contact with black workers in the wine industry. Farm operations, where almost all manual labor is performed by blacks, are much less visible to tourists. In a way, wine tourism provides the image of a "blacker" industry, a symbolic value creation on its own. In the next section, we further develop this aspect of symbolic value management.

"Black Economic Empowerment"

A final element in efforts to improve and/or manage symbolic value in South Africa relates to "Black Economic Empowerment" (BEE) initiatives. At least until the 2010 Fédération Internationale de Football Association (FIFA) World Cup, and other than tourism and fresh fruit, South African wine was one of the few ways in which consumers of the wealthy North encountered South Africa. In the context of the charged history of apartheid and the international struggle against it—a struggle in which the call to boycott South African products played a key part—BEE is seen in the industry as potentially repositioning South Africa in the Northern "consumer imaginary." These images of a "New South Africa" constitute part of the cultural wealth portfolio of the country.

As du Toit has eloquently argued (1993; 1998), the history of the South African wine industry is intricately linked with the social history of slavery. Above all, slavery thoroughly shaped the habits and expectations of the small white elite who owned most of the farms of the Western Cape. Land ownership was embedded in a racialized and authoritarian discourse of mastery that linked blackness and servility and that reduced black people to the status of minor children. This was entrenched on wine farms in a myriad of institutions that worked to ensure the powerlessness, subjection, and dependency of slaves and, after the abolition of slavery, of farm servants (du Toit, Kruger, and Ponte 2008).

As we have already seen, the end of apartheid brought major changes in the wine industry—such as the opening of the export market, the adoption of new methods and technologies in vineyard management and winemaking, more attention to marketing, and more demand-driven product design. In parallel to these, farm owners reduced their permanent workforce, adopted technologies that minimized the need for permanent workers, and restricted job security on farms by hiring younger workers. Such restructuring, as du Toit and Ewert (2002) have argued, has created a "double divide" in the industry: between "winners" and "losers" among cellars and farmers, depending on how they were positioned to take advantage of export opportunities, and between permanent workers and casual or outsourced laborers. The movement toward the minimization of a permanent labor force and the casualization of unskilled and low-skilled labor is part of a wider process in the western Cape and elsewhere in South Africa, especially in labor-intensive branches of farming (du Toit and Ewert 2002; Kritzinger, Barrientos, and Rossouw 2004). Casual workers are excluded from the basic entitlements that permanent workers have gained. Despite reporting wages that may not be lower than those of permanent workers, casual workers face greater employment insecurity (Kritzinger et al. 2004).

Against this background, industry-level and individual company BEE initiatives were conceived as tools to address the plight of farm workers in the wine industry. But, as du Toit, Kruger, and Ponte (2008) chronicle in detail, the industry managed to cast BEE as a managerial exercise through the Wine BEE Charter and its codes and reduced "transformation" to a marketing exercise—through "black branding," "black winemaker showcasing," or a focus on "nature." This way, while attempting to "clean" its symbolic value sheet, it has been able to avoid facing more potentially uncomfortable outcomes of transformation such as land redistribution, import boycotts, and much improved working conditions for grape pickers that would go much further to redress persistent racialized inequalities.

What commitment to farm worker interest remains in BEE initiatives is couched solidly in discourses of self-improvement (education, training, combating alcoholism) rather than on labor regimes that entrench exploitative power relations and on how farm worker organization might challenge them. At the same time, the marketing and codification technologies deployed help move restructuring from a political to a managerial terrain where a small cohort of black entrepreneurs can operate. This terrain is characterized by branding, advertising, and image building on the one side and by codes of conduct, a sectoral BEE charter, scorecards, and auditing on the other. These tools allow both the standardization and the apparent deracialization of labor and social relations in a wine industry originally established on slavery and more recently characterized by more or less benign forms of paternalism (du Toit et al. 2008). The symbolic value of BEE is being created and controlled by a small group of black entrepreneurs who make, or more often just market, "empowered" wines. Brand South Africa attempts to clean its record, while those who toil the fields do not obtain any tangible benefits.

Conclusion

In this chapter, we proposed that upgrading in global value chains can be understood as the ability or inability of producers in the South to create and control the value embedded not only in material but also in the symbolic quality attributes of a product. Many countries in the global South are stuck in producing and exporting goods that are valued for their material quality attributes. Symbolic quality attributes are generated and controlled elsewhere in the value chain. Traditionally, the main strategies for improving welfare for agrofood producers in the South entailed creating relative material scarcity of a product in an international market. While some of these strategies worked well in specific historical circumstances and for a limited time, the terms of trade for primary commodities, and increasingly for labor-intensive manufactures as well, have been deteriorating. Creating and controlling symbolic value has become an important element in avoiding a race to the bottom.

In the second part of the chapter, we examined how symbolic value has been created in the South African wine industry and the regulatory and institutional components of such production. We also highlighted the struggles around the appropriation of different kinds of symbolic value. In general, one can argue that the South African wine industry has upgraded substantially through enhancing symbolic value. But the picture of who has been able to control which symbolic value is much more varied. Value creation through geographic origin has been modest but broadly distributed. The use of "diversity" as a symbolic device has been contested and seems to have yielded modest outcomes. Value addition through branding is taking place, but many of these brands are controlled by agents outside South Africa. Fair trade, organic, and biodynamic wine sales and wine tourism are thriving and improving the image of South African wine, but WIETA is faltering. Black Economic Empowerment is helping small groups of black entrepreneurs to succeed but is failing the majority of farm workers; plus the industry remains essentially dominated by a white elite.

This case study shows that, while there is indeed potential in efforts to create and control symbolic value in the South, the road is fraught with obstacles. Symbolic value creation requires fairly sophisticated institutions and industry associations, collective action by industry actors, substantial financial investment, and appropriate regulatory support. These are difficult to mobilize, especially in least-developed countries. Moreover, possessing the potential to create symbolic value from natural, geographic, cultural, or social resources is not equal to being able to control such a value or to distribute it in politically acceptable ways.

10 Cultural Brokers, the Internet, and Value Chains

The Case of the Thai Silk Industry

Mark Graham

THIS CHAPTER WILL ADDRESS THE ROLE OF THE INTERNET in bringing producers of Thai silk into global marketplaces. Scholars studying the role that networks play in perpetuating inequalities have noted that entrepreneurs who successfully cut out intermediaries can achieve economic success in the global marketplace. It would therefore seem that small-scale cultural producers would experience an economic boom as they reap the full economic benefits from global trade; however, this has not always been the case.

The imaginary of an "Internet revolution" has been readily adopted in discussions of economic development, as development practitioners have imagined that information and communications technologies (ICTs) can be deployed to invigorate otherwise weak economic actors to traverse geographic boundaries in search of new markets (Graham 2008; 2011a). For cultural industries more generally, it is imagined that people can take advantage of their local practices and their cultural heritage to construct themselves as the purveyors of tradition and can thereby make for themselves a market niche. The cultural portfolio that local producers have to draw on makes them attractive, but for buyers to become aware of and then act on this sense of attraction, both producers and buyers need to be linked.

Development scholars have often placed a large amount of emphasis on the physical forms of linkage and have largely ignored symbolic boundaries, cultural affinities, and the dynamic processes of culture work that make linkage possible. In development discourse, for example, linkage is achieved through paved roads, passable waterways, and now Internet connections. Unlike past links between Southern producers and Northern consumers, the Internet initially appears almost free of spatial constraints: Any two computers can connect to one another irrespective of geographic location.

In cultural and economic sociology, the notion of linkage is anything but straightforward. There are strongly held understandings about what makes a producer good, and these understandings include but surpass the technical specifications of what is being produced. Good producers have to be "presented" dramaturgically as such. Producers from some countries or regions will find themselves placed on a pedestal, while others will be marked with shame by virtue of where they live and the narrative histories attached to those places (Wherry 2008b). Moreover, buyers will feel a greater sense of comfort and closeness with people representing similar cultural traditions and styles of interaction than with others (Bandelj 2008a). These nonphysical aspects of trade may likely attenuate the proposed liberating effects of the Internet on trade.

This chapter challenges the assumption that the availability of Internet access necessarily leads to revolutionary reorganizations of commodity chains and economic relations for small-scale producers in the global South. The chapter's first section examines unsuccessful attempts to use the Internet as a tool of economic development in the Thai silk industry. Value within the Thai silk industry is most often created by cultural brokers with a detailed knowledge of foreign customer tastes, marketing strategies, and distribution outlets, and the Internet alone has not been able to bring about significant topological alterations to commodity chains that would benefit the producers of silk. The lessons learned from the Thai silk industry ultimately suggest that a rethinking of the relationships between geography and ICTs is needed for alternate discourses and practices of development to be envisioned.

The "Internet Revolution," E-Commerce, and Reconfigured Commodity Chains

The concept of disintermediation has been advanced to describe the potential of the Internet to threaten the existence of middlemen, brokers, and intermediaries in any commodity chain and to reorganize economic spaces and relations (Benjamin and Wigland 1995; Janelle and Hodge 2000; Javalgi and Ramsey 2001). Direct economic links between producers and consumers are often argued to provide large benefits to both producers and consumers because the surpluses that were once extracted by middlemen can be redivided into the disintermediated commodity chain. Figures 10.1, 10.2, and 10.3 depict the potential reorganization of commodity chains by the Internet. Figure 10.1 is a highly simplified representation of a commodity chain involving a product that is partially sold abroad with a number of intermediaries between the producers and consumers. Figure 10.2, in contrast, represents a partially disintermediated chain in which a foreign merchant is the link between producers and international consumers. Figure 10.3 represents a full state of disintermediation: Consumers can buy directly from producers (Graham 2008).

Disintermediation is an oft-repeated notion in economic development discourse. In place of large-scale modernization projects of the past, many proponents of development projects in "underdeveloped" areas are now proposing smaller, microscale projects that combine disintermediation (or reductions in spatial barriers and transaction costs), e-commerce, and the use of new and

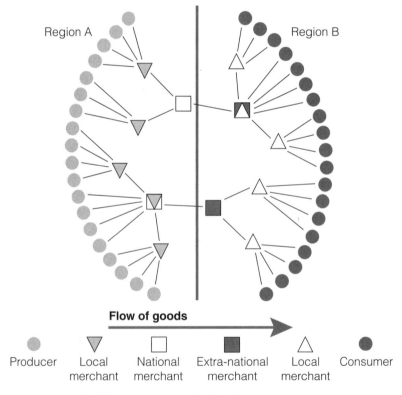

Figure 10.1 Simplified representation of a value chain.
SOURCE: Graham, "Warped Geographies of Development."

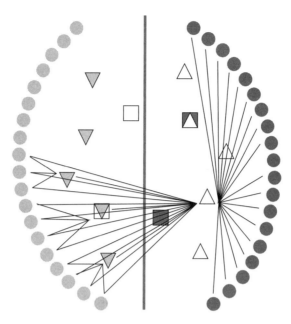

Figure 10.2. Partially disintermediated chain.
SOURCE: Graham, "Warped Geographies of Development."

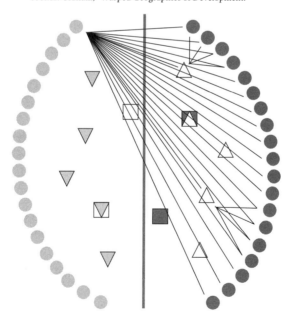

Figure 10.3. Disintermediated chain.
SOURCE: Graham, "Warped Geographies of Development."

often virtual marketplaces (Chandrasekaran 2001; Purcell and Toland 2004; Rhodes 2003). Purcell and Toland (2004: 241) claim: "ICT[s] offer the opportunity to reduce the barriers of distance, and give . . . countries better access to the global economy." Romero (2000), for example, has reported on a group of rural Guyanese weavers who, with newfound connections to the Internet, began successfully selling hammocks online. Despite being economically successful, the project fell apart because existing village relations were disrupted, and the social infrastructure for mobilizing resources became defunct. This brief example illustrates that the structure of relations may be advantageous for low-cost trade but that cultural understandings about how work, money, and social life should be organized within a community may mean that what looks to be a better technical arrangement for the production and distribution of woven hammocks may instead be unworkable.

This cautionary tale contrasts strongly with Poon and Jevons (1997: 34), who state that "the Internet creates a 'borderless' virtual business platform on which suppliers, customers, competitors and network partners can freely interact without going through the pre-defined channels on the value chain, members of the same business network or of different networks can by-pass the traditional interaction patterns and form virtual value chains" (for a similar argument see Benjamin and Wigland 1995). In a borderless world, it is argued that historical competitive advantages, such as firm size, become irrelevant because the Internet can "level the competitive playing field by allowing small companies to extend their geographical reach and secure new customers in ways formerly restricted to much larger firms" (Organization for Economic Cooperation and Development 1999: 153).

The "Internet revolution" and e-commerce often rely on reconfigured, and usually disintermediated, commodity chains. Reconfigured commodity chains, in turn, are based on an inherently geographic metaphor: the idea that eliminating a divide in digital space will bring people into the same virtual space or marketplace, thus facilitating trade. While some of the nuanced understandings of the relationships between the Internet and geography that were outlined in the previous section have been incorporated into writings about the ability of the Internet to affect commodity chains, it is rather more simplistic formulations (that is, the ability of the Internet to disintermediate chains and thereby render previously distant people and places in relative concursion with one another) that frequently are used to justify the theory and practice of much Internet-led economic development. By setting up the idea that relative or virtual concursion can occur between geographically separated producers and consumers of commodities due to the space-transcending powers of the Internet and e-commerce, a counterargument also comes into being. Namely, that an absence of ICTs will create a "digital divide" that makes the coming together of producers and consumers into shared virtual marketplaces impossible (Graham 2011a). The following section of this chapter now turns to the idea of a digital divide and examines how the exaggerated understandings of the ability of the Internet to change geography that are wrapped up in discussions of disintermediation have been integrated into discourses of development.

Development and the Internet

By invoking the idea of a digital divide, many actors (state, private, and individual) are able to have powerful economic and political effects. The digital divide has sparked a U.N. summit (the World Summit on the Information Society), countless articles and reports (for example: United Nations 2003a; U.N. Development Programme [UNDP] 2005), and most significantly, a range of programs and plans designed to reduce the divide and bring disconnected people into an information society.

In its description of the digital divide, the U.S. Department of Commerce (in Selwyn 2004: 344) notes that while some individuals "have the most powerful computers, the best telephone service and fastest Internet service, as well as a wealth of content and training relevant to their lives . . . Another group of people don't have access to the newest and best computers, the most reliable telephone service or the fastest or most convenient Internet services. The difference between these two groups is the . . . Digital Divide." The World Bank, in support of investments in ICTs in developing countries, similarly points out that "infrastructure is a major bottleneck to growth and poverty alleviation in developing countries" (World Bank 2005).

ICTs such as the Internet are seen to be the panacea that can breach this digital gap. Reducing the digital divide is thought to increase education and access to public services by allowing users to harness the supposed spacelessness of Internet, to transcend their geographic constraints (such as lack of education and distance from government representatives), and to become citizens of the informational society (Katz, Rice, and Aspden 2001; Servon and Nelson 2001). Others have argued that narrowing the digital divide will increase economic equality, social mobility, social equality, democracy, and economic growth (Golding 1996; Marine and Blanchard 2004).

Discussions of digital divides usually draw on only selective understandings of the relationships between cyber- and physical space; specifically, the ability of the Internet to create an ontologically independent cyberspace removed from geographic influences and to thereby diminish the importance of absolute, physical distance. By reducing a digital divide, a spatial divide is also transcended, thus bringing students closer to teachers, citizens closer to government, and, perhaps most significantly, producers closer to consumers. By altering positionalities, and thereby bringing producers and consumers into virtual proximity, practitioners of development hope to facilitate a disintermediation of commodity chains. From this perspective, proximity is material, not symbolic (Graham 2011a).

Such ideas have been used to argue that a shrinking of the digital divide can bring increased commerce and wealth to the previously disconnected. To return to the example of silk, we can observe the desire to break through a digital divide, participate in the "Internet revolution," and disintermediate traditional commodity chains in the website of a development agency working with the Cambodia village of Robib. They state: "The Internet now offers leapfrogging opportunities to take . . . villages out of their isolation and poverty into our global village" (Krisher, 2011a). Then they move on to claim that:

> One of the gaps which concerns those of us in the big cities and rich countries who are experiencing the digitalization of our lives, who are witnessing the rapid development of the Internet along with its ability to bring us greater knowledge, freedom and economic benefits, is the pitfall that little of this may be benefiting the developing world. Villages like Robib, unless we do something, are destined never to catch up. . . . Join us in succeeding to bring cyber commerce through the Internet to remote villages like Robib everywhere in the world. (Krisher, 2011b)

The Sat-ed group in Northeastern Thailand, while operating a similar project, specifically highlight their use of the Internet to disintermediate commodity chains and achieve virtual copresence: "The problem is that, before now, they have never had access to the world's markets. Instead middlemen come in and buy up the silk from them for a pittance and then take it to Bangkok and beyond, marking it up often 4 to and 6 times . . . Until now" (Sat-Ed, 2011). This vision of intermediaries is one of power based on capital and technology but not on the cultural affinities that buyers and intermediaries may have or the social skills that intermediaries exhibit as they act as cultural brokers.

If distance is no longer what is used to be, and if ICTs can radically disintermediate commodity chains, then what are the consequences for the producers of goods in transnational commodity chains? Throughout the history of trade there have been countless stories of middlemen and intermediaries leveraging their topological and geographic positionalities to capture the bulk of profits made throughout a commodity chain at the expense of producers. But, to many people, the Internet offers a fundamentally different vision. To explore this theme in more detail, the role and limitations of the Internet in shaping commodity chains in the Thai silk industry are now presented as a case study.

The Internet and Commodity Chains in the Thai Silk Industry

The Thai silk industry is specifically chosen because it offers an ideal setting to examine some of the themes discussed in this chapter. Thailand has a millennia-old tradition of silk production that has survived up to the present day and thereby constitutes a part of Thailand's cultural wealth portfolio. While the country's silk industry is significantly more developed than those of other Southeast Asian nations, Thailand lags behind China and India in terms of total raw and finished silk production (Datta 1996; UNCTAD/WTO 1997). Although statistics vary considerably on the matter, it is estimated that there are between 150,000 and 500,000 households, mostly in northeastern Thailand, that are dependent on the production of silk for supplemental income (Pye 1988; Rani 1998; UNCTAD/WTO 2002). While no specific study on the production chains of the Thai silk industry exists to date, Cohen's (2000) study of crafts in Thailand indicates that an increasing amount of profit is made at each step away from the producer in the production chain. In other words, the making of the craft itself is the least profitable step, while foreign importers set the highest markups.

The Thai silk industry is distinct in Southeast Asia in its predominant use of handlooms (Rani 1998). Reeling and weaving are most often performed by hand by rural women and elderly household members (Charsombut and Islam 1992; Ohno and Jirapatpimol 1998). This is in part because native and hybrid varieties of Thai yarn cannot be machine reeled, but the persistence of handloom silk can also be attributed to the commercial viability of traditional fabrics that are not mass produced (Montlake 2007).

Thai silk producers are currently in a worrying economic position. The old global Multi-Fiber Arrangement (MFA), which expired in 2005, set export limits to wealthy countries on textiles (Suphachalasai 1994; Yearman and Gluckman 2005). However, with its expiration, Thailand's National Economic and Social Development Board and the World Bank (2005) warn that Thai silk is highly uncompetitive in comparison to Chinese and other imported fabrics. They estimate that either large reductions in labor costs or increases in productivity are needed. Lower labor costs are clearly not a desirable option, and although increases in productivity at first sound appealing, the necessary adoption of hybrid or foreign higher-yield silk would eliminate domestic varieties that are the basis for traditional Thai handwoven silk products. In response to these dilemmas, a number of commentators have proposed using the Internet as an effective strategy to bring economic wealth into impoverished regions of Thailand, often with an explicit goal of disintermediating commodity chains (Graham 2010; Sambandaraksa 2006; Thuvasethakul and Koanantakool 2002; United Nations 2003b).

Thus, given the perilous state of the Thai silk industry (and the nature of many of the proposed solutions), a multiyear study was carried out to analyze the production chains of Thai silk as it moves from yarn to a finished product and on to the end consumer. A four-step methodology was used. First, a content analysis of websites and policy documents put forth by economic actors who use the Internet to sell silk was performed. Second, institutional surveys were completed by silk merchants, producers, and managers of cooperatives that use the Internet. Third, face-to-face surveys with a sample of merchants and producers who do not necessarily use ICTs were conducted. Finally, in-depth interviews with a select set of silk producers at sampled firms and cooperatives were carried out.

The content analysis of websites found that many of the producers and merchants who sell silk make bold claims about the effects that the Internet has on their economic positionalities. Many websites claimed to be playing a crucial role in disintermediating chains and reducing the topological distances between producers and consumers. Below is a selection of quotations from some of those websites (with words relating to altered spatial positionalities in italics):

> World of Thai Silk online fabric shop *connects you directly* to Thailand's rural village weavers as well as the wholesale fabric of the largest weaving mills. No

matter how *distant* you are from these villages, now you have *access* to them online. [bangkok-thailand.com]

We also aim to provide a platform for the skillful Thai craft people. Many of those live in *remote villages* and do not have *access to the world market.* [thailandfashion.net]

We make the world smaller than ever so you can *reach* Thailand everywhere you are. [thaisilversilk.com]

The crafts that you see on our site are supplied *direct from source* which helps us to keep our prices very competitive, against other Thai and non Thai suppliers. [chiangmaicraft.com]

Asian Silks deals **direct** with the manufactures in CHINA and THAILAND. *We cut out the middle man* (several) and pass the SAVINGS on to YOU! We are constantly updating our website to bring you NEW STYLES and products. We have satisfied thousands of people from all over the world. [asiansilks.com]

So that we can ensure to all buying agents or any other international traders that you are now getting *in touch directly* with the manufacturer online right now. [dechsuwan.com]

What the buyer gets closer to is not a cheaper product but rather the product's source. The source takes on multiple meanings as place, tradition, and ritual. Touch it yourself, the websites implore. There is no need to remain at a symbolic distance, too far away to feel it. These websites simultaneously claim that physical barriers have come down even as symbolic barriers—the difference between what is available "here" versus "there" by "them" versus "us—remain erect.

Interestingly, the users of the Internet in the Thai silk industry are predominantly merchants and intermediaries in Bangkok rather than producers in the northeast of the country. In my survey of 173 economic actors, I found that 61 percent of Bangkok merchants have a website and 66 percent use e-mail. This stands in sharp contrast to the dearth of websites run by northeastern merchants (only 5 percent use e-mail) and the low level of Internet use among northeastern producers (7 percent of whom operate a website and 17 percent of whom use e-mail).

Surprisingly, instead of fulfilling one of the most widely touted benefits of the Internet (that it directly connects producers with consumers, thus eliminating intermediaries), we see Internet adopters occupying mediating roles. The Internet does not seem to be transcending, or allowing a jumping-over, of the commodity chain positions occupied by intermediaries (Graham 2011b). These results thus raise the question: Why is Internet use associated with mediation rather than disintermediation in the commodity chains of Thai silk?

Enter Culture and Its Brokers

To address this question, it is helpful to briefly discuss the geography of the silk industry in Pakthongchai, Thailand, and the power that cultural brokers have in linking buyers to suppliers. Pakthongchai is a small town situated thirty-five kilometers south of the city of Nakhon Ratchasima. The town has long been a center of silk production and specializes in the production of plain-colored cloth (although almost all varieties of silk are woven in the area). Very few shops and markets in Bangkok are without at least some silk from Pakthongchai in their displays, and many retailers almost exclusively stock Pakthongchai silk. Despite this, Pakthongchai has not been able to establish a well-known geographic brand among either Thai or foreign consumers. In Bangkok, many Thai residents (who are not originally from the Northeast) know that silk generally comes from the Northeast. However, only a few of the locals that I spoke with knew the names of any towns that specialized in particular types of silk.

My discussion with numerous foreign nationals in Thailand suggests that they are generally even less knowledgeable about the geography of Thai silk. Many know that silk comes from "somewhere up north" and frequently assume silk production to be based in the northern provinces (as opposed to the northeast). On numerous occasions when I told either Thais or foreigners about my project, they insisted that I should have been spending more time in Chiang Mai (under the assumption that the majority of Thai silk is produced there). Some of the silk merchants in Pakthongchai even joke about the fact that both residents of Bangkok and foreigners will take trips to Chiang Mai (a city that, by road, is at least eight hours from the northeast and eleven from Bangkok) just to buy silk in the hope of obtaining a bargain.

Because buyers have little detailed knowledge about the universe of producers making Thai silk, they rely on cultural brokers to broker knowledge and on their own impressions of where beautiful silk is most likely sourced. The northeast is known as the poorest province, not as the most culturally rich area of the country. That designation goes to Chiang Mai. Chiang Mai–based merchants know that they are given the benefit of the doubt by virtue of where they operate. Some even engage in the practice of rebranding silk from Pakthongchai so that it appears as if it is made in Chiang Mai.

Throughout the commodity chains of Thai silk there are abundant amounts of confusion and misinformation, resulting in an almost absolute lack of transparency. Yet, it is not only end consumers who are lacking a complete picture of the flows of silk within Thailand. Very few producers, cultural brokers (intermediaries), or consumers know about what happens more than one link in the silk commodity chain away from their own position. Consumers often do not know exactly where their silk comes from, and weavers usually know little about what intermediaries do with their silk. For example, when asked about the end customers that use her silk, Ms. Worawan, the head of a weaving group that sells large amounts of silk to local merchants, told me: "There is such a long chain of people, and I really just don't know where it goes. I don't know if the retailers that buy from us export our silk." By contrast, some of the producers and merchants I interviewed in the northeast had either a vague idea about the sites at which their silk was ultimately consumed or at least a general understanding about the directions in which their silk moved after it was sold. Ms. Boonsin, head of another weaving group, explained: "Some of the people who buy from me export my silk, but I have no idea to where."

Although Ms. Boonsin has some knowledge about the movement of her silk after it is sold, there is a lack of any specific information about sites in the commodity chain beyond one node removed from her own position. Her statement is symptomatic of the lack of transparency through the entire network. People are highly unlikely to be able to see past the haze created by each successive node in the chain, even if only small absolute distances separate those nodes: a point that can be best seen by returning to the geography of weaving and selling in Pakthongchai.

Pakthongchai is comprised of a series of settlements built beside narrow walled streets. These settlements are sited outside the central business district for a few kilometers in most directions and for the most part are set back from the main roads leading through the town. One of the roads that transects Pakthongchai is a major north–south artery, and almost all of the local silk shops are sited on it. These shops all have large signs on the road, ample parking space, and glossy cabinets filled with rolls of silk categorized by pattern or color. Most of the shops have air-conditioning, elaborate decorations, and furnishings; they employ neatly dressed employees who offer customers water or coffee, while leading them through the displays.

Some of the shops on the main road employ weavers in small spaces behind their shops. However, most buy from producers who live in small villages on the outskirts of the town. To reach these areas, one must navigate a somewhat labyrinthine street network. Houses in these settlements tend to have tall walls made of concrete, brick, or sheet metal fronting the public roads. The narrow roads that snake through the area (connecting to the main arteries in only a few spots) turn the villages into mazes for anyone not thoroughly familiar with the area.

Other than locals, few end customers ever visit the weavers who work in the Pakthongchai villages, and so the weavers and their representatives sell almost the entirety of their silk to intermediaries. Mr. Thai, who lives in Noinakeh village (a village sited behind the Pakthongchai high school), is one of these producers. His house contains a platform for spinning and three looms that are operated by his wife and two neighbors. Mr. Thai deals with financial issues for the group and has a number of concerns about the group's economic situation. Early in our discussion, he touched on a theme that was repeated by many of the weavers and heads of weaving groups with whom I spoke: namely, that the price of silk fabric was too low. Mr. Thai stated that his group weaves as much as they physically can and would be unable to increase production if they wanted to. I therefore asked him why he chose not to raise prices. He replied:

> If I sell in Pakthongchai district, I can't control the price. The middlemen fix the price. I worry about this, but I have no choice; I need money to buy the raw materials. In the past I gathered a group of weavers to fix the price, but there was conflict, and people stopped weaving, and the group stopped. So it is better to work for yourself anyway. Some companies come to visit. But I can't sell to them because I can't increase production.

His resource constraints keep him from increasing production for more lucrative contracts and from decreasing the costs of distribution. Raw materials are expensive; he has no savings; and he lacks access to low-cost credit for working capital; moreover, he cannot rely on collective action to bring down the costs of production or to facilitate distribution. He does not know where his silk is being sold. He only knows who the merchants are who come to his village, where he sometimes sells his cloth for as little as 100 Baht per yard (just under the cost of production).

At the crux of Mr. Thai's problems is the fact that he is locked into exploitative economic relations. Intermediaries know the price at which they are able to buy silk from producers and are generally unwilling to pay more. If Mr. Thai were to attempt to raise his prices, his customers could easily buy from other producers. This threat is so powerful that Mr. Thai is occasionally convinced to sell his silk below the cost of production. While examples of weavers selling silk below production costs is rare, the lack of resources, lack of access to working capital, and lack of market information is unfortunately extremely common.

The absolute spatial positionality of Mr. Thai and other weavers in relation to large population centers (Bangkok is 250 km away) seems not to be the most important factor contributing to their economic woes. The silk shops located on the Pakthongchai main road are equally as removed from Bangkok and other important markets, yet they are kept in business by end customers and purchasing agents for other intermediaries who travel long distances to buy silk at its source. Mr. Thai's physical distance from the main road is not the problem. Customers could have access to him, but they do not seem to "frame" (evaluate) his shop as being as easily accessible as other shops less than a kilometer away. Convenience is being enacted and accomplished on a day-to-day basis with tangible economic consequences.

While this example does not involve any virtual commodity chains, its relevance for the economic actors attempting to sell silk on the Internet is clear. The example illustrates that Mr. Thai's problems might not be solely borne out of his remote geographic positionality. Pakthongchai and the surrounding villages are equally as far removed from important distant markets, and yet visiting buyers in many cases prefer to buy silk from intermediaries rather than producers who are a mere few hundred meters away. Internet connections used to alter relative distance might therefore mean little to producers if there are significant linguistic, educational, and resource divides.

Mr. Thai's inability to reach alternate (higher-paying) customers perhaps rests on a relative distance from new markets that is unbridgeable with any space-altering technologies. The intermediaries who purchase from him keep him in the dark about how they convert, market, and distribute his silk, leaving him with little practical knowledge about how to accomplish such tasks if he were to attempt to do so himself on the main road. The commodity chain positions into which Mr. Thai and his group are locked thus make him invisible in a way that his absolute distance from markets cannot. These acts of conversion, marketing, and distribution require cultural skills that have to be learned and deployed for the actors to reap the full benefits of information and communications technologies.

The filtering of market transparency through intermediaries not only prevents producers from developing detailed understandings of downstream consumer tastes and preferences but also inhibits the flow of knowledge about producers to the consumers of silk. Merchants throughout the world are generally loath to reveal their sources for fear of losing a competitive advantage, and intermediaries within the Thai silk industry are no exception. Some intermediaries were straightforward about their reasons for not wanting to allow end customers to communicate with producers. For instance, Mrs. Wongpituk of the Ganez company in Bangkok (an intermediary) professed: "Information can be dangerous to villagers because if there is direct contact with foreigners then foreigners will also want low prices."

It is not only intermediaries who actively try to prevent customers from achieving an uninterrupted overview of the silk commodity chains. A commonly repeated complaint that I heard from a majority of producers with whom I spoke related to the poor state of the economy since the military coup in 2006. Some told me sales were down to 50 or 75 percent of what they had been in previous years. Others, however, had much more dramatic stories, telling me that they were selling only 20 or 30 percent of the silk they had the previous year. Producers are thus careful to maintain any customer relationships in which they are involved and are naturally worried about competition. Ms. Laong, the head of a weaving group in the Chonnabot area, affirmed: "We take our products to the retailers who buy from us. I don't like it when they come here because they bargain and see the competition . . . After that I don't know what the retailers do with the silk, and I don't care."

The desire to maintain the status quo is common throughout the industry; but, interestingly, some of the least transparent commodity chains I encountered involve companies that use the Internet. Four separate producers and merchants recounted stories of third-party companies that had set up online consignment stores in association with their own businesses. Kantima Yatsangkad, the owner of Rattanasuran Thai Silk (a small silk shop at a Bangkok market), told me: "Some company takes pictures of my silk and puts them on the Internet. They only pay me if it sells . . . I don't know the name of the company though."

In summary, in all of the cases discussed in the preceding paragraphs, sellers not only have no information about end customers but also know very little about the Internet-based companies who sell their silk. Value within the Thai silk industry is most often created and captured by those possessing detailed knowledge of multiple nodes on the commodity chains of silk. Due to the lack of transparency within commodity chains, producers rarely possess much knowledge of customer tastes, marketing strategies, and distribution outlets, and no amount of technological resources and Internet connectivity is able to transgress these essential barriers to trade. Successful cultural brokers possess the savoir faire to make the purchases attractive and "doable" for buyers. Simply having what customers are said to want is simply not sufficient to succeed in global markets for cultural goods.

An Alternate Groundwork for Development

The Internet has come to shape many of the ways in which economic development is conceptualized. Imaginations of the space-transcending effects of the Internet underpin a host of projects that seek to transform those potentials into actualities. The concepts and practices of disintermediation and e-commerce, in particular, have led some practitioners of development to attempt to replicate the successes of Western firms such as Amazon.com. Yet successes have thus far not been forthcoming. There are countless shells of websites, unused computers, and traditional commodity chains linking networks of intermediaries in defiance of development projects attempting to foster participation in the "Internet revolution."

Despite the existence of nuanced understandings of the relationships between technology and geography, much development discourse continues to rely on technological deterministic formulations of the effects of the Internet on space and distance. Under such formulations it is frequently argued that by reducing a digital divide, a spatial divide can also be diminished. Bringing the previously divided "closer" to the connected will create economic benefits by allowing the former to share a marketplace with the latter.

The example of the Thai silk industry suggests that for the disintermediation of commodity chains to occur, more than Internet copresence is required. Distance is complex, multidimensional, and culturally mediated. It simply cannot be bridged by communication technologies alone. Cultural brokers and other intermediaries occupy essential positions in commodity chains and are able to use their embedded knowledge to capture, enact, and create value. Producers, on the other hand, are hindered by a lack of economic transparency and possess little knowledge about any nonproximate nodes on the chains that their silk will ultimately pass through. Where they have some knowledge of these processes, producers have rarely embodied that knowledge so that they can perform their roles as skilled artisans in ways attractive to their target audiences.

The precise effects that the Internet will have on global commodity chains remain unknown. It therefore seems unwise to build both the discourses and the implementations of development around such narrow conceptualizations of the relationships between geography and the Internet. Alternate imaginations of the relationships between space and ICTs could be used as the groundwork for implementations of economic development that seeks to rearrange commodity chains. Thinking about the relationships between geography and the Internet in terms of hybrid spaces has the potential to add much to this discussion. In place of monocausal and unidirectional influences, we can begin to understand the situationally specific ways in which the Internet does influence space and economic positionality. Doing so would undoubtedly lead to more nuanced types of development.

If applied to the example of Thai silk: A development agency would not necessarily expect villagers to sell their silk directly through disintermediated channels on the global marketplace. Although a digital divide may have been technologically bridged, thus in theory allowing producers access to virtual marketplaces, myriad barriers (physical distance, linguistic distance, cultural distance, technical skill distance, distance from capital resources, and so on) continue to hinder efficient trade between producer and consumer. What may be needed is a series of cybermediaries, each intimately familiar with their adjacent nodes on the commodity chain, each aware of the symbols and narratives animating action on both sides of the marketplace. Or perhaps certain commodities are simply unsuitable for e-commerce, and no amount of knocking down of digital divides will spark interaction between Thai weavers and potential customers in London, Tokyo, and New York.

In summary, many of the theoretical debates presented in this paper have decidedly powerful outcomes. The Internet is touted as the engine of a new revolution and as a way to eliminate poverty and bring prosperity to all participants. It is also considered to be a tool of oppression and economic slavery with the power to disrupt goals of self-sufficiency and displace traditions. The Internet is a highly disruptive technology, and it is frequently argued that, like the Industrial Revolution, the Internet Age will be the cause of fundamental economic and social changes. As this chapter has shown, the effects of the Internet in the contexts of economic development can also fail to live up its potential. At least in the context of the Thai silk industry, the Internet is most often used as an effective communication tool by skilled cultural brokers rather than a radical bridge between producers and consumers. The conclusions of this chapter are not meant to suggest that the Internet cannot have significant positive effects in the lives of impoverished economic actors around the world. However, for those potentials to be unlocked, it is important to move away from exaggerated assumptions and instead focus on the meanings, the embodied knowledge, and the skilled dramaturgical performances that must be coupled with these communications technologies in the cultural industries.

Notes

Introduction

The authors are listed alphabetically and contributed equally to this chapter and to the editing of this volume.

Chapter 1

1. Interview with Saul Bellow in *The New Yorker*, March 7, 1988.

2. A middle ground of sorts exists in the celebration of "pluralistic" variety, but this often merely obscures the underlying dominance of either the cultural universalism or relativism views.

3. UNESCO's World Heritage List portrayed on an interactive map retrieved on February 17, 2011, from http://whc.unesco.org/en/list.

4. We are cognizant of the culture reception literature that points to differences in audiences' reception of seemingly "universal" cultural products launched by American media conglomerates (for review, see Crane 2002). Therefore, we agree that globalization creates *potentialities* for hybridization of culture, but what our data show is that there is a significant Western bias in media production.

5. Princeton graduate student Victoria Reyes is exploring the precise network structure of global tourism.

6. The Branding Thailand Project was initiated in 2001 by the government of Thailand in cooperation with the Sasin Graduate Institute of Business Administration at Chulalongkorn University in Bangkok and the Kellogg School of Management at Northwestern University.

Chapter 2

I would like to thank the editors very much for helping me to recast this chapter into their own creative perspective of a cultural wealth of nations.

1. Talcott Parsons does not appear to have found Adam Smith very interesting, to judge from *The Structure of Social Action* (1937) and (with Neil Smelser) *Economy and Society* (1956). In the latter work, Adam Smith is described as a proponent of "traditional economics" (Parsons and Smelser 1956: 311).

2. According to Frédéric Lebaron, one of Bourdieu's students who specializes in economic sociology, Bourdieu "was rather far from classical economics [like] Smith, Ricardo . . . he was more interested in microeconomics and empirical (post-) Marxism than macroeconomics," as conveyed to the author in an e-mail correspondence on March 1, 2009.

3. For a very similar view of the market, see "Markets as Politics: A Political-Cultural Approach to Market Institutions" by Neil Fligstein (1996).

Chapter 4

1. Bruno Vecchio, *Siena. Tendenze Evolutive del Territorio Provinciale nel Dopoguerra, University of Siena,* 1979, held by the Istituto Regionale per la Programmazione Economica e Territoriale (IRPET) library in Florence, Italy.

2. Archivio Storico del Movimento Operaio Senese (Siena), Fondo Peris Brogi, box XIII 1, folder 4, Convegno per la Casa Rurale, October 31, 1959.

3. Data from ISTAT (Istituto Centrale di Statistica), Censimento Generale della Popolazione 1981, Provincia di Siena, table 29.

4. Marcello Cellerini, "Proposte per uno sviluppo democratico dell'agricoltura chiantigiana nel quadro del piano regionale di sviluppo economico," paper presented at the Union Conference of August 4, 1963, in Radda. Archivio della CGIL Toscana, Florence, Fondo Federterra, Busta 206 Chianti.

5. Amministrazione Provinciale di Siena, *Convegno per lo Sviluppo Economico della Provincia di Siena,* June 25, 1960, held at the IRPET library in Florence, Italy.

6. Data from Assessorato all'Agricultura della Provincia di Siena, *Il Punto sull'Agricoltura. Documento Riassuntivo sui Mutamenti Avvenuti nell'Agricultura Senese nel Decennio 1961–1971 e Programmi di Investimento Previsti per gli Anni Futuri,* Siena, 1971, held at the IRPET library in Florence, Italy.

7. Sebastian Schweizer and Mario Falciai, "Siccità e ripristino degli invasi collinari minori. Un'analisi GIS," retrieved on October 22, 2009, from www1.unifi.it/AIIA2007/Comunicazioni%20A3.pdf.

8. In the early 1960s, the production of Chianti wine was less than half what it had been in the late 1920s. Ente Autonomo per la Bonifica, l'Irrigazione e la Valorizzazione Fondiaria nelle Provincie di Arezzo, Siena, Perugia e Terni, *Contributo per lo Sviluppo dell'Agricoltura del Chianti Senese,* 1971, held at the IRPET library in Florence, Italy.

9. "Tempo d'agonia nel Chianti," *Giornale del Mattino,* October 13, 1956.

10. "Remodeled Hideaway in Chianti Is Europe's Latest Vacation Chic," *International Herald Tribune*, September 27, 1968.

11. Toskanafraktion. Retrieved on February 11, 2011, from www.toskanafraktion .de/index2.html.

12. Data provided by Luca Rossi at the Parco Artistico Naturale e Culturale della Val d'Orcia, San Quirico d'Orcia.

13. Val d'Orcia. UNESCO World Heritage Centre. Retrieved on February 11, 2011, from whc.unesco.org/en/list/1026.

14. Parco della Val d'Orcia. Retrieved on February 11, 2011, from www .parcodellavaldorcia.com/indexb.asp.

Chapter 5

Portions of Chapter 5 reprinted with the permission of the American Sociological Association. Lauren A. Rivera, "Managing 'Spoiled' National Identity: War, Tourism, and Memory in Croatia," *American Sociological Review* 73: 613–634. Copyright 2008 American Sociological Association.

1. The privately run Homeland War Museum in Karlovac, opened in 2009, is now advertised on the county tourist office's website although not the CNTB's. The Sponza Palace memorial room, erected in Dubrovnik by local citizens in 2005, is not yet listed in either country or national tourism publications.

2. These figures represent the percentage of all mentions of primary attractions in brochures.

3. Although the war did increase religious homogeneity, Croatia still exhibits some religious diversity. Croatia is 90 percent Catholic, 5 percent Eastern Orthodox, 1 percent Muslim, and 4 percent other compared to 78 percent, 12 percent, and less than 1 percent before of war (Central Bureau of Statistics 2007). Experts suggest that these figures underestimate the percentage of non-Catholics who may not disclose their affiliation for fear of discrimination or persecution.

4. See "The Official Tourism Site for Malta, Gozo and Comino," at www.visitmalta .com/, retrieved on March 18, 2007, and "Welcome to Latvia" at www.latviatourism .lv/, retrieved on March 18, 2007.

Chapter 7

The author gratefully acknowledges her adviser, Dr. Ulrike Schuerkens (EHESS) for her moral and intellectual support; the kindhearted Professor Emeritus Nelson Graburn (UC Berkeley) for his extensive support, whose works, as well as his teaching, have been invaluable in the analysis of this topic; the Conseil Général of Mayotte for its financial support; and all the people who agreed to be interviewed (policy makers, tourists, and craftspeople).

1. For 2008, the number of tourist arrivals was around 38,000 in Mayotte and more than 380,000 visitors in Reunion. Nevertheless, these figures have to be explained and completed by noting that Mayotte (144 square miles) is much smaller than Reunion (969.9 square miles) and that there is no direct flight to Mayotte from the French mainland.

2. ODIT France is the official agency in charge of the French tourism policy.

3. Graburn shows how the Mexican government has promoted a favorable image of regional Mexico using a distinction with European Spain and other Latin American countries (1976: 117–118). The fact that the Mexican government glorified the arts of the local civilizations and supported various exhibitions, collections, or museums is motivated by a strong need to promote the local cultural aspects in opposition to the culture of the colonizer imposed by the past.

4. In other words, these local people don't feel as if they are in their own land anymore.

5. In 2008, the *"tourists affinitaires"* were half of the tourists coming to La Réunion (source: survey INSEE/IRT). The same year, these tourists also represented almost half of the tourist arrivals in Mayotte (source: INSEE). For La Réunion, see www.insee.fr/fr/regions/reunion/default.asp?page=themes/infos_rapides/tourisme/irtour93/irtour93.htm; for Mayotte, see www.insee.fr/fr/insee_regions/mayotte/themes/dossiers/tem/tem_12-1-frequentation-touristique.pdf

6. This French term is used to describe tourism practiced by persons who visit friends or family.

Chapter 8

I am grateful to the editors, Nina Bandelj and Frederick Wherry, and the press's reviewers for helpful comments.

1. For purposes of this chapter, I will refer to the global value chains (GVC) framework as the most policy-oriented of the extant chain or network approaches to globalization, and the one that most squarely addresses the relationship between the dynamics of industrial sectors and processes of economic development.

2. The global South's share of total tourist receipts has been increasing, reaching approximately one-third of the total by 1997 (Clancy 2009).

3. An importance exception to this observation is Michael Clancy's work on the political economy of tourism, which has frequently employed a commodity chain perspective (1998; 2002; 2008). Other recent studies of tourism that use the commodity chain concept are Judd (2006) and Mosedale (2006). Clancy (2009) notes that the British Department for International Development (DFID), which has been developing and promoting the concept of "pro-poor tourism," has commissioned a number of case studies that employ value chain analysis to track the distribution of tourist dollars in developing countries.

4. GVC analysts have identified four different types of upgrading, although in practice these frequently overlap. They are: (1) process upgrading (increasing productivity or otherwise improving the production process); (2) functional upgrading (adding new activities or links in the chain); (3) product upgrading (moving to higher value-added products within the same chain); and (4) interchain upgrading (moving from a less capital- or technology-intensive chain, like clothing, to one that is more capital- or technology-intensive, such as autos) (Gereffi 1999). Upgrading within the tourism chain from sun, sea, and sand to heritage tourism is primarily an example of product upgrading, though it may include elements of functional upgrading as well.

5. A similar point was made by Terrence Hopkins and Immanuel Wallerstein in one of the first discussions of commodity chains. Hopkins and Wallerstein (1986) argued that those links in a chain that are characterized by a high rate of profit are typically monopolized by a small number of producers and are usually located in core countries, but that any highly profitable link is subject to competitive pressures that tend toward its demonopolization over time.

6. In this chapter, I am focusing narrowly on the value chain for heritage tourism as a particular form of marketing cultural wealth. Consequently, I do not address the broader question of the relationship between culture and value chains. However, a growing literature is devoted to showing that cultural practices and meanings shape consumer preferences, and that this, in turn, shapes the organization and geography of value chains (for example, Friedberg 2004; Pratt 2008; Schurman and Munro 2009).

7. One fascinating aspect of heritage tourism in Mexico is the extent to which it challenges the ideology of *mestizaje*, which is built on valorizing Mexico's pre-Conquest indigenous past while simultaneously asserting a modern national identity that minimizes ethnic differences in the present. Thus while government officials may valorize the "Mayan-ness" of Mexicans of Mayan descent for the purposes of promoting heritage tourism, the same government rejects the principle of ethnic ancestry in counting and classifying its citizenry. Mayans, like other indigenous Mexicans, are recorded as nonindigenous in the Mexican census unless they speak an indigenous language (van den Berghe 1995). In the state of Yucatán, for example, about one-third of the inhabitants of Mayan descent speak Yucatec Mayan.

Chapter 9

1. Value chains are the full range of resources and activities involved in bringing a product from its conception to its end use.

2. At the same time that political economy expands its interest in "culture," anthropology is becoming more concerned with the political economy of culture, ethnicity, and identity. This is epitomized in Comaroff and Comaroff's (2009) coinage of the concept "Ethnicity, Inc.," an overlap of institutional processes, marketing, and branding created to create, re/discover, manage, and re/distribute the symbolic value

embedded into "ethnicity." Ethnicity, Inc., epitomizes a double process of cultural commodification and the incorporation (as in "Inc.") of identity.

3. Although international coffee prices increased substantially in the second half of the first decade of the 2000s, thus easing the pressure on coffee farmers, the main challenge for producers in the South still remains how to create and control the symbolic value of coffee.

4. In our earlier work (Daviron and Ponte 2005), we also examined in-person service quality attributes. These are the product of interpersonal relations between producers or providers and consumers. Most of in-person services imply some physical transformation of a good (for example, preparing a drink) or, directly, of the consumer (such as cutting hair). All in-person services include emotional work. This third kind of quality attribute will not be examined in this chapter due to lack of space.

5. As argued elsewhere (Ponte and Ewert 2009), the trajectory of upgrading in the South African wine industry has been a complex one, combining value addition with volume growth in basic quality wines. By focusing on symbolic aspects in this chapter, we do not mean to underestimate the importance of economies of scale and improvements in the material quality of South African wine.

6. It should be noted, however, that the wine industry is changing in France as well, with new consumer-friendly brands taking root and an increased use of cultivar names on bottles. The AOC system is going through reform to make it more flexible.

Chapter 10

The author gratefully acknowledges that portions in the chapter's sections on "The 'Internet Revolution,' E-Commerce, and Reconfigured Commodity Chains" and "Development and the Internet" (along with the three figures) come from his previously published article "Warped Geographies of Development," *Geography Compass* 2 (2008): 771–789, and are used here with permission.

References

Abbott, Andrew. 2001. *Time Matters: On Theory and Method*. Chicago: University of Chicago Press.

Abolafia, Mitchell. 1996. *Making Markets: Opportunism and Restraint on Wall Street*. Cambridge, MA: Harvard University Press.

Abrams, Philip. 1983. *Historical Sociology*. Ithaca, NY: Cornell University Press.

Adams, Julia, Elisabeth S. Clemens, and Ann Shola Orloff. 2005. *Remaking Modernity: Politics, History and Sociology*. Durham, NC: Duke University Press.

Adelson, Naomi. 2001. "A Rocky Road for the *Ruta Maya*." *Business Mexico* 11(6): 56–57.

Agnew, John. 2002. *Place and Politics in Modern Italy*. Chicago: University of Chicago Press.

Akerlof, George A. 1970. "The Market for 'Lemons': Qualitative Uncertainty and the Market Mechanism." *Quarterly Journal of Economics* 84: 488–500.

Alexander, Jeffrey C. 2003. *The Meanings of Social Life: A Cultural Sociology*. New York: Oxford University Press.

Alexander, Jeffrey C. 2004a. "Cultural Pragmatics: Social Performance between Ritual and Strategy." *Sociological Theory* 22 :527–573.

Alexander, Jeffrey C. 2004b. "Toward a Theory of Cultural Trauma." In *Cultural Trauma and Collective Identity*, edited by J. C. Alexander, R. Eyerman, B. Giesen, N. J. Smelser, and P. Sztompka, pp. 1–29. Berkeley: University of California Press.

Alexander, Jeffrey C., and Philip Smith. 1993. "The Discourse of American Civil Society: A New Proposal for Cultural Studies." *Theory and Society* 22: 151–207.

Amin, Ash, and Nigel Thrift. 2003. *The Blackwell Cultural Economy Reader*. Oxford, UK: Blackwell Publishing.

Angiolini, Sandro. 1989. *Agriturismo in Toscana. Protagonisti, Tendenze, Problemi*, Montepulciano: Edizioni del Grifo.

Anholt, Simon. 2004. *Brand America: The Mother of All Brands*. London: Cyan Books.

Aoyama, Yuko. 2009. "Artists, Tourists, and the State: Cultural Tourism and the Flamenco Industry in Andalusia, Spain." *International Journal of Urban and Regional Research* 33(1): 80–104.

Apostolakis, Alexandros. 2003. "The Convergence Process in Heritage Tourism." *Annals of Tourism Research* 30(4): 795–812.

Appadurai, Arjun. 2001. *Après le colonialisme. Les conséquences culturelles de la mondialisation*. Paris: Payot.

Apter, David. 1967. *The Politics of Modernization*. Chicago: University of Chicago Press.

Arden, Traci. 2002. "Conversations about the Production of Archaeological Knowledge and Community Museums at Chunchucmil and Kochol, Yucatán, México." *World Archaeology* 34(2): 379–400.

Arrighi, Giovanni. 2007. *Adam Smith in Beijing: Lineages of the Twenty-First Century*. London: Verso.

Arrighi, Giovanni, Beverly J. Silver, and Benjamin D. Brewer. 2003. "Industrial Convergence, Globalization and the Persistence of the North–South Divide." *Studies in Comparative International Development* 38(1): 3–31.

Augé, Marc. 1992. *Non-lieux, introduction à une anthropologie de la surmodernité*. Paris: Le Seuil.

Bair, Jennifer. 2005. "Global Capitalism and Commodity Chains: Looking Back, Going Forward." *Competition and Change* 9(2): 153–180.

Bair, Jennifer. 2009. "Commodity Chains: Genealogy and Review." In *Frontiers of Commodity Chain Research*, edited by Jennifer Bair, pp. 1–34. Stanford, CA: Stanford University Press.

Bair, Jennifer, and Gary Gereffi. 2001. "Local Clusters in Global Chains: The Causes and Consequences of Export Dynamism in Torreon's Blue Jeans Industry." *World Development* 29(11): 1885–1903.

Bair, Jennifer, and Gary Gereffi. 2003. "Upgrading, Uneven Development, and Jobs in the North American Apparel Industry." *Global Networks* 3(2): 143–169.

Bakhtin, Mikhail. 1981. *The Dialogic Imagination: Four Essays*. Translated by Caryl Emerson and Michael Holquist. Edited by Michael Holquist. Austin: University of Texas Press.

Ballini, Pier Luigi, Luigi Lotti, and Mario G. Rossi. 1991. *La Toscana nel Secondo Dopoguerra*. Milan: Franco Angeli.

Bandelj, Nina. 2002. "Embedded Economies: Social Relations as Determinants of Foreign Direct Investment in Central and Eastern Europe." *Social Forces* 81: 411–444.

Bandelj, Nina. 2008a. "Economic Objects as Cultural Objects: Discourse on Foreign Investment in Post-Socialist Europe." *Socio-Economic Review* 6(4): 671–702.

Bandelj Nina. 2008b. *From Communists to Foreign Capitalists: The Social Foundations of Foreign Direct Investment in Postsocialist Europe.* Princeton, NJ: Princeton University Press.

Baranowski, Shelley, and Ellen Furlough, eds. 2001. *Being Elsewhere: Tourism, Consumer Culture, and Identity in Modern Europe and North America.* Ann Arbor: University of Michigan Press.

Barbalet, Jack. 2005. "Smith's *Sentiments* (1759) and Wright's *Passions* (1601): The Beginnings of Sociology." *British Journal of Sociology* 56(2): 171–189.

Barham, Elizabeth. 2003. "Translating Terroir: The Global Challenge of French AOC Labeling." *Journal of Rural Studies* 19(1): 127–138.

Barjolle, Dominique, and Bertil Sylvander. 2000. *PDO and PGI Products: Market, Supply Chains and Institutions.* Brussels: European Commission: FAIR 1–CT 95-0306.

Barjolle, Dominique, and Bertil Sylvander. 2002. "Some Factors of Success for Origin Labelled Products in Agri-Food Supply Chains in Europe: Market, Internal Resources and Institutions." *Economies et Sociétés* 25(9–10): 1441–1461.

Barrère, Christian. 2005. *Reinventer le Patrimoine: De la Culture à l'Economie. Une Nouvelle Pensée de le Patrimoine?* Paris: L'Harmattan.

Batisse, Michel, and George Bolla. 2003. *L'invention du Patrimoine Mondial.* Paris: UNESCO.

Beckert, Jens. 2008. *Inherited Wealth.* Princeton, NJ: Princeton University Press.

Bek, David, Cheryl McEwan, and Karen Bek. 2007. "Ethical Trading and Socioeconomic Transformation: Critical Reflections on the South African Wine Industry." *Environment and Planning A* 39: 301–319.

Bellah, Robert N. 1958. "Religious Aspects of Modernization in Turkey and Japan." *American Journal of Sociology* 64: 1–5.

Belting, Hans. 1994. *Likeness and Presence: A History of the Image before the Era of Art.* Chicago: University of Chicago Press.

Benjamin, Robert, and Robert Wigland. 1995. "Electronic Markets and Virtual Value Chains on the Information Superhighway." *Sloan Management Review* 36: 62–72.

Bennett, Tony. 1995. *The Birth of the Museum: History, Theory, Politics.* London and New York: Routledge.

Biernacki, Richard. 1995. *The Fabrication of Labor: Germany and Britain 1640–1914.* Berkeley: University of California Press.

Biffoli, Guido. 1966. *La Casa Colonica in Toscana.* Florence: Vallecchi.

Biggart, Nicole Woolsey. 1989. *Charismatic Capitalism: Direct Selling Organizations in America.* Chicago: University of Chicago Press.

Boissevain, Jeremy. 1979. "The Impact of Tourism on a Dependant Island, Gozo, Malta." *Annals of Tourism Research* 6: 76–90.

Bonifazi, Emo. 1979. *Lotte Contadine in Val d'Orcia.* Siena: Nuovo Corriere Senese.

Borrione, Paola. 1999. *Analisi Economica e Istituzionale di un Distretto Culturale: I Diritti di Proprietà e il Caso delle Langhe*. Laurea Thesis, University of Turin.

Borrus, Michael, Dieter Ernst, and Stephan Haggard. 2000. *International Production Networks in Asia: Rivalry or Riches?* London: Routledge.

Bourdieu, Pierre. 1977. *Outline of a Theory of Practice*. New York: Cambridge University Press.

Bourdieu, Pierre. 1984. *Distinction: A Social Critique of the Judgment of Taste*. Cambridge, MA: Harvard University Press.

Bourdieu, Pierre. 1986. "The Forms of Capital." In *Handbook of Theory and Research for the Sociology of Education*, edited by J. G. Richardson, pp. 241–258. Westport, CT: Greenwood Press.

Bourdieu, Pierre. 1990. "The Interest of the Sociologist." In *In Other Words: Essays Towards a Reflexive Sociology*, edited by P. Bourdieu et al., pp. 87–93 Palo Alto, CA: Stanford University Press.

Bourdieu, Pierre. 1993a. *The Field of Cultural Production: Essays on Art and Literature*. Edited and translated by Randal Johnson. New York: Columbia University Press.

Bourdieu, Pierre. 1993b. "A Science That Makes Trouble." In *Sociology in Question*, pp. 8–20. Translated by Richard Nice. London: Sage.

Bourdieu, Pierre. 1998a. *Acts of Resistance: Against the Tyranny of the Market*. New York: New Press.

Bourdieu, Pierre. 1998b. "Is a Disinterested Act Possible?" In *Practical Reason: On the Theory of Action*, pp. 75–91. Translated by Randal Johnson. Stanford, CA: Stanford University Press.

Bourdieu, Pierre. 2005. *The Social Structures of the Economy*. Translated by Chris Turner. Cambridge, UK: Polity Press.

Bourdieu, Pierre. 2007. *Sketch for a Self-Analysis*. Translated by Richard Nice. Chicago: University of Chicago Press.

Bourdieu, Pierre, Luc Boltanski, and Jean-Claude Chamboredon. 1963. *La banque et sa clientèle. Eléments d'une sociologie du crédit*. "Etude réalisée sous la direction de Pierre Bourdieu par Luc Boltanski et Jean-Claude Chamboredon." Unpublished manuscript. Paris: Centre de Sociologie Européenne.

Bourdieu, Pierre, and Loic Wacquant. 1992. *An Invitation to Reflexive Sociology*. Chicago: University of Chicago Press.

Boy, Laurence. 2002. "Propriété Intellectuelle: L'agriculture en Première Ligne avec L'accord ADPIC." In *Economie et Strategies Agricoles: Nouveaux Enjeux pour l'Agriculture*, pp. 67–110. Paris: Armand Colin/VUEF.

Brannon, Jeffery, and Eric Baklanoff. 1984. "The Political Economy of Agrarian Reform in Yucatán, Mexico." *World Development* 12(11–12): 1131–1141.

Braudel, Fernand. 1972. *The Mediterranean and the Mediterranean World in the Age of Philip II*. London: Collins.

Breglia, Lisa. 2006. *Monumental Ambivalence: The Politics of Heritage*. Austin: University of Texas Press.

Brown, Denise Fay. 1999. "Mayas and Tourists in the May World." *Human Organization* 58(3): 295–304.

Burke, Peter, 2001. *Eyewitnessing: The Use of Images as Historical Evidence*. Ithaca, NY: Cornell University Press.

Burtner, Jennifer Carol. 2004. "Travel and Transgression in the *Mundo Maya*: Spaces of Home and Alterity in a Guatemalan Tourist Market." PhD dissertation, University of Texas, Austin.

Calhoun, Craig. 1997. *Nationalism*. Minneapolis: University of Minnesota Press.

Cano, Lucero Morales, and Avis Mysyk. 2004. "Cultural Tourism, the State, and Day of the Dead." *Annals of Tourism Research* 31(4): 879–898.

Cardoso, Fernando Henrique, and Enzo Faletto. 1979. *Dependency and Development in Latin America*. Berkeley: University of California Press.

Cardwell, Michael. 2004. *The European Model of Agriculture*. Oxford, UK: Oxford University Press.

Castañeda, Quetzil E. 2004. "'We Are *Not* Indigenous': An Introduction to the Maya Identity of Yucatan." *The Journal of Latin American Anthropology* 9(1): 36–63.

Čavlek, Nevenka. 2002. "Tour Operators and Destination Safety." *Annals of Tourism Research* 29: 478–496.

Centeno, Miguel A., and Joseph N. Cohen. 2010. *Global Capitalism*. London: Polity.

Central Bureau of Statistics. 2005. *Statistical Yearbook 2004*. Zagreb, Croatia: Central Bureau of Statistics.

Central Bureau of Statistics. 2007. *Statistical Yearbook 2006*. Zagreb, Croatia: Central Bureau of Statistics.

Central Bureau of Statistics. 2009. *Statistical Yearbook 2008*. Zagreb, Croatia: Central Bureau of Statistics.

Chamber of Economy. 2006. "Tourism." Zagreb, Croatia: Chamber of Economy. Retrieved on March 15, 2007, from www2.hgk.hr/en/depts/tourism/Turizam_2006 .pdf.

Chamber of Economy. 2009. "Tourism." Zagreb, Croatia: Chamber of Economy. Retrieved on February 5, 2010, from www2.hgk.hr/en/depts/tourism/Turizam_ brosura_2009.pdf.

Chamberlin, Edward. 1933. *The Theory of Monopolistic Competition*. Cambridge, MA: Harvard University Press.

Chandrasekaran, Rajiv. 2001. "Cambodian Village Wired to Future." *Washington Post*, p. A01.

Charmaz, Kathy. 2001. "Grounded Theory." In *Contemporary Field Research*, 2nd ed., edited by R. M. Emerson, pp. 335–352. Prospect Heights, IL: Waveland.

Charsombut, Pradit, and Rizwanul Islam. 1992. "Adoption and Diffusion of New Technology in Cottage Industries of Rural Thailand: A Case Study of Basketry and Silk." In *Transfer, Adoption, and Diffusion of Technology for Small and Cottage Industries*, edited by Rizwanul Islam, pp. 256–282. Geneva, Switzerland: International Labour Organization.

Chase-Dunn, Christopher, and Richard Rubinson. 1977. "Toward a Structural Perspective on the World-System." *Politics and Society* 7(4): 453–476.

Choay, Francoise. [1991] 2001. *The Invention of the Historic Monument.* Translated by Lauren M. O'Connell. Cambridge, UK, and New York: Cambridge University Press.

Cifrić, Ivan. 2004. *Modernization and Identity in Croatian Society.* Working Paper, University of Zagreb.

Cini, Michelle. 2001. "The Europeanization of Malta." In *Europeanization and the Southern Periphery*, edited by K. Featherstone and G. Kazamias, pp. 261–276. London: Frank Cass.

Clancy, Michael. 1998. "Commodity Chains, Services and Development: Theory and Preliminary Evidence from the Tourism Industry." *Review of International Political Economy* 5(1): 122–148.

Clancy, Michael. 2002. "The Globalization of Sex Tourism and Cuba: A Commodity Chains Approach." *Studies in Comparative International Development* 36(4): 63–88.

Clancy, Michael. 2008. "Cruisin' to Exclusion: Commodity Chains, the Cruise Industry and Development in the Caribbean." *Globalizations* 5(3): 405–418.

Clancy, Michael. 2009 "Global Commodity Chains and Tourism: Past Research and Future Promise." Paper presented at the International Studies Association Convention, New York.

Cohen, Erik. 1988. "Authenticity and Commoditization in Tourism." *Annals of Tourism Research* 15: 371–386.

Cohen, Erik. 2000. "The Study of Commercialized Crafts in Thailand." In *The Commercialized Crafts of Thailand: Hill Tribes and Lowland Villages*, edited by Erik Cohen, pp. 1–24. Honolulu: University of Hawaii Press.

Coleman, James S. 1990. *Foundations of Social Theory.* Cambridge, UK: Belknap Press of Harvard University Press.

Coleman, James. 1993. "Social Capital in the Creation of Human Capital." *American Journal of Sociology* 94: S95–121.

Collins, Randall. 2004. *Interaction Ritual Chains.* Princeton, NJ: Princeton University Press.

Colloredo-Mansfeld. Rudi. 2002. "An Ethnography of Neoliberalism: Understanding Competition in Artisan Economies," *Current Anthropology* 43: 113–137.

Comtrade. 2011. United Nations Commodity Trade Statistics Database. Retrieved on February 17, 2011, from http://comtrade.un.org.

Commission of the European Communities. 2006. "Progress Report." Brussels, Belgium: Commission of the European Communities. Retrieved on March 18, 2007, from ec.europa.eu/enlargement/key_documents/reports_nov_2006_en.hm.

Cosgrove, Denis. 1984. *Social Formation and Symbolic Landscape*. London: Croom Helm.

Crane, Diana. 2002. "Culture and Globalization: Theoretical Models and Emerging Trends." In *Global Culture: Media, Arts, Policy and Globalization*, edited by D. Crane, N. Kawashima, and K. Kawasaki, pp. 1–25. New York: Routledge.

Crick, Malcolm. 1989. "Representations of International Tourism in the Social Sciences: Sun, Sex, Sights, Savings, and Servility." *Annual Review of Anthropology* 18: 307–344.

Croatian National Tourist Board (CNTB). 2003a. *Croatia Like a Picture, A Picture Like Croatia*. Zagreb, Croatia: CNTB.

Croatian National Tourist Board (CNTB). 2003b. *Magical Croatia*. Zagreb, Croatia: CNTB.

Croatian National Tourist Board (CNTB). 2003c. *The Wondrous Natural Heritage of Croatia*. Zagreb, Croatia: CNTB.

Croatian National Tourist Board (CNTB). 2004a. *Croatia*. Zagreb, Croatia: CNTB.

Croatian National Tourist Board (CNTB). 2004b. *Croatian Cultural Heritage*. Zagreb, Croatia: CNTB.

Cusmano, Lucia, Andrea Morrison, and Roberta Rabelloti. 2010. "Catching Up Trajectories in the Wine Sector: A Comparative Study of Chile, Italy and South Africa." *World Development* 38: 1588–1602.

Dahles, Heidi. 1998. "Redefining Amsterdam as a Tourist Destination." *Annals of Tourism Research* 25: 55–69.

Dalama, Marie-Gisèle. 2005. "Les Hauts de l'île de La Réunion et le tourisme: Les facteurs en jeu dans le processus complexe qui associe le patrimoine et la modernité dans les Hauts." In J. M. Jauze and J. L. Guebourg, eds., *Inégalités et Spatialité dans l'océan Indien*. Paris: L'Harmattan.

Dalisi, Riccardo. 1964. "Nota per una Lettura Segnica del Paesaggio." *Bollettino di Italia Nostra* 56: 22–26.

Dann, Graham. 1996. "The People of Tourist Brochures." In *The Tourist Image*, edited by T. Selwyn, pp. 61–82. Chichester, UK: John Wiley.

Darby, Michael R., and Edi Karni. 1973. "Free Competition and Optimal Amount of Fraud." *Journal of Law and Economics* 16(1): 67–88.

Datta, Rajat K., ed. 1996. *Global Silk Scenario 2001*. New Delhi: Oxford and IBH Publishing.

Davies, James, Susanna Sandström, Anthony Shorrocks, and Edward Wolff. 2006. "World Distribution of Hosuehold Wealth." In *World Institute for Development Economics Research of the United Nations University*. New York: United Nations.

Daviron, Benoit. 2002. "Small Farm Production and the Standardization of Tropical Products." *Journal of Agrarian Change* 2(2): 162–184.

Daviron, Benoit, and Stefano Ponte. 2005. *The Coffee Paradox: Global Markets, Commodity Trade and the Elusive Promise of Development*. London: Zed Books.

Dikhanov, Yuri. 2005. "Trends in Global Income Distribution, 1970–2000, and Scenarios for 2015." In UNDP Human Development Report. New York: United Nations Development Programme.

Direction of Tourism of the French Ministry of Economy, Finance and Employment. 2007. "Le tourisme dans l'Outre-mer français." Retrieved on February 5, 2010, from www.tourisme.gouv.fr/fr/z2/stat/etudes/att00017746/outre-mer_octobre07 .pdf.

Dobbin, Frank. 1994. *Forging Industrial Policy: The United States, Britain, and France in the Railway Age*. Cambridge, UK: Cambridge University Press.

Du Gay, Paul. 1997. *Production of Culture, Cultures of Production*. London: Sage.

du Toit, Andries. 1993. "The Micropolitics of Paternalism: Discourses of Management and Resistance on Western Cape Fruit and Wine Farms." *Journal of Southern African Studies* 19(3): 314–336.

du Toit, Andries. 1998. "The Fruits of Modernity: Law, Power and Paternalism in Western Cape Fruit and Wine Farms." In *South Africa in Transition: New Theoretical Perspectives*, edited A. Norval and D. Howarth, pp. 149–164. London: Macmillan.

du Toit, Andries. 2002. "Globalising Ethics: Social Technologies of Private Regulation and the South African Wine Industry." *Journal of Agrarian Change* 2(3): 356–380.

du Toit, Andries, and Joachim Ewert. 2002. "Myths of Globalisation: Private Regulation and Farm Worker Livelihoods on Western Cape Farms." *Transformation* 50: 77–104.

du Toit, Andries, Sandra Kruger, and Stefano Ponte. 2008. "De-Racialising Exploitation: 'Black Economic Empowerment' in the South African Wine Sector." *Journal of Agrarian Change* 8(1): 6–32.

Duncan, Carol, and Alan Wallach. 1980. "The Universal Survey Museum." *Art History* 3: 448–469.

Durkheim, Emile. [1893] 1984. *The Division of Labor in Society*. Translated by W. D. Halls. New York: The Free Press.

Durkheim, Emile. [1895] 1986. *Les Règles de la Méthode*. Paris: Presses Universitaires de France.

Durkheim, Emile. [1912] 1995. *The Elementary Forms of Religious Life*. New York: The Free Press.

Durkheim, Emile. 2004. *Durkheim's Philosophy Lectures: Notes from the Lycée de Sens Course, 1883–1884*. Translated by N. Gross and R. A. Jones. Cambridge, UK: Cambridge University Press.

Eco, Umberto. 2009. *The Infinity of Lists*. Translated by Alastair McEwen. London: MacLehose.

Eglitis, Daina. 2002. *Imagining the Nation: History, Modernity, and Revolution in Latvia*. University Park: Pennsylvania State University Press.

Enloe, Cynthia. 1989. *Bananas, Beaches and Bases: Making Feminist Sense of International Politics*. London: Pandora Books.

Espeland, Wendy N., and Michael Sauder. 2007. "Rankings and Reactivity: How Public Measures Recreate Social Worlds." *American Journal of Sociology* 113(1): 1–40.

Espeland, Wendy N., and Mitchell L. Stevens. 1998. "Commensuration as a Social Process." *Annual Review of Sociology* 24: 313–343.

Ethington, Philip, and Vanessa Schwartz. 2006. "Introduction: An Atlas of the Urban Icons Project." *Urban History* 33: 5–19.

Evans, Graeme. 2005. "*Mundo Maya*: From Cancún to City of Culture. World Heritage in Post-Colonial Mesoamerica." In *The Politics of World Heritage: Negotiating Tourism and* Conservation, edited by David Harrison and Michael Hitchcock, pp. 35–49. Bristol, UK: Channel View Publications.

Evans, Peter. 1979. *Dependent Development: The Alliance of Multinational, State and Local Capital in Brazil*. Princeton, NJ: Princeton University Press.

Ewert, J., Yuna Chiffoleau, Fabrice Dreyfus, C. Martin, Jean-Marc Touzard, and G. Williams. 2002. "Qualité et Solidarité dans les Coopératives Viticoles: Des Enjeux pour l'Ancien et le Nouveau Monde?" *Revue Internationale de l'Economie Sociale* 285.

Feenstra, Robert C. 1998. "Integration of Trade and Disintegration of Production in the Global Economy." *Journal of Economic Perspectives* 12(4): 31–50.

Fine, Gary Alan. 1996. "Reputational Entrepreneurs and the Memory of Incompetence: Melting Supporters, Partisan Warriors, and Images of President Harding." *American Journal of Sociology* 101: 1159–1193.

Fiorentini, Antonio, and Marcello Massa. 1979. *La Collina Fiorentina tra Speculazione Edilizia e Investimenti Multinazionali*. Florence: Pappagallo.

Firebaugh, Glenn. 2003. *The New Geography of Global Income Inequality*. Cambridge, MA: Harvard University Press.

Fligstein, Neil. 1996. "Markets as Politics: A Political-Cultural Approach to Market Institutions." *American Sociological Review* 61(4): 656–673.

Florida, Richard. 2002. *The Rise of the Creative Class: And How It's Transforming Work, Leisure, Community and Everyday Life*. New York: Basic Books.

Flower, Raymond. 1979. *Chianti: The Land, the People and the Wine*. London: Croom Helm.

Francioni, Francesco, ed. 2008. *The 1972 World Heritage Convention*. Oxford, UK: Oxford University Press.

Friedberg, Suzanne. 2004. *French Beans and Food Scares: Culture and Commerce in an Anxious Age*. Oxford, UK: Oxford University Press.

Frobel, Folker, Jurgen Heinrichs, and Otto Kreye. 1980. *The New International Division of Labor.* Cambridge, UK: Cambridge University Press.

Fuma, Sudel. 2004. "Aux Origines Ethno-historiques du Maloya Réunionnais Traditionnel." *Kabaro* 2: 207–218.

Garrett, Wilbur. 1989. "La Ruta Maya." *National Geographic* (October): 424–479.

Gereffi, Gary. 1978. "Drug Firms and Dependency in Mexico: The Case of the Steroid Hormone Industry." *International Organizations* 32: 237–286.

Gereffi, Gary. 1983. *The Pharmaceutical Industry and Dependency in the Third World.* Princeton, NJ: Princeton University Press.

Gereffi, Gary. 1999. "International Trade and Industrial Upgrading in the Apparel Commodity Chain." *Journal of International Economics* 48(1): 37–70.

Gereffi, Gary, John Humphrey, Raphael Kaplinsky, and Timothy Sturgeon. 2001. "Introduction: Globalisation, Value Chains, and Development." *IDS Bulletin* 32(3): 1–8.

Gereffi, Gary, John Humphrey, and Timothy Sturgeon. 2005. "The Governance of Global Value Chains." *Review of International Political Economy* 12(1): 78–104.

Gereffi, Gary, and Miguel Korzeniewicz, eds. 1994. *Commodity Chains and Global Capitalism.* Westport, CT: Praeger.

Gianfrate, Giovanni, 1988. "Il Chianti: Trasformazione e degrado del paesaggio agrario." *Genio Rurale* 5: 21–32.

Gibbon, Peter. 2001. "Upgrading Primary Production: A Global Commodity Chain Approach." *World Development* 29(2): 345–363.

Gibbon, Peter, and Stefano Ponte. 2005. *Trading Down: Africa, Value Chains and the Global Economy.* Philadelphia: Temple University Press.

Giesen, Bernhard. 2004. "The Trauma of Perpetrators." In *Cultural Trauma and Collective Identity,* edited by J. C. Alexander, R. Eyerman, B. Giesen, N. J. Smelser, and P. Sztompka, pp. 112–154. Berkeley: University of California Press.

Giorgetti, Giorgio. 1974. *Contadini e Proprietari nell'Italia Moderna.* Turin: Einaudi.

Giuliani, Elisa, Carlo Pietrobelli, and Roberta Rabellotti. 2005. "Upgrading in Global Value Chains: Lessons from Latin American Clusters." *World Development* 33(4): 549–573.

Goffman, Erving. 1959. *The Presentation of Self in Everyday Life.* Garden City, NY: Doubleday.

Goffman, Erving. 1961. *Encounters: Two Studies in the Sociology of Interaction.* Indianapolis: Bobbs-Merrill.

Goffman, Erving. 1963. *Stigma: Notes on the Management of Spoiled Identity.* New York: Prentice Hall.

Golding, Peter. 1996. "World Wide Wedge: Division and Contradiction in the Global Information Infrastructure." *Monthly Review* 48: 70–86.

Gori-Montanelli, Lorenzo. 1961. "Difesa Dell'architettura Colonica." *Bollettino di Italia Nostra* 21: 9–12.

Gori-Montanelli, Lorenzo. 1978. *Architettura Rurale in Toscana*. Florence: Edam.

Graburn, Nelson. 1983. "The Anthropology of Tourism." *Annals of Tourism Research.* 10: 9–34.

Graburn, Nelson. 1976. *Ethnic and Tourist Arts: Cultural Expressions from the Fourth World*. Berkeley: University of California Press.

Graburn, Nelson. 2000. "Foreword." In *Souvenirs: The Material Culture of Tourism*, edited by M. Hitchcock and K. Teague, pp. xii–xvii. Aldershot, UK: Ashgate.

Graham, Mark. 2008. "Warped Geographies of Development: The Internet and Theories of Economic Development." *Geography Compass* 2: 771–789.

Graham, Mark. 2010. "Justifying Virtual Presence in the Thai Silk Industry: Links between Data and Discourse." *Information Technologies and International Development* 6(4): 57–70.

Graham, Mark. 2011. "Time Machines and Virtual Portals: The Spatialities of the Digital Divide." *Progress in Development Studies* 11 (3).

Grandia, Liza. 2007. "Between Bolivar and Bureaucracy: The Mesoamerican Biological Corridor." *Conservation & Society* 5(4): 478–503.

Granovetter, Mark. 1985. "Economic Action and Social Structure: The Problem of Embeddedness." *American Journal of Sociology* 91: 481–510.

Grazian, David. 2003. *Blue Chicago: The Search for Authenticity in Urban Blues Clubs*. Chicago: Chicago University Press.

Greathouse Amador, Louisa M. 1997. "Ethnic, Cultural and Eco-Tourism." *American Behavioral Scientist* 40(7): 936–943.

Greene, Graham. [1958] 1970. *Our Man in Havana*. London: The Bodley Head.

Greenwood, Davydd J. 1977. "Culture by the Pound: An Anthropological Perspective on Tourism as Cultural Commoditization." In *Hosts and Guests. The Anthropology of Tourism*, edited by V. L. Smith, pp. 171–188. Philadelphia: University of Pennsylvania Press.

Guillen, Mauro. 2001. "Is Globalization Civilizing, Destructive, or Feeble? A Critique of Five Key Debates in the Social Science Literature." *Annual Review of Sociology* 27: 235–260.

Guthman, Julie. 2009. "Unveiling the Unveiling: Commodity Chains, Commodity Fetishism, and the 'Value' of Voluntary, Ethical Food Labels." In *Frontiers of Commodity Chain Research*, edited by Jennifer Bair, pp. 190–206. Stanford, CA: Stanford University Press.

Guy, Kolleen. 2003. *When Champagne Became French: Wine and the Making of a National Identity*. Baltimore: Johns Hopkins University Press.

Harvey, David. 2001. *Spaces of Capital*. Edinburgh, UK: Edinburgh University Press.

Heilbron, Johan. 1999. "Book Translations as a Cultural World-System." *European Journal of Social Theory* 2: 429–444.

Henderson, Jeffery, Peter Dicken, Martin Hess, Neil Coe, and Henry Wai-chung Yeung. 2002. "Global Production Networks and the Analysis of Economic Development." *Review of International Political Economy* 9(3): 436–464.

Hernandez Cruz, Rosa E., Eduardo Bello Baltazar, Guillermo Montoya Gomez, and Erin I. J. Estrada Lugo. 2005. "Social Adaptation: Ecotourism in the Lacandon Forest." *Annals of Tourism Research* 32(3): 610–627.

Herrero, Marta. 2010. "Performing Calculation in the Art Market." *Journal of Cultural Economy* 3(1): 19–34.

Herzfeld, Michael. 2002. "The Absent Presence: Discourses of Crypto-Colonialism." *South Atlantic Quarterly* 101: 899–926.

Hess, Martin, and Neil M. Coe. 2006. "Making Connections: Global Production Networks, Standards, and Embeddedness in the Mobile-Telecommunications Industry." *Environment and Planning A* 38: 1205–1227.

Hill, Lisa. 2007. "Adam Smith, Adam Ferguson and Karl Marx on the Division of Labour." *Journal of Classical Sociology* 7(3): 339–366.

Hirsch, Paul. 2000. "Cultural Industries Revisited." *Organizational Science* 11(3): 356–361.

Hobsbawm, Eric, and Ranger, Terence, eds.. 1983. *The Invention of Tradition*. Cambridge, UK: Cambridge University Press.

Hočevar, Barbara. 2006. "Bomo čutili srčnost, veliko kot Triglav? Turizem zadovoljen, stroka zgrožena." [Shall we feel heartiness, as big as Triglav? Tourism happy, professionals outraged.] *Delo* November 10. Retrieved on November 20, 2010, from www.delo.si/clanek/0170406.

Holt, James. 2004. *How Brands Become Icons: The Principles of Cultural Branding*. Boston: Harvard Business School Press.

Honoré, Daniel. 2003. *Contes creoles* (Tome 1 and Tome 2). Saint Denis de La Réunion: Udir.

Hopkins, Terence, and Immanuel Wallerstein. 1986. "Commodity Chains in the World-Economy prior to 1800." *Review* 10(1): 157–170.

Hudson, Robert. 2005. *Economic Geographies*. London: Sage.

Hughes, George. 1995. "Authenticity in Tourism." *Annals of Tourism Research* 22(4): 781–803.

Humphrey, John, and Olga Memdovic. 2003. *The Global Automotive Industry Value Chain: What Prospects for Upgrading by Developing Countries?* Vienna: U.N. Industrial Development Organization.

Humphrey, John, and Hubert Schmitz. 2002. "How Does Insertion in Global Value Chains Affect Upgrading in Industrial Clusters?" *Regional Studies* 36(9): 1017–1028.

Huntington, Samuel P. 1996. *The Clash of Civilizations and the Remaking of the World Order*. New York: Simon and Schuster.

Hymer, Stephen H. 1976. *The International Operation of National Firms: A Study of Direct Investment.* Cambridge, MA: MIT Press.

Ilbery, Brian W., and Moya Kneafsey. 1999. "Niche Markets and Regional Specialty Food Products in Europe." *Environment and Planning A* 31: 2223–2238.

Imperato, Pascal James. 1988. "Art of the Dogon: Selections from the Lester Wunderman Collection." *African Arts* 22: 87–88.

Institute of International Education. 2009. "Atlas of Student Mobility: Global Destinations for International Students at the Post-Secondary (Tertiary) Level." Retrieved on February 18, 2011 from www.atlas.iienetwork.org/page/Country_Profiles/;jsessionid= 3dhoromqp56uf.

Institute for Tourism. 2000. "Effects of Tourism on the Croatian Economy." Zagreb, Croatia: Institute for Tourism. Retrieved on March 18, 2007 from www.iztzg.hr/ iztzg-eng/iztzg-eng/croatian-tourism/effects.htm.

Integrated Production of Wine (IPW). 2004. *The South African System of Integrated Production of Wine (IPW).* Stellenbosch, SA: IPW.

Inter-American Development Bank (IADB). 2000. "IDB and Mundo Maya Sign Documents for Grant to Support Sustainable Growth Program for Guatemala, Honduras, El Salvador, Belize and Mexico." Retrieved on March 28, 2010, from www .iadb.org/news/detail.cfm?language=English&id=1633.

Inter-American Development Bank (IADB). 2003. "Initiative Launched to Promote Sustainable Tourism in Mayan Region of Central America." Retrieved on January 16, 2010, from www.iadb.org/news/detail.cfm?language=English&id=56.

Interbrand. 2010. "Best Global Brands 2010." Retrieved November 20, 2010, from www. interbrand.com/en/best-global-brands/best-global-brands-2008/best-global-brands-2010.aspx.

Irwin-Zarecka, Iwona. 1994. *Frames of Remembrance: The Dynamics of Collective Memory.* New Brunswick, NJ: Transaction.

Janelle, Donald G., and David C. Hodge, eds. 2000. *Information, Place, and Cyberspace: Issues in Accessibility.* Berlin: Springer.

Javalgi, Rajshekhar, and Rosemary Ramsey. 2001. "Strategic Issues of E-commerce as an Alternative Global Distribution System." *International Marketing Review* 18: 376–391.

Jensen, Michael, and William Meckling. 1976. "Theory of the Firm: Managerial Behavior, Agency Costs and Ownership Structure." *Journal of Financial Economics* 3(4): 305–360.

Joseph, Gilbert. 1988. *Revolution from Without: Yucatan, Mexico, and the United States, 1880–1924.* Durham, NC: Duke University Press.

Judd, Dennis R. 2006. "Commentary: Tracing the Commodity Chain of Global Tourism." *Tourism Geographies* 8(4): 323–336.

Judt, Tony. 2005. *Postwar: A History of Europe since 1945.* New York: Penguin.

Kaplinsky, Raphael. 1993. "Export Processing Zones in the Dominican Republic: Transforming Manufactures into Commodities." *World Development* 21(11): 1851–1865.

Kaplinsky, Raphael. 2005. *Globalization, Poverty and Inequality: Between a Rock and a Hard Place.* London: Polity.

Kaplinsky, Raphael, Mike Morris, and Jeff Readman. 2002. "The Globalization of Product Markets and Immiserizinng Growth: Lessons from the South African Furniture Industry." *World Development* 30(7): 1159–1177.

Katz, James E., Ronald E. Rice, and Philip Aspden. 2001. "The Internet, 1995–2000: Access, Civic Involvement, and Social Interaction." *American Behavioral Scientist* 45: 405–419.

Kerr, Clark, John T. Dunlop, Frederick H. Harbison, and Charles A. Myers. 1960. *Industrialism and Industrial Man. The Problems of Labor and. Management in Economic Growth.* London: Heinemann.

Kindleberger, Charles P. 1970. *The International Corporation: A Symposium.* Cambridge, MA: MIT Press.

Knickerbocker, Frederick T. 1973. *Oligopolistic Reaction and Multinational Enterprise.* Cambridge, MA: Harvard University Press.

Kopytoff, Igor. 1986. "The Cultural Biography of Things: Commoditization as Process." In *The Social Life of Things: Commodities in Cultural Perspective,* edited by Arjun Appadurai, pp. 64–91. Cambridge, UK: Cambridge University Press.

Kotler, Philip, Somkid Jatusripitak, and Suvit Maesincee. 1997. *The Marketing of Nations: A Strategic Approach to Building National Wealth.* New York: The Free Press.

Krisher, Bernard. 2011a. "Robib Is One Village and Also Every Village in the World." Retrieved on February 7, 2011, from www.camnet.com.kh/cambodiaschools/villageleap/intro.htm.

Krisher, Bernard. 2011b. "Robib Products." Retrieved on February 7, 2011, from www.camnet.com.kh/cambodiaschools/villageleap/products.htm.

Kritzinger, Andrienetta, Stephanie Barrientos, and Hester Rossouw. 2004. "Global Production and Flexible Employment in South African Horticulture: Experiences of Contract Workers in Fruit Exports." *Sociologia Ruralis* 44(1): 17–39.

Kruger, Sandra, and Andries du Toit. 2007. "Reconstructing Fairness: Fair Trade Conventions and Worker Empowerment in South African Horticulture." In *Fair Trade: The Challenges of Transforming Globalization,* edited by Laura T. Raynolds, Douglas Murray, and John Wilkinson, pp. 200–220. London and New York: Routledge.

Krugman, Paul. 2004. Plenary Speech at the "Future of Neoliberalism" Panel at the Annual Meeting of the American Sociological Association. San Francisco, August 14–17.

Kunovich, Robert, and Randy Hodson. 1999. "Civil War, Social Integration, and Mental Health in Croatia." *Journal of Health and Social Behavior* 40: 323–343.

L'Abate, Alberto. 1964. "L'esodo Rurale." *La Regione* 10: 71–91.

Lagarde, Benjamin. 2007. "Un Monument Musical à la Mémoire des Ancêtres Esclaves: le Maloya (île de La Réunion)." *Conserveries Mémorielles* 3: 27–46.

Lagrange, Louis, Hervé Briand, and Laurent Trogon. 2000. "Importance Économique des Filières Agro-Alimentaires de Produits Sous Signes Officiels de Qualité." *Economie Rurale* 258: 6–18.

Lamont, Michèle, and Virag Molnar. 2002. "The Study of Boundaries in the Social Sciences." *Annual Review of Sociology* 28: 167–195.

Landes, David S. 1998. *The Wealth and Poverty of Nations: Why Some Are So Rich and Some So Poor.* New York: W. W. Norton.

Landry, Charles. 1998. "From Barriers to Bridges: Re-Imagining Croatian Cultural Policy." *Report to the Council of Europe.* Strasbourg, France: Council of Europe.

Lanfant, Marie-Françoise. 1995. *International Tourism: Identity and Change.* London: Sage Publications.

Lash, Scott, and John Urry. 1994. *Economies of Signs and Spaces.* London: Sage.

Lee, Cheol-Sung, Francois Nielsen, and Arthur Alderson. 2007. "Income Inequality, Global Economy and the State." *Social Forces* 86(1): 77–111.

Leloup, Hélène, William Rubin, and Richard Serra. 1994. *Dogon Statuary.* Strasbourg, France: D. Amez.

Lennon, John, and Malcolm Foley. 2002. *Dark Tourism.* London: Continuum.

Lepenies, Wolf. 1988. *Die Drei Kulturen. Soziologie zwischen Literatur und Wissenschaft.* Munich: Hanser.

Levy, Marion J. 1962. "Some Aspects of 'Individualism' and the Problem of Modernization in China and Japan." *Economic Development and Cultural Change* 10: 225–240.

Lewis, Jack. 1985. "The birth of the EPA." *EPA Journal*, November 1985. Retrieved on October 5, 2010, from www.epa.gov/history/topics/epa/15c.htm.

Lie, John. 1993. "Visualizing the Invisible Hand: The Social Origins of 'Market Society' in England, 1550–1750." *Politics and Society* 21(3): 275–303.

Link, Bruce, and Jo Phelan. 2001. "Conceptualizing Stigma." *Annual Review of Sociology* 27: 363–385.

Little, Walter E. 2008. "Living within the *Mundo Maya* Project: Strategies of Maya Handicraft Vendors." *Latin American Perspectives* 35(3): 87–102.

Longman Dictionary of English Language and Culture. 1993. Longman Publishing.

Loubser, S. S. 2001. *The Wine Business: A Strategic Marketing Framework.* Stellenbosch, SA: Winetech.

Lury, Celia. 2004. *Brands: The Logos of the Global Economy.* London: Routledge.

Lury, Celia. 2005. "The Objectivity of the Brand: Marketing, Law, and Sociology." In *The Technological Economy,* edited by Andrew Barry and Don Slater, pp. 183–205. London: Routledge.

MacCannell, Dean. 1973. "Staged Authenticity: Arrangements of Social Space in Tourist Settings." *American Journal of Sociology* 79(3): 589–603.

MacCannell, Dean. 1976. *The Tourist: A New Theory of the Leisure Class.* New York: Schocken Books.

Macleod, Donald V. L., and James G. Carrier. 2010. *Tourism, Power and Culture. Anthropological Insights.* Bristol, UK: Channel View Publications.

Magnoni, Aline, Traci Arden, and Scott Hutson. 2007. "Tourism in the *Mundo Maya*: Inventions and (Mis)Representations of Maya Identities and Heritage." *Archaeologies* 3(3): 353–383.

Marine, Souheil, and Jean-Marie Blanchard. 2004. "Bridging the Digital Divide: An Opportunity for Growth in the 21st Century." Retrieved on November 20, 2010, from www.key4biz.it/files/000051/00005126.pdf.

Marn, Ursa. 2006. "Zaljubljena Slovenia [Slovenia in Love]." *Mladina* 46. Retrieved on November 20, 2010, from www.mladina.si/tednik/200646/clanek/slo--promocija-ursa_marn/.

Marx, Karl. [1859] 1978. "Preface to A Contribution to the Critique of Political Economy." In *The Marx-Engels Reader,* edited by Robert C. Tucker, pp 3–6. New York: W. W. Norton Company.

Marx, Karl. [1867] 1906. *Capital: A Critique of Political Economy.* New York: The Modern Library.

Marx, Karl. [1844] 1964. *Economic and Philosophic Manuscripts of 1844.* New York: International.

Mayer, Jörg. 2002. "The Fallacy of Composition: A Review of the Literature." *The World Economy,* 25(6): 875–894.

McKercher, Bob, and Hilary du Cros. 2002. *Cultural Tourism: The Partnership between Tourism and Cultural Heritage.* Binghamton, NY: The Haworth Hospitality Press.

McMichael, Philip. 2000. *Development and Social Change: A Global Perspective.* Thousand Oaks, CA: Pine Forge Press.

McMorran, Chris. 2008. "Understanding the 'Heritage' in Heritage Tourism: Ideological Tool or Economic Tool for a Japanese Hot Spring Resort?" *Tourism Geographies* 10(3): 334–354.

Medina, Laurie Kroshus. 2003. "Commoditizing Culture: Tourism and Maya Identity." *Annals of Tourism Research* 30(2): 353–368.

Merridale, Catherine. 1999. "War, Death, and Remembrance in Soviet Russia." In *War and Remembrance in the Twentieth Century,* edited by J. Winter and E. Sivan, pp. 61–83. Cambridge, UK: Cambridge University Press.

Meyer, John, John Boli, George M. Thomas, and Francisco Ramirez. 1997. "World Society and the Nation-State." *American Journal of Sociology* 103: 144–181.

Miele, Mara, and Jonathan Murdoch. 2002. "The Practical Aesthetics of Traditional Cuisines: Slow Food in Tuscany." *Sociologia Ruralis* 42: 312–328.

Mitchell, Clare J. A. 1998. "Entrepreneurialism, Commodification and Creative Destruction: A Model of Postmodern Community Development." *Journal of Rural Studies* 14(3): 273–286.

Mitchell, Timothy. 2001. "Making the Nation: The Politics of Heritage in Egypt." In *Consuming Tradition, Manufacturing Heritage: Global Norms and Urban Forms in the Age of Tourism*, edited by N. AlSayyad, pp. 212–239. London: Routledge.

Montlake, Simon. 2007. "Uncertain Future Looms for Ancient Thai Silk." *The Christian Science Monitor*, July 31. Retrieved in November 2010 from www.csmonitor .com/2007/0731/p20s01-alar.html.

Moretti, Italo. 1988. "Qualche Considerazione Sulla Nascita e Sull'evoluzione del Paesaggio Chiantigiano." In *Il Paesaggio del Chianti: Problemi e Prospettive*, edited by Italo Moretti, pp 15–41. Florence: Associazione Intercomunale 10.

Mori, Giorgio. 1986. *La Toscana*. Turin: Einaudi.

Mosedale, Jan. 2006. "Tourism Commodity Chains: Market Entry and Its Effects on St. Lucia." *Current Issues in Tourism* 9(4): 436–458.

Musso, Isabelle. 2005. "Les pratiques touristiques affinitaires à La Réunion: un phénomène post-migratoire." In J. M. Jauze and J. L. Guebourg, eds., *Inégalités et Spatialité dans l'océan Indien*. Paris: L'Harmattan.

Naimark, Norman. 2001. *Fires of Hatred: Ethnic Cleansing in Twentieth-Century Europe*. Cambridge, MA: Harvard University Press.

Neilson, Jeff, and Bill Pritchard. 2009. *Value Chain Struggles: Institutions and Governance in the Plantation Districts of South India*. Chichester, UK: Wiley-Blackwell.

Nelson, Phillip. 1970. "Information and Consumer Behavior." *The Journal of Political Economy* 78(2): 311–329.

Nora, Pierre. 1984. *Les lieux de mémoire*. Paris: Quarto Gallimard. [3 volumes, 1984–1992]

North Atlantic Treaty Organization (NATO). 1998. "Trip Report: Visit to Croatia." Brussels, Belgium: Sub-Committee on NATO Enlargement and the New Democracies. Retrieved on April 8, 2007, from www.nato-pa.int/archivedpub/trip/ar67cc984-croatia.asp.

Nuryanti, Wiendu. 1996. "Heritage and Postmodern Tourism." *Annals of Tourism Research* 23(2): 249–260.

Nuttavuthisit, Krittinee. 2007. "Branding Thailand: Correcting the Negative Image of Sex Tourism." *Place Branding and Public Diplomacy* 3: 21–30.

Ohno, Akihiko, and Benja Jirapatpimol. 1998. "The Rural Garment and Weaving Industries in Northern Thailand." In *Toward the Rural-Based Development of Commerce and Industry: Selected Experiences from East Asia*, edited by Yujiro Hayami, pp. 131–159. Washington DC: The World Bank.

Olick, Jeffrey. 2007. *The Politics of Regret*. New York: Routledge.

Ong, Aiwa, and Stephen Collier. 2004. *Global Assemblages*. Malden, MA: Blackwell.

Organization for Economic Cooperation and Development (OECD). 1999. *The Economic and Social Impact of Electronic Commerce*. Paris, France: OECD Publications.

Orlandini, Alessandro, and Giorgio Venturini. 1980. *Padrone Arrivedello a Battitura: Lotte Mezzadrili nel Senese nel Secondo Dopoguerra*. Milan: Feltrinelli.

Pagni, Roberto. 2005. *Il Turismo e la Valorizzazione delle Aree Protette. Analisi dell'Esperienza Toscana*. Florence: IRPET.

Parco della Val d'Orcia. Retrieved on February 11, 2011, from www.parcodellavaldorcia.com/indexb.asp.

Parsons, Talcott. 1937. *The Structure of Social Action*. New York: The Free Press.

Parsons, Talcott, and Neil Smelser. 1956. *Economy and Society: A Study in the Integration of Economic and Social Theory*. London: Routledge & Kegan Paul.

Persky, Joseph. 1989. "Adam Smith's Invisible Hands." *Journal of Economic Perspectives* 3(4): 195–201.

Picard, David. 2005. "Gardening the Past and Being in the World: A Popular Celebration of the Abolition of Slavery in La Réunion." In *Remaking Worlds: Festivals, Tourism and Change*, edited by David Picard and Mike Robinson. pp. 46–70. Clevedon, UK: Channel View Publications.

Picard, Michel. 1992. *Bali. Tourisme Culturel et Culture Touristique*. Paris: L'Harmattan.

Picard, Michel. 2008. "Balinese Identity as Tourist Attraction: From 'Cultural Tourism' (Pariwisata Budaya) to 'Bali Erect' (Ajeg Bali)." *Tourist Studies* 8(2): 155–173.

Pieterse, Jan Nederveen. 1994. "Globalization as Hybridization." *International Sociology* 9: 161–184.

Pizam, Abraham, and Yoel Mansfeld, eds. 1996. *Tourism, Crime, and International Security Issues*. Chichester, UK: John Wiley.

Podolny, Joel. 2005. *Status Signals: A Sociological Study of Market Competition*. Princeton, NJ: Princeton University Press.

Polanyi, Karl. [1944] 1957. *The Great Transformation*. Boston, MA: Beacon Press.

Polanyi, Karl. [1947] 1971. *Primitive, Archaic and Modern Economies: Essays of Karl Polanyi*. George Dalton, ed. Boston: Beacon Press.

Pomian, Krzysztof. [1987] 1990. *Collectors and Curiosities: Paris and Venice, 1500–1800*. Translated by Elizabeth Wiles-Portier. Cambridge, UK: Polity Press.

Ponte, Stefano. 2002. "The 'Latte Revolution'? Regulation, Markets and Consumption in the Global Coffee Chain." *World Development* 30(7): 1099–1122.

Ponte, Stefano. 2008. "Greener than Thou: The Political Economy of Fish Ecolabeling and Its Local Manifestations in South Africa." *World Development* 36(1): 159–175.

Ponte, Stefano. 2009. "Governing through Quality: Conventions and Supply Relations in the Value Chain for South African Wine." *Sociologia Ruralis* 49(2): 236–257.

Ponte, Stefano, and Joachim Ewert. 2009. "Which Way Is 'Up' in Upgrading? Trajectories of Change in the Value Chain for South African Wine." *World Development* 37(10): 1637–1650.

Ponte, Stefano, and Peter Gibbon. 2005. "Quality Standards, Conventions and the Governance of Global Value Chains." *Economy and Society* 34(1): 1–31.

Poon, Simpson, and Colin Jevons. 1997. "Internet-Enabled International Marketing: A Small Business Network Perspective." *Journal of Marketing Management* 13: 29–41.

Portes, Alejandro. 2010. *Economic Sociology: A Systematic Inquiry.* Princeton, NJ: Princeton University Press.

Portes, Alejandro, and Patricia Landolt. 2000. "Social Capital: The Promise and Pitfalls of Its Role in Development." *Journal of Latin American Studies* 32: 529–547.

Portes, Alejandro, and Julia Sensenbrenner. 1993. "Embeddedness and Immigration: Notes on the Social Determinants of Economic Action." *American Journal of Sociology* 98: 1320–1350.

Potter, Evan. 2009. *Branding Canada: Projecting Canada's Soft Power through Public Diplomacy.* Montreal, PQ, and Kingston, ON: McGill-Queen's University Press.

Pratt, Andrew. 2004. "The Cultural Economy: A Call for Spatialized 'Production of Culture' Perspective." *International Journal of Cultural Studies* 7(1): 117–128.

Pratt, Andrew. 2008. "Cultural Commodity Chains, Cultural Clusters, or Cultural Production Chains." *Growth and Change* 39(1): 95–103.

Prior, Nick. 2002. *Museums and Modernity: Art Galleries and the Making of Modern Culture.* Oxford, UK: Berg.

Prost, Antoine. 1999. "The Algerian War in French Collective Memory." In *War and Remembrance in the Twentieth Century,* edited by Jay Winter and Emmanuel Sivan, pp. 161–176. Cambridge, UK: Cambridge University Press.

Purcell, Fuati, and Janet Toland. 2004. "Electronic Commerce for the South Pacific: A Review of E-Readiness." *Electronic Commerce Research* 4: 241–262.

Putnam, Robert D. 1993. *Making Democracy Work: Civic Traditions in Modern Italy.* Princeton, NJ: Princeton University Press.

Pye, Ellwood A., ed. 1988. *Artisans in Economic Development: Evidence from Asia.* Ottawa: IDRC.

Rabobank. (2004). *The South African Wine Industry: Between Past and Future.* Utrecht: Rabobank.

Raikes, Philip, Michael Friis Jensen, and Stefano Ponte. 2000. "Global Commodity Chain Analysis and the French *Filière* Approach: Comparison and Critique." *Economy and Society* 29(3): 390–417.

Ramet, Sabrina P. 2005. *Thinking about Yugoslavia.* Cambridge, UK: Cambridge University Press.

Rangnekar, Dwijen. 2004. "The Socio-Economics of Geographical Indications." UNCTAD-ICTSD Project on IPRs and Sustainable Development Issue Paper. Geneva: UNCTAD.

Rani, Sandhya G. 1998. *Sericulture and Rural Development.* New Delhi: Discovery Publishing House.

Rauch, André. 2002. "Le Tourisme ou la Construction de l'Étrangeté." *Ethnologie Française* Tome XXXVII: 389–392.

Regnault, Madina. 2009. "Politique Culturelle et Départementalisation à Mayotte." *Revue Juridique de l'Océan Indien*, Special Edition Mayotte 2009: 145–174.

Reisman, David A. 1976. *Adam Smith's Sociological Economics*. London: Croom Helm.

Rekom, Johan van, and Frank Go. 2006. "Cultural Identities in a GlobalizingWorld." In *Tourism and Social Identities*, edited by P. M. Burns and M. Novelli, pp. 79–90. Oxford, UK: Elsevier.

Rhodes, Jo. 2003. "Can E-Commerce Enable Marketing in an African Rural Women's Community Based Development Organisation?" *Informing Science Journal* 6: 157–172.

Ricardo, David. 1817. *On the Principles of Political Economy and Taxation*. London: John Murray.

Richey, Lisa A., and Stefano Ponte. 2011. *Brand Aid: Shopping Well to Save the World*. Minneapolis: University of Minnesota Press.

Ritzer, George. 2003. "Rethinking Globalization: Glocalization/Grobalization and Something/Nothing." *Sociological Theory* 21: 193–209.

Rivera, Lauren A. 2008. "Managing 'Spoiled' National Identity: War, Tourism and Memory in Croatia." *American Sociological Review* 73: 613–634.

Roeck, Bernd. 2009. *Florence 1900: The Quest for Arcadia*. New Haven, CT: Yale University Press.

Rose, Gillian. 1995. "Place and Identity: A Sense of Place." In *A Place in the World? Places, Cultures and Globalization*, edited by Doreen Massey and Pat Jess, pp. 87–132. Oxford, UK: Oxford University Press.

Ross, Ian. 1995. *The Life of Adam Smith*. Oxford, UK: Oxford University Press.

Rostow, Walt. 1960. *The Stages of Economic Growth: A Non-Communist Manifesto*. Cambridge, UK: Cambridge University Press.

Rothschild, Emma. 2001. *Economic Sentiments: Adam Smith, Condorcet and the Enlightenment*. Cambridge, MA: Harvard University Press.

Rowlands, Michael, and Ferdinand DeJong. 2007. *Reclaiming Heritage: Alternative Imaginaries of Memory in West Africa*. Walnut Creek, CA: Left Coast Press.

Sallaz, Jeffrey, and Jane Zavisca. 2007. "Bourdieu in American Sociology, 1980–2004." *Annual Review of Sociology* 33: 21–41.

Sambandaraksa, Don. 2006. "Bringing the Market to the Village." *Bangkok Post*, May 3. Retrieved on November 20, 2010, from www.sat-ed.com/bangkok_post_news.html.

Sat-Ed. 2011. "Buy from the Villages." Retrieved on February 7, 2011, from www.sat-ed.com/Buyfromthevillage.htm.

Schmitz, Hubert. 2006. "Learning and Earning in Global Garment and Footwear Chains." *European Journal of Development Research* 18(4): 546–571.

Schudson, Michael. 1989. "How Culture Works: Perspectives from Media Studies on the Efficacy of Symbols." *Theory and Society* 18: 153–180.

Schuerkens, Ulrike. 2003. "The Sociological and Anthropological Study of Globalization and Localization." *Current Sociology* 51: 209–222.

Schumpeter, Joseph A. 1934. *The Theory of Economic Development.* Cambridge, MA: Harvard University Press.

Schumpeter, Joseph A. 1954. *History of Economic Analysis.* London: Allen & Unwin.

Schurman, Rachel, and William Munro. 2009. "Targeting Capital: A Cultural Economy Approach to Understanding the Efficacy of Two Anti-Genetic Engineering Movements." *American Journal of Sociology* 115(1): 155–202.

Schweizer, Sebastian, and Mario Falciai, "Siccità e ripristino degli invasi collinari minori: Un'analisi GIS." Retrieved on October 22, 2009, from www1.unifi.it/AIIA2007/Comunicazioni%20A3.pdf.

Scott, Allen. 1999. "The Culture Economy: Geography and the Creative Field." *Media, Culture & Society* 21(6): 807–817.

Screen Digest. 2006. "World Film Production/Distribution." Retrieved on November 20, 2010, from www.fafo.at/download/WorldFilmProduction06.pdf.

Secretaría de Turismo, Gobierno de México. 2007. "Se consolida Mundo maya como product túristico," Boletín Informativo 083/2007. Retrieved on August 12, 2010, from www.presidencia.gob.mx/prensa/comunicados/?contenido=34594.

Selwyn, Neil. 2004. "Reconsidering Political and Popular Understandings of the Digital Divide." *New Media & Society* 6: 341–362.

Sereni, Emilio. 1997. *History of the Italian Agricultural Landscape.* Princeton, NJ: Princeton University Press.

Servon, Lisa J., and Marla K. Nelson. 2001. "Community Technology Centers: Narrowing the Digital Divide in Low-Income, Urban Communities." *Journal of Urban Affairs* 23: 279–290.

Sewell, William. 1992. "A Theory of Structure: Duality, Agency and Transformation." *American Journal of Sociology* 98(1): 1–29.

Sewell, William. 1996. "Three Temporalities: Toward an Eventful Sociology." In *The Historic Turn in the Human Sciences*, edited by Terence J. McDonald, pp. 245–280. Ann Arbor: University of Michigan Press.

Shapiro, Carl. 1982. "Consumer Information, Product Quality, and Seller Reputation." *Bell Journal of Economics* 13(1): 20–35.

Singh, J. P. 2007. "Culture or Commerce? A Comparative Assessment of International Interactions and Developing Countries at UNESCO, WTO, and Beyond." *International Studies Perspectives* 8: 36–53.

Simmel, Georg. [1907] 1978. *The Philosophy of Money.* Translated by T. Bottomore and D. Frisby. London: Routledge.

Simons, Marlise. 2005. "War Crimes Case Revives Passions in a Divided Croatia." *New York Times*, December 12. Retrieved on April 9, 2008, from www.nytimes .com/2005/12/12/international/europe/12croat.html?scp=1&sq=War+Crimes+ Case+Revives+Passions+in+a+Divided+Croatia&st=nyt.

Singer, Brian. 2004. "Montesquieu, Adam Smith and the Discovery of the Social." *Journal of Classical Sociology* 4(1): 31–57.

Slater, Don. 1997. *Consumer Culture and Modernity*. London: Polity.

Small, Albion. 1907. *Adam Smith and Modern Sociology: A Study in the Methodology of the Social Sciences*. Chicago: University of Chicago Press.

Smith, Adam. [1795] 1980. "History of Astronomy." In W. P. D. Wightman, J. C. Bryce, and I. S. Ross, eds., *Essays on Philosophical Subjects*, pp. 5–32. Oxford, UK: Clarendon Press.

Smith, Adam. [1759] 1876. *The Theory of Moral Sentiments*. Indianapolis: Liberty Classics.

Smith, Adam. [1776] 2000. *The Wealth of Nations*. Introduction by Robert Reich. New York: Modern Library.

Smith, Charles. 1990. *Auctions: The Social Construction of Values*. Berkeley: University of California Press.

Smith, Laura-Jeanne. 2006. *The Uses of Heritage*. London: Routledge.

Smith, Melanie K. 2003. *Issues in Cultural Tourism Studies*. London: Routledge.

Soilihi, Zaharia, and Sophie Blanchy. 2002. *Furukombe—Et autres contes de Mayotte*. Paris: L'Harmattan.

Somers, Margaret, and Fred Block. 2005. "From Poverty to Perversity: Ideas, Markets, and Institutions over 200 Years of Welfare Debate." *American Sociological Review* 70 (2): 260–287.

Sonnino, Roberta. 2004. "For a 'Piece of Bread'? Interpreting Sustainable Development through Agritourism in Southern Tuscany." *Sociologia Ruralis* 44: 285–300.

Spillman, Lyn. 1999. "Enriching Exchange: Cultural Dimensions of Markets." *American Journal of Economics and Sociology* 58: 1047–1071.

Spillman, Lyn. 2003. "When Do Collective Memories Last? Founding Moments in the United States and Australia." In *States of Memory*, edited by J. Olick, pp. 161–192. Durham, NC: Duke University Press.

Spillman, Lyn. 2010. "Culture and Economic Life." In *Oxford Handbook of Cultural Sociology*, edited by Jeffrey C. Alexander, Philip Smith, and Ronald Jacobs. New York: Oxford University Press.

Steedman, Carolyn. 1984. *Landscape for a Good Woman. A Story of Two Lives*. New Brunswick, NJ: Rutgers University Press.

Stopford, John M., and Louis T. Wells. 1972. *Managing the Multinational Enterprise*. New York: Basic Books.

Sturgeon, Timothy. 2002. "Modular Production Networks. A New American Model of Industrial Organization." *Industrial and Corporate Change* 11(3): 451–496.

Sturgeon, Timothy, Van Biesebroeck, and Gary Gereffi. 2008. "Value Chains, Networks, and Clusters: Reframing the Global Automotive Industry." *Journal of Economic Geography* 8: 297–321.

Summerby-Murray, Robert. 2002. "Interpreting Deindustrialised Landscapes of Atlantic Canada: Memory and Industrial Heritage in Sackville, New Brunswick." *The Canadian Geographer* 46(1): 48–62.

Suphachalasai, Suphat. 1994. *Thailand's Clothing and Textile Exports*. Singapore: Institute of Southeast Asian Studies.

Swedberg, Richard. 1997. "New Economic Sociology: What Has Been Accomplished, What Is Ahead?" *Acta Sociologica* 40: 161–182.

Swidler, Ann. 1986. "Culture in Action: Symbols and Strategies." *American Sociological Review* 51: 273–286.

Tajnikar, Maks. 2010. "Commentary." Omizje: Blagovne Znamke, Kje ste? [Roundtable: Brands, Where Are You?]. Slovenian National Radio and Television, Channel 1, aired on September 29, 2010.

Talbot, John. 2004. *Grounds for Agreement: The Political Economy of the Coffee Commodity Chain*. New York: Rowman & Littlefield.

Tanner, Marcus. 2001. *Croatia: A Nation Forged in War*, 2nd ed. New Haven, CT: Yale University Press.

Taylor, John P. 2001. "Authenticity and Sincerity in Tourism." *Annals of Tourism Research* 28: 7–26.

Taylor, Mary N. 2009. "Intangible Heritage Governance, Cultural Diversity, Ethnonationalism." *Focaal* 55(3): 41–58.

Thailand's National Economic and Social Development Board and the World Bank. 2005. "Thailand Northeast Economic Development Report." Retrieved on November 20, 2010, from siteresources.worldbank.org/INTTHAILAND/Resources/333200-1097667766090/need_report-2005-eng.pdf.

Thuvasethakul, Chadamas, and Thaweesak Koanantakool. 2002. "National ICT Policy in Thailand." In *Africa-Asia Workshop: Promoting Co-operation in Information and Communications Technologies Development*. Kuala Lumpur and Penang, Malaysia. Retrieved on November 20, 2010, from www.nectec.or.th/users/htk/publish/20020302-National-ICT Policy-v16-word.pdf.

Tilly, Charles. 1999. *Durable Inequality*. Berkeley: University of California Press.

Titchen, Sarah. 1995. "On the Construction of Outstanding Universal Value." PhD dissertation, Department of Archeology and Anthropology, Australian National University, Canberra, Australia.

Toesca, Pietro, 2004. "Tecnologia, Civiltà, Paesaggio." *Eupolis* 33/34: 8–21.

Torres, Rebecca Marie, and Janet D. Momsen. 2005. "Gringolandia: The Construction of a New Tourist Space in Mexico." *Annals of the Association of American Geographers* 95(2): 314–335

Toskanafraktion. Retrieved on February 11, 2011, from www.toskanafraktion.de/index2.html

Train, Russell E. 1972. "A World Heritage Trust." In *Action for Wilderness*, edited by E. R. Gillette, pp. 172–176. Washington, DC: Sierra Club.

Tribe, Keith. 1999. "Adam Smith: Critical Theorist?" *Journal of Economic Literature* 37: 609–632.

Truong, Thanh-Dam. 1990. *Sex, Money and Morality: Prostitution and Tourism in Southeast Asia*. London: Zed Books.

Tucker, Robert (ed.). 1978. *The Marx-Engels Reader*, 2nd ed. New York: W. W. Norton & Company.

Turnbridge, John E., and Gregory J. Ashworth. 1996. *Dissonant Heritage: The Management of the Past as a Resource in Conflict*. Ottawa: Carleton University.

Turri, Eugenio. 2003. *Il Paesaggio Come Teatro. Dal Territorio Vissuto al Territorio Rappresentato*. Venice: Marsilio.

TVbytheNumbers. 2010. "CSI: Crime Scene Investigation Is the Most Watched Show in the World." Retrieved on June 11, 2010, from http://tvbythenumbers.com/2010/06/11/csi-crime-scene-investigation-is-the-most-watched-show-in-the-world/53833.

United Nations. 2003a. "E-commerce and Development Report 2003." New York: United Nations.

United Nations. 2003b. "Poverty Reduction Practices: Information and Communication Technology For Rural Poverty Reduction," edited by Committee on Poverty Reduction. Bangkok: United Nations Economic and Social Council. Retrieved on November 20, 2010, from www.unescap.org/pdd/CPR/CPR2003/English/CPR_4E.pdf.

U.N. Conference on Trade and Development (UNCTAD). 2002. *Trade and Development Report 2002*. Geneva: UNCTAD.

U.N. Conference on Trade and Development/World Trade Organization (UNCTAD/WTO). 1997. "Silk Review 1997: A Survey of International Trends in Production and Trade." Geneva: International Trade Centre UNCTAD/WTO.

U.N. Conference on Trade and Development/World Trade Organization (UNCTAD/WTO). 2002. "Silk Review 2001: A Survey of International Trends in Production and Trade." Geneva: International Trade Centre UNCTAD/WTO.

U.N. Development Programme (UNDP). 2005. "Do Governments Actually Believe That ICT Can Help Alleviate Poverty?" *Poverty Reduction Strategy Papers*. Geneva: United Nations. Retrieved on November 20, 1010, from www.apdip.net/apdipenote/2.pdf.

U.N. Educational, Scientific and Cultural Organization (UNESCO). 1990. "The World Heritage Convention: A New Idea Takes Shape." *Courier* 43(10): 44–45.

U.N. Educational, Scientific and Cultural Organization (UNESCO). 2011. "World Heritage List." Accessed on February 17, 2011 from http://whc.unesco.org/en/list/

U.N. World Tourism Organization. 2011. "Tourism Highlights: International Tourist Arrivals." Accessed on February 17 from http://www.unwto.org/facts/menu.html.

Urry, John. 1990. *The Tourist Gaze*. London: SAGE Publications.

Urry, John. 1995. *Consuming Places*. London: Routledge.

US Department of State. 2009. *Human Rights Report*. http://www.state.gov/g/drl/rls/hrrpt/2009/eap/136010.htm, accessed February 14, 2011.

Valceschini, Egizio, and Armelle Mazé. 2000. "La Politique de la Qualité Agro-Alimentaire dans le Contexte International." *Economie Rurale* 258: 30–41.

Val d'Orcia. UNESCO World Heritage Centre. Retrieved on February 11, 2011, from whc.unesco.org/en/list/1026

Van den Berghe, Pierre L. 1995. "Marketing Maya: Ethnic Tourism Promotion in Mexico." *Annals of Tourism Research* 22: 568–588.

Velthuis, Olav. 2005. *Talking Prices: Symbolic Meanings of Prices on the Market for Contemporary Art*. Princeton, NJ: Princeton University Press.

Vigna, Anne. 2006. "Fair Trade and Fair Tourism." *Le Monde Diplomatique* (English edition), August 11, p. 8.

Villages Créoles. 2010. "About us." Retrieved in June 2010 from www.villagescreoles.re.

Vinitzky-Seroussi, Vered. 2002. "Commemorating a Difficult Past: Yitzhak Rabin's Memorials." *American Sociological Review* 67: 30–51.

Vink, Nick, Gavin Williams, and Johann Kirsten. 2004. "South Africa." In *The World's Wine Markets: Globalization at Work*, edited by K. Anderson, pp. 227–251. Cheltenham, UK: Edward Elgar.

Wade, Robert. 2004. "Is Globalization Reducing Poverty and Inequality?" *World Development* 32, 4: 567–589.

Wallerstein, Immanuel. 1974a. *The Modern World System*. New York: Academic Press.

Wallerstein, Immanuel. 1974b. "The Rise and Future Demise of the World Capitalist System: Concepts for Comparative Analysis." *Comparative Studies in Society and History* 16: 387–415.

Wallerstein, Immanuel. 1990. "Culture as the Ideological Battleground of the Modern World-System." *Theory, Culture and Society* 7: 31–55.

Wallerstein, Immanuel. 2004. *World-Systems Analysis: An Introduction*. Durham, NC: Duke University Press.

Ward, Stephen. 1998. *Selling Places: The Marketing and Promotion of Towns and Cities, 1850–2000*. London: Routledge.

Weber, Max. [1898] 1990. *Grundriss zu den Vorlesungen über Allgemeine ('theoretische') Nationalökonomie*. Tübingen: J. C. B. Mohr.

Weber, Max. [1903-1906] 1975. *Roscher and Knies: The Logical Problems of Historical Economics*. Translated by Guy Oakes. New York: The Free Press.

Weber, Max. [1905] 2002. *The Protestant Ethic and the Spirit of Capitalism*. Los Angeles, CA: Roxbury.

Weber, Max. [1922] 1978. *Economy and Society: An Outline of Interpretive Sociology*. Berkeley: University of California Press.

Wells, Allen. 1985. *Yucatan's Gilded Age: Haciendas, Henequen, and International Harvester, 1860–1915*. Albuquerque: University of New Mexico Press.

Wherry, Frederick F. 2005. "The Limits and Possibilities of Branding Culture in Handicraft Economies." *Consumers, Commodities & Consumption*. Retrieved February 4, 2010, from https://netfiles.uiuc.edu/dtcook/www/CCCnewsletter/7-1/wherry.htm.

Wherry, Frederick F. 2006. "The Social Sources of Authenticity in Global Handicraft Markets: Evidence from Northern Thailand." *Journal of Consumer Culture* 6: 5–32.

Wherry, Frederick F. 2007. "Trading Impressions: Evidence from Costa Rica." *The Annals of the American Academy of Political and Social Science* 610: 217–231.

Wherry, Frederick F. 2008a. "The Export of Cultural Commodities as Impression Management: The Case of Thailand." In *Globalization and Transformations of Local Socio-economic Practices*, edited by Ulrike Schuerkens, pp. 120–137. London: Routledge.

Wherry, Frederick F. 2008b. *Global Markets and Local Crafts: Thailand and Costa Rica Compared*. Baltimore: Johns Hopkins University Press.

White, Harrison. 1981. "Where Do Markets Come From?" *American Journal of Sociology* 87(3): 517–541.

Williams, G. 2005. "Black Economic Empowerment in the South African Wine Industry." *Journal of Agrarian Change* 5(4): 476–504.

Williams, Raymond. 1977. *Marxism and Literature*. Oxford, UK: Oxford University Press.

Wines of South Africa (WOSA). 2005. "The Wines of South Africa: Variety is in Our Nature." Stellenbosch, SA: WOSA.

Wood, Eric, and David Kaplan. 2005. "Innovation and Performance in the South African Wine Industry." *International Journal of Technology and Globalization* 1(3/4): 381–399.

Woolcock, Michael. 1998. "Social Capital and Economic Development: Toward a Theoretical Synthesis and Policy Framework." *Theory and Society* 27(2): 151–208.

World Bank. 2005. "Equity and Development: World Development Report 2006." Washington DC: The World Bank.

World Bank. 2007. *World Development Indicators 2007*. CD-ROM. Washington, DC: The World Bank.

World Tourism Organization. 2010. "UNWTO World Tourism Barometer January 2010." Retrieved on November 19, 2010, from www.unwto.org/facts/eng/pdf/barometer/UNWTO_Barom10_1_en.pdf.

World Trade Organization (WTO). 2010. "WTO in Brief." Retrieved on November 20, 2010, from www.wto.org/english/res_e/doload_e/inbr_e.pdf.

World Travel and Tourism Council (WTTC). 2002. *Croatia: The Impact of Travel and Tourism on Jobs and the Economy*. London: WTTC.

Wylie, John. 2007. *Landscape*. London: Routledge.

Yang, Mary, ed. 2000. *Investing in World Heritage: A Guide to International Assistance*. Paris: UNESCO.

Yearman, Keith, and Amy Gluckman. 2005. "Falling off a Cliff." *Dollars & Sense*. September/October, 126: 8–36.

Young, Craig, and Sylvia Kaczmarek. 2008. "The Socialist Past and Postsocialist Urban Identity in Central and Eastern Europe." *European Urban and Regional Studies* 15: 53–70.

Zelizer, Viviana. 1979. *Morals and Markets: The Development of Life Insurance in the United States*. New York: Columbia University Press.

Zelizer, Viviana. 1987. *Pricing the Priceless Child: The Changing Social Value of Children*. New York: Basic.

Zelizer, Viviana. 1994. *The Social Meaning of Money*. New York: Basic.

Zelizer, Viviana. 2001. "Circuits of Commerce." In *Self, Social Structure, and Beliefs: Explorations in the Sociological Thought of Neil Smelser*, edited by Jeffrey Alexander, Gary T. Marx, and Christine Williams, pp. 122–144. Berkeley: University of California Press.

Zelizer, Viviana. 2003. "Enter Culture." In *The New Economic Sociology: Developments in an Emerging Field*, edited by M. Guillen et al., pp. 101–128. New York: Russell Sage Foundation.

Zelizer, Viviana. 2005a. "Circuits within Capitalism." In *The Economic Sociology of Capitalism*, edited by Victor Nee and Richard Swedberg, pp. 289–322. Princeton, NJ: Princeton University Press.

Zelizer, Viviana. 2005b. *The Purchase of Intimacy*. Princeton, NJ: Princeton University Press.

Zelizer, Viviana. 2010. *Economic Lives: How Culture Shapes the Economy*. Princeton, NJ: Princeton University Press.

Zouain, George. 1997. "Words and Deeds." *Courier* 50(9): 28–31.

Index

Note: Figures are indicated by *f* following the page number.

Abu Simbel, temple of, 78
Agrotourism, 108–9, 111
Aguilera, Christine, 41
Alexander, Jeffrey, 41
Amadou and Miriam, 150
Andrew Mellon Foundation, 149
Anthropology, 5–6
Arrighi, Giovanni, 54
Arrow, Kenneth, 48
Aswan Dam, Egypt, 78
Augé, Marc, 164
Austen, Jane, 26
Australia, 213
Authenticity: handicrafts and, 171–73; of Reunion Island, 166; social/political factors in, 8–9, 94, 156–57; in tale telling, 158; of Tuscany, 94, 106, 111–13

Bair, Jennifer, 15, 16–17, 19, 197–98
Bali, 169
Bandelj, Nina, 13, 185
Banks, 55–56
Barbalet, Jack, 54
Beaches and bars tourism, 13, 16, 39
BEE initiatives. *See* Black Economic Empowerment (BEE) initiatives
Belize, 185
Bellow, Saul, 25
Bells tourism, 13, 16–17, 39–42
Belting, Hans, 92

Biodiversity and Wine Initiative (BWI), 215
Black Economic Empowerment (BEE) initiatives, 218–20
Boissevain, Jeremy, 112–13
Boltanski, Luc, 55
Bosnia, 126
Bounded solidarity, 153
Bourdieu, Pierre, 12, 14, 24–25, 47–48, 54–69, 145, 156; background on, 57; *The Bank and Its Customers*, 55–56; on firms, 65–68; on interests, 58–61; on markets, 61–65; *The Social Structures of the Economy*, 63–64, 67; stereotypical view of, 48, 55
Brand, 4, 92, 197, 206–207; Brand South Africa, 214, 220; coffee, 199; development of, 182; global value chain and, 11; iconic brands, 90, 93, 103, 111, 113; private brands, 214, 216; silk and, 232; Slovenian brands, 43; symbolic capital and, 67; wine brands, 102, 212–213, 216–217
Branding, 9; defined, 92; iconicity and, 92–95; of landscape, 93–95; Slovenia, 42–43; as social performance, 44; of South African wine, 214–17; Thailand, 40–42; Tuscany, 90, 91. *See also* Global brands; Impression management
Branding Thailand Project, 40
Braque, Georges, 149
Bridget Jones: The Edge of Reason (film), 41
Brokers, in Thai silk industry, 232–37

Cambodia, 121, 126, 228
Capital, conversion of, 147–49. *See also* Cultural capital; Social capital; Symbolic capital
Capitalism, and personal finances, 56
Cárdenas, Lázaro, 192
Carrier, James G., 173
Centeno, Miguel A., 13
Chamberlin, Edward, 206
Chamboredon, Jean-Claude, 55
Charter of Athens (1931), 77
Chiang Mai, Thailand, 232–33
Chianti: farm in, 101*f*; tourism in, 106; wine of, 102–3
China, 229, 230
Chirac, Jacques, 149, 169
Chocolate, 34–35, 35*f*
Christian Democrats, in Italy, 97
Chunchucmil, Yucatán, Mexico, 192–94
Circuits, 154
Class. *See* Global class
CNTB. *See* Croatian National Tourist Board
Cocoa, 34–35
Coffee, 198
Cohen, Erik, 229
Cold War, 3, 75, 96
Coleman, James, 145
Colloredo-Mansfeld, Rudi, 171
Comité Départemental du Tourisme de Mayotte (CDTM), 167, 170–71
Committee on National Resources, Conservation and Development, 75
Commodification, 6, 93
Commodity chains, 224, 224*f*, 225*f*, 226, 229–32, 235–37, 245*n*5
Commodity management, 200–201
Communist Party (Italy), 96–97, 99, 102, 105, 108, 112
Comte, Auguste, 49
Conservation International, 187
Contingency. *See* Historical contingency
Convention for the Safeguarding of Intangible Cultural Heritage (2003), 157–62
Cooley, Charles Horton, 54
Co-partneries, 66
Corporations, 66
Council on Environmental Quality (CEQ), 76
Counterpart International, 187
Covering, of stigma, 115, 125–32, 134

Crafts. *See* Handicrafts
Credence attributes, 203
Credit applications, 55–56
Credit morality, 56
Creole Villages, Reunion Island, 166
Crime Scene Investigation (CSI) television programs, 36
Croatia, 15, 19, 114–36; background on, 117–18; "covering" strategy in, 125–32, 134; economic conditions in, 127–29; marketers' representations of, 121–25, 132–34; narrative control in, 130–32; political conditions in, 129–30; religion in, 122, 243*n*3; tourism in, 117–36, 120*f*; and war, 120–21, 128–29, 134
Croatian National Tourist Board (CNTB), 118–25, 129–35
Crosby, Todd, 15–16, 19
Cultural and heritage tourism, 6, 39–42; Croatia and, 15, 19, 114–36; and economic development, 156; global value chain analysis of, 184–85, 195; Mayotte and, 16, 19, 156–62, 167–74; *Mundo Maya* and, 16–17, 177–78, 185–96; Reunion Island and, 16, 156–66, 171–74. *See also* Bells tourism
Cultural capital, 24–25, 156, 158
Cultural capitalization, 74, 85–87, 157, 174
Cultural economic sociology, 5, 6, 20
Cultural economy perspective, 5–6
Cultural heritage: concept of, 14, 86–87; intangible, UNESCO definition of, 157–62
Cultural heritage management, 6, 7
Cultural imperialism, 27, 30, 45
Cultural relativism, 25–26
Cultural sociology, 10, 12–13
Cultural wealth of nations: activation of, 8; aspects of, 4; authenticity in, 8–9; defining, 7–9, 26; and economic development, 4, 16, 19; empirical trends in, 13; evaluations of, 8; implications of, 19–20; perspectives on, 10–13; reception of, 8. *See also* Global system of cultural wealth
Culture: in cultural sociology perspective, 12–13; and economy, 5–6, 20, 23–25; geography and, 31–37; global class and, 30; ideological use of, 24; in political economy perspective, 10–11; universalism concerning, 24–25; value chains and, 245*n*6

Culture Bank of Mali, 15–16, 139–50, 154–55; and cultural preservation, 147–49; origins and operations of, 140–45; and symbolic capital, 139, 147–49

Dalama, Marie-Gisèle, 166
Dark tourism, 121, 126
Daviron, Benoit, 17, 19, 195
Dendur, temple of, 78
Dependency theory, 3–4
Digital divide, 227–28
Disintermediation, 223–24, 224f, 225f, 226
Division of labor, 30, 50, 51, 53
Djenné, Mali, 149
Dogon culture, 139–50
Durkheim, Emile, 3, 48–50, 150–52, 154
Du Toit, Andries, 218, 219

East India Company, 66
E-commerce, 18, 223–227, 237–238. *See also* Internet
Ecomusée de l'Habitat, Mayotte, 170–71
Economic development: cultural intermediaries and, 232–37; cultural wealth and, 4, 16, 19; in global economy, 178–81; Internet and, 222–23, 227–28, 237–39; linkage in, 222–23; symbolic capital and, 140; theories of, 3–4; tourism and, 180–81
Economic geography, 6
Economic Man. See *Homo economicus*
Economic sociology, 5, 14, 20, 47, 54
Economy: culture and, 5–6, 20, 23–25; symbolic resources as contributor to, 1–2. *See also* Economic development
Ejidal system, 191–92
El Salvador, 185
Engels, Friedrich, *The Communist Manifesto* (with Karl Marx), 153
English language, 36–37
Environmental Protection Agency (EPA), 76
Ethnicity: income distribution by, 28, 29f; political economy of, 245n2
Eurocentrism, 31–32, 88
European Agricultural Guidance and Guarantee Fund (EAGGF), 100
European Model of Agriculture, 107
European Union (EU), 129–30, 207
Evans, Graeme, 193
Evans, Peter, *Dependent Development*, 4

Eventful sociology, 74
Ewert, Joachim, 219
Exclusive companies, 66
Experience attributes, 203
Experts, 85–86, 88
Export-oriented production, 33–34, 34f, 178–79, 200–201

Fair trade, 35–36, 217
Fairtrade Labelling Organization International (FLO), 217
Feno, Raissa, 171
Festive events, 159
Film, 36
Firms, 65–68
Fischer, Joseph, 75, 76
Florida, Richard, *The Rise of the Creative Class*, 44–45
Food and Agriculture Organization (FAO), 76, 80
France, 63–64, 167–69, 207, 211, 213
Free market economy, 2–3

Gaggio, Dario, 14–15
Garrett, Wilbur, 186
Gates, Bill, 149
Gates, Henry Louis, 149
Geography: cultural production and, 31–37; discipline of, 5–6; income distribution by, 29f
Gereffi, Gary, 182–84, 197, 202
Germany, 121
Global brands, 32–33, 33f
Global class: income distribution and, 27–28, 28f, 29f; indications of, 27–30
Global system of cultural wealth, 9, 27. See *also* North vs. South, global
Global tourism, 178–81; distribution of, 38, 39f; expenditures on, 37; Slovenia, 42–43; Thailand, 40–42; types of, 39
Global value chains: culture and, 245n6; defined, 181; governance structures in, 182; *Mundo Maya* and, 16–17, 185–96; South Africa and, 17, 19; studies of, 10, 11, 179–80; symbolic value in, 195, 199; Thailand and, 18; tourism and, 181, 184, 195; upgrading in, 182–85, 195–97, 201–3, 245n4; value creation in, 195–96
Goffman, Erving, 11, 15, 44, 115–17, 127; *Stigma*, 115–17

Graburn, Nelson H. H., 159, 161, 172, 244*n*3
Graham, Mark, 18, 19
Grameen Bank, 16, 139, 140
Greene, Graham, *Our Man in Havana*, 29
Greenwood, Davydd J., 166
Guatemala, 185, 191

Handicrafts, 161, 170–73, 172*f*
Heilbron, Johan, 37
Herder, J. G., 23
Heritage. *See* Cultural heritage
"Heritage in danger," 81, 84–85
Heritage tourism. *See* Cultural and heritage tourism
Higher education, study abroad in, 37, 38*f*
Historical contingency, 83–85
Hobsbawm, Eric, 173
Homo economicus, 53, 56
Honduras, 185
Hopkins, Terrence, 245*n*5
Housing, 63–64, 170–71
Human rights, 29
Humphrey, John, 202
Hybridity, 27

ICOMOS. *See* International Council on Monuments and Sites
Iconic brands, 93
Iconicity, 92–95
Impression management, 10–12, 15, 16; of countries' images, 44; in Croatia, 114–36; international, 115–17; in Mayotte, 167–70; tourism and, 114. *See also* Branding
Income, global distribution of, 28*f*, 29*f*
India, 36, 66, 229
Indication of geographical origin (IGO), 206–9, 214
Institut National des Appellations d'Origine (INAO), 207
Intangible cultural heritage, 157–62
Integrated Production of Wine (IPW) scheme, 215, 217
Intellectual property rights, 206–8
Inter-American Development Bank, 187
Interests, Smith and Bourdieu on, 58–61. *See also* Self-interest
Intermediaries, in Thai silk industry, 18, 232–37
International Council of Museums (ICOM), 76

International Council on Monuments and Sites (ICOMOS), 77, 79, 81, 83, 86
International Criminal Tribunal for the Former Yugoslavia (ICTY), 130, 131
International Union for the Conservation of Nature (IUCN), 74, 76, 80, 81, 83, 86
Internet, 18; and disintermediation, 223–24, 224*f*, 225*f*, 226–27; and economic development, 222–23, 227–28, 237–39; Thai silk industry and, 228–39
Invisible hand, 48, 49, 58, 62
Islam, 122, 168, 169
IUCN. *See* International Union for the Conservation of Nature

Jensen, Michael, "Theory of the Firm" (with William Meckling), 65
Jevons, Colin, 226
Johnson, Lyndon B., 75
Joint-stock companies, 66

Kaplinsky, Raphael, 201
Keita, Salif, 150
Kennedy, John F., 78
Koöperatieve Wijnbouwers Vereniging van Zuid-Afrika (KWV), 211–12
Kosovo, 126
Kowalski, Alexandra, 14, 32
Kruger, Sandra, 219
Krugman, Paul, 47

Labels, 209–10
Labor. *See* Division of labor
Landes, David, 23–24
Landolt, Patricia, 24
Landscape: iconicity and branding of, 93–95; symbolic value of, 15; Tuscan, 95–101, 103–11
Language: dominance of European, 36–37; global hierarchy of, 37
Latvia, 133
Law, and symbolic value, 206–9
Lazaret, Reunion Island, 164, 165*f*
League of Nations, 77
Life, value of, 28
Linkage, 222–23
Lists, 86–87
Localization of the global, 27
Local knowledge, 160
Local populations: and tourism, 166, 170, 189–94; and Tuscany's cultural wealth, 112–13

Lorenzetti, Ambrogio, *Allegory of Good and Bad Government*, 104
Lury, Celia, 93

MacCanell, Dean, 94
Macleod, Donald V. L., 173
Madagascar, 172, 172*f*
Maheu, René, 74, 77, 79, 84, 85
Malaysia, 205
Mali, 1–2; cultural wealth of, 149–50; Culture Bank of, 15–16, 139–50, 154–55
Malta, 133
Markets, Smith and Bourdieu on, 61–65
Marx, Karl, 3, 23, 47, 50–51; *The Communist Manifesto* (with Friedrich Engels), 153
Material attributes of products, 200–205
Mayan people. See *Mundo Maya*
Mayotte, 15, 16, 19, 156–62, 167–74
McIntosh, Roderick and Susan, 149
Measurement of value, 204–5
Meckling, William, "Theory of the Firm" (with Michael Jensen), 65
Mercantilism, 2
Metropolitan Museum of Art, New York City, 150
Mexico, 185, 189, 190–94, 244*n*3, 245*n*7
Microcredit, 139, 140
Mill, John Stuart, 53
Mode of value production, 82–83, 86–89
Modernization, Tuscany and, 98–103
Modernization theory, 3, 23
Morality: personal finance-related, 56; Smith and, 50–52
Multi-Fiber Arrangement (MFA), 230
Mundo Maya, 15, 16–17, 177–78, 185–96, 190*f*
Mundo Maya Organization, 187, 189
Music, 158–59

Napoleon, 211
Narratives, 7–8
Nasser, Gamal Abdel, 78
National Geographic (magazine), 149, 177, 186, 189
National Geographic Society, 187
Nationalism, 125
Nation branding. See Branding
Neoclassical economics, 3
Neoliberalism, 62
New economic sociology, 5
New York Herald Tribune (newspaper), 106
New York Times (newspaper), 40
Niche tourism, 184, 188

Nixon, Richard, 75, 82, 83
Non-lieux, 164
Nora, Pierre, 164
North Atlantic Treaty Organization (NATO), 128
North vs. South, global, 9, 10, 73, 83, 179, 183, 198
Nuttavuthisit, Krittinee, 40

Oral traditions, 158
Orcia valley, 109–10, 109*f*

Pakthongchai, Thailand, 232–35
Performing arts, 158–59
Persky, Joseph, 48
Philae, temple of, 78
Picard, Michel, 161, 169
Picasso, Pablo, 149
Place: iconic branding of, 93–95; *sur-lieux* and *non-lieux*, 164; symbolic capital and, 149–50
Plan Puebla Panama, 187–88
Poland, 121
Polanyi, Karl, 53–54
Political economy perspective, 10–11, 20
Ponte, Stefano, 17, 19, 195, 219
Poon, Simpson, 226
Popular culture, U.S. influence on, 36
Portes, Alejandro, 24, 153
Power, historical contingency and, 83–85
Preservation: of Dogon culture, 147–49; of Tuscan landscape, 107–11
Protected designation of origin (PDO), 207–8
Protected geographical indication (PGI), 207–8
Protected Natural Zones of Local Interest (ANPILs), 110–11
Purcell, Fuati, 226
Putnam, Robert, 145

Quality, material vs. symbolic, 203–11

Race, income distribution by, 28, 29*f*. See also Ethnicity
Ranger, Terence, 173
Rangnekar, Dwijen, 206
Rauch, André, 166
Regnault, Madina, 15, 16, 19
Regulated companies, 66
Relativism, 25–26
Reputation: of Thailand, 40–41; value of, 1–2, 32–33, 206

Restricted companies, 66
Reunion Island, 16, 156–66, 171–74
Ricardo, David, 3
Ricasoli, Baron, 102
Rivera, Lauren, 15, 19
Robinson, Jancis, 214
Ross, Ian, 57
Rubber, 205
Ruta Maya. See *Mundo Maya*
Rwanda, 121

Salinas de Gortari, Carlos, 191
Sangare, Oumou, 150
Savings morality, 56
Schmitz, Hubert, 202
Schumpeter, Joseph, 52–53
Search attributes, 203
Self-interest, 50–51, 54, 58
Sensenbrenner, Julia, 153
Serbia, 117, 128
Sewell, William, 74
Sex, in Thailand, 40–41
Sharecropping, 95–98
Simmel, Georg, *The Philosophy of Money*, 51
Slater, Don, 198
Slavery, 162, 164, 218–19
Slovenia, 42–43
Small, Albion, 51–52
Smith, Adam, 2–3, 14, 47–54, 56–69;
    background on, 57; on firms, 65–68;
    "History of Astronomy," 62; on interests,
    58–61; *The Lectures on Rhetoric*, 49; on
    markets, 61–65; sociologists on, 49–54;
    stereotypical view of, 48, 58; *The Theory
    of Moral Sentiments*, 49, 50, 54, 57, 62;
    The Wealth of Nations, 49, 50, 51, 54, 57,
    58, 61, 62, 65–66
Smith, Philip, 41
Social capital, 139
Social justice, 35
Sociology, Adam Smith and, 49–54. *See also*
    Cultural economic sociology; Economic
    sociology; New economic sociology
South Africa: black economic empowerment
    in, 218–20; branding in, 214–17;
    certification systems in, 212–14, 217–18;
    tourism in, 121, 218; wine of, 1–2, 17, 19,
    211–21
Souvenirs, 171–74
Specialty tourism, 184, 188
Stigma management, 15
Stigmatized nations, 15, 115–17

Stockholm Conference (1972), 76
Study abroad, 37, 38f
Summer, Donna, 43
Sur-lieux, 164
Sustainability labels, 209–10
Symbolic attributes of products, 205–6
Symbolic capital: characteristics of, 145–47;
    Culture Bank and, 139, 147–49; and
    economic development, 140; place and,
    149–50; totems and, 150–54
Symbolic resources, 1–2. *See also* Cultural
    wealth of nations
Symbolic value: creating and controlling,
    205–11; global value chain analysis and,
    195, 199; significance of, 197–98; South
    African wine and, 211–21; struggles
    over, 199

Tale telling, 158
Tastes, 24–25
Thailand: branding in, 40–42; silk industry
    in, 18, 228–39
Third World, 35–36
Timbuktu, Mali, 149
Tobacco, 35
Togliatti, Palmiro, 96
Togola, Téréba, 149
Toland, Janet, 226
Totems, 150–54
Toure, Ali Farka, 150
Tourism: in Croatia, 117–36, 120f; cultural
    policies in relation to, 162–64; as
    development strategy, 180–81; global
    value chain analysis of, 181, 184; iconic
    branding and, 94; impressions projected
    through, 114; local populations and, 166,
    170, 189–94; niche/specialty, 184, 188;
    and South African wine, 218; Tuscan
    landscape and, 103–11; war and, 121,
    126; wine, 218. *See also* Beaches and bars
    tourism; Bells tourism; Cultural and
    heritage tourism; Global tourism
Tourism affinitaire, 174
Trademarks, 206
Trade-Related Intellectual Property Rights
    (TRIPS), 206–8
Train, Russell E., 75, 76, 85
Translations, 36–37
Tribe, Keith, 49
Tuscany, 1–2, 15, 90–113; authenticity of, 94,
    106, 111–13; branding of, 90, 91; cultural
    wealth accumulation of, 90–91, 111–12;

exodus from, 97–98; history of landscape of, 95–101; landscape as resource in, 103–11; locals' role in cultural wealth of, 112–13; modernization and, 98–103; photography of, 99; politics in, 96–97, 99, 104–5, 107–8, 112; preservation of landscape in, 107–11; tourism in, 103–11; World War II and the Resistance in, 96

U.N. Conference on the Human Environment (1972), 76
U.N. Industrial Development Organization, 183
U.N. International Criminal Tribunal, 117
United Nations Educational, Scientific, and Cultural Organization (UNESCO). See Convention for the Safeguarding of Intangible Cultural Heritage (2003); World Heritage Convention (1972); World Heritage Sites
United States: environmentalist project of, 75–76; and Mundo Maya, 187–88; popular culture distributed and influenced by, 36; and World Heritage Sites, 75–76, 78–82, 84
Universalism, 24–26, 30
Upgrading, 182–85, 195–97, 201–3, 245n4
Urry, John, 112, 160
U.S. National Park Service, 75, 83, 86

Value creation: in global value chains, 195–96; material attributes and, 204–5; symbolic attributes and, 205–11
Van den Berghe, Pierre L., 194
Venice Charter for the Conservation and Restoration of Monuments and Sites, 77, 78
Village Tobé, Mayotte, 170

Wallerstein, Immanuel, 24, 245n5
War, and tourism, 121, 126
Weber, Max, 3, 5, 51, 59, 63; The Protestant Ethic and the Spirit of Capitalism, 23

Wedding ceremonies, 159, 160f
Wherry, Frederick, 13, 15–16, 19, 94, 164, 170, 185
White, Harrison, 63
Wine: Italian, 102–4; South African, 1–2, 17, 19, 211–21
Wine and Spirits Board (WSB), 212, 214
Wine Industry Ethical Trade Association (WIETA), 217
Wine of origin (WO) scheme, 212–14
Wines of South Africa (WOSA), 214–15
Wine tourism, 218
The Wonders of the African World (television show), 149
World Bank, 183, 227, 230
World Heritage Convention (1972), 14, 73–89; genesis of, 32, 74–82, 86; global character of, 73; historical contingencies of, 83–85; impact of, 73; intentions and effects of, 84–85; rules and resources associated with, 86–89
World Heritage Sites: distribution of, 83–84, 88; economics and, 83–84; in Mundo Maya, 188–89; politics and, 7, 83–84, 87–88; by region, 31, 31f; registry of, 7, 87
World Heritage Trust, 75–76, 79, 81
World music, 36
World systems theory, 3, 24
World Trade Organization (WTO), 208–9
WOSA. See Wines of South Africa
WO system. See Wine of origin (WO) scheme
WSB. See Wine and Spirits Board
WTO. See World Trade Organization (WTO)
Wunderman, Lester, 150

Yucatán, Mexico, 192–94
Yugoslavia, 124–26, 128
Yugoslavia National Tourist Organization, 118, 121

Zapatista movement, 191
Zelizer, Viviana, 5, 154